CULTURE AND AUTHORITY IN THE BAROQUE

Edited by
Massimo Ciavolella and Patrick Coleman

Despite the recent revival of interest in baroque art, architecture, and music, a common and clear definition of what constitutes the baroque has remained somewhat elusive and problematic. This collection of original essays challenges conventional understandings of the baroque and its place in history and contemporary society. In *Culture and Authority in the Baroque* editors Massimo Ciavolella and Patrick Coleman have brought together an eminent group of scholars from a wide range of disciplines to explore many aspects of the baroque, from poetics to politics, to the rituals of musical, dramatic, and religious performance.

The cultural forms referred to as baroque are often described as 'transcendent,' and in effect are the most spectacular expressions of early modern Europe's efforts to mediate between knowledge and authority at a time of political, religious, and social upheaval. During this period, political authority was being centralized, the authority of religion was being undermined by the division of Christianity, and science and poetry were increasingly seen as rival forms of intellectual authority. This volume concentrates on an area known as the 'baroque crescent,' stretching from Spain through Italy to Russia, but it also examines the relevance of Shakespeare and English cosmological poetry to baroque world-views within continental Europe. Through discussion of diverse examples the authors investigate baroque modes of persuasion, paying careful attention to the complexity of particular cultural phenomena and their political and aesthetic implications.

(UCLA Clarke Memorial Library)

MASSIMO CIAVOLELLA is professor and chair in the Department of Italian at the University of California, Los Angeles.

PATRICK COLEMAN is a professor in the Department of French and Francophone Studies at the University of California, Los Angeles.

CULTURE AND AUTHORITY IN THE BAROQUE

Edited by
Massimo Ciavolella and Patrick Coleman

UNIVERSITY OF TORONTO PRESS
Toronto Buffalo London

© The Regents of the University of California 2005
Toronto Buffalo London
utorontopress.com

Reprinted in paperback 2021

ISBN 978-0-8020-3838-8 (cloth)
ISBN 978-1-4875-4471-3 (paper)

UCLA Centre / Clark Series

Library and Archives Canada Cataloguing in Publication

Title: Culture and authority in the baroque / edited by Massimo Ciavolella and Patrick Coleman.

Names: Ciavolella, Massimo, 1942– editor. | Coleman, Patrick, editor.

Series: UCLA Clark Memorial Library series ; 3.

Description: Series statement: UCLA Center/Clark series ; 3 | Paperback reprint.
Originally published 2005. | Includes bibliographical references and index.

Identifiers: Canadiana 20210229853 | ISBN 9781487544713 (softcover)

Subjects: LCSH: Baroque literature – History and criticism. | LCSH: Civilization, Baroque.

Classification: LCC PN56.B3 C84 2021 | DDC 940.2/52–dc23

This book has been published with the help of a grant from the UCLA Center for Seventeenth- and Eighteenth-Century Studies

University of Toronto Press acknowledges the financial assistance to its publishing program of the Canada Council for the Arts and the Ontario Arts Council, an agency of the Government of Ontario.

 Canada Council for the Arts   Conseil des Arts du Canada

 ONTARIO ARTS COUNCIL
CONSEIL DES ARTS DE L'ONTARIO
an Ontario government agency
un organisme du gouvernement de l'Ontario

Funded by the Government of Canada   Financé par le gouvernement du Canada

Contents

Introduction 3
MASSIMO CIAVOLELLA AND PATRICK COLEMAN

1 'Believing and Not Believing': Shakespeare and the Archaeology of Wonder 12
PETER G. PLATT

2 Philosophical Tours of the Universe in British Poetry, 1700–1729, Or, The Soaring Muse 30
LORNA CLYMER

3 Marino and the *Meraviglia* 63
PAOLO CHERCHI

4 I Would Rather Drown, Than Not Find New Worlds 73
PAOLO FASOLI

5 Truth and Wonder in Naples circa 1640 85
JON R. SNYDER

6 'Particolar gusto e diletto alle orecchie': Listening in the Early *Seicento* 106
ANDREW DELL'ANTONIO

7 From Liturgy to Literature: Prayer and Play in the Early Russian Baroque 122
RONALD VROON

8 Reconciling Divine and Political Authority in Racine's *Esther*   138
ANN DELEHANTY

9 Apostles and Apostates: The Court of Peter the Great as a Chivalrous Religious Order   159
ERNEST A. ZITSER

10 Self-Knowledge and the Advantages of Concealment: Pierre Nicole's 'On Self-Knowledge'   193
JOHN D. LYONS

11 The Baroque Social Bond in the *Memoirs* of the Cardinal de Retz   208
MALINA STEFANOVSKA

12 A Different Kind of Wonder? Women's Writing in Early Modern Spain   229
LISA VOLLENDORF

Contributors   245

Index   249

CULTURE AND AUTHORITY IN THE BAROQUE

Introduction

MASSIMO CIAVOLELLA AND PATRICK COLEMAN

Baroque is back. In architecture, recent preoccupation with enhancing feelings of community has sparked renewed appreciation for the 'expansive and inclusive' use of space in baroque buildings, and more generally in perspectives that 'order urban distribution and circulation through avenues, vistas and foci' in order to complicate and intensify the subject's relation to the more elusive aspects of social experience.[1] Reflections on changing, 'postmodern' conceptions of space, real and virtual, commonly refer to baroque aesthetics.[2] Over the last two decades, cinematic re-imaginations of seventeenth-century Europe such as Peter Greenaway's *Draughtsman's Contract* (1982) and Alain Corneau's *Tous les matins du monde* (1991) have probed the contemporary resonance of the baroque tension between sensuality, intellectuality, and the sacred. In philosophy, Gilles Deleuze's path-breaking *The Fold: Leibniz and the Baroque* (1988), by showing the interpenetration of mathematical rigour and metaphorical imagery in early modern argumentation, has exerted considerable influence on postmodern thinking. It has also spawned more detailed historical investigations into thinkers such as Hobbes and Spinoza, the rhetorical strategies of whose writings cannot be captured by the terms of 'modern' scientific rationality, and whose materialism cannot be framed by secular categories alone.[3]

The essays in this volume originated from a similar need to question conventional narratives of cultural development across a wider range of disciplines, from poetics to politics to the rituals of musical, dramatic, and religious performance. The geographical range of the essays is equally wide. They span what has been called the 'baroque crescent' stretching from Spain through Italy to Russia, but they also bring Shakespeare and English cosmological poetry into productive dialogue with continental Europe in the reinterpretation of baroque worldviews.[4]

Like other terms, such as 'romantic' and 'modern,' that cover a historical period, a characteristic style, and an underlying world-view, 'baroque' has had its usefulness for identifying and appreciating cultural phenomena weighed against worries about its conceptual coherence. An additional difficulty is that although scattered aesthetic uses of the word 'baroque' can be found within the period it now names – from the early seventeenth to the early eighteenth century, with some national variations – the term only came into common critical use in the late nineteenth century, as historians of art and architecture debated the merits of a distinctive post-Renaissance style. Characterized by the multiplication and metamorphosis of figures and perspectives (sometimes to grotesque extremes), this style seemed designed less to advance the cause of the new humanism than to sweep the disoriented viewer into a indefinite movement of transcendence. And yet the technical sophistication and overt emphasis on rhetorical effect suggested a worldliness apparently at odds with its transcendent aims – a paradox summed up in references to the baroque as the 'Jesuit style.' A similar ambiguity can be found in the identification of baroque music as originating in the reaction against polyphony in the time of Monteverdi. Individualized and increasingly ornamented voices are the hallmarks of this music, and, as Andrew Dell'Antonio explains in his essay, so is a new role for the individual listener as educated *connaisseur*, but the new genre of opera in which they were heard represented what could be called a new kind of sacred music, even if its space of representation was no longer that of the church. The 'increasing "delay" of resolutions, and an increasing generation of new developments out of temporary resolutions'[5] that characterize Bach's fugues, which have been called the ultimate baroque instrumental form, stand in equally problematic relationship to a modernity defined by a view of the universe as open and yet fully graspable by mathematical certainty.

In one sense, therefore, arguments about the baroque were from the start part of a larger debate about the relationship between secularization and the reconfiguration of religious and political authority in early modern Europe. For a while this argument seemed to have been settled by the triumph of a liberal historiography that dissolved the puzzle of the baroque into separate stories about scientific progress and political rationalization, on the one hand, and religious and artistic quarrels increasingly relegated to the margins of mainstream cultural history.

Today, criticism of the reductiveness of the 'Enlightenment project' and suspicion of grand historical narratives, including the very idea of a main stream, have become pervasive features of the thinking we call postmodern. In this context, the problematic nature of the baroque label, the fact that it marks a question rather than the presumption of an answer, becomes a virtue rather than a fault. Indeed, appeals to the baroque as an indirect way of articulating the self-understanding of contemporary culture has been a constant feature in baroque scholarship and criticism in the century since the term first came into common use.

Thus, musicians opened up to diverse cultural influences in the Jazz Age rediscovered the value of 'period' instruments for capturing the flavour of baroque music, while expressionist and surrealist writers exploring the limits of poetic language rehabilitated the bold rhetorical figures of baroque poets such as Sponde, Marino, and Gryphius, whose work violated neoclassical norms of good taste. For some writers and critics, 'baroque' came to label almost any kind of stylistic 'excess.' Yet, as Claude-Gilbert Dubois has pointed out, early-twentieth-century interest in identifying a specific baroque culture was not just an echo of modernist experiments in style. It was also rooted in the political crisis of the time.[6] The major wave of German and Italian scholarship in the 1920s and 1930s coincided with the rise of totalitarianism, and the study of baroque theatrical effects reflected a fascination with the strategies of persuasion made possible by the self-conscious appropriation of the new mass media by Fascist regimes. For critics such as Walter Benjamin, however, the stylistic devices of the baroque also signalled a crisis in consciousness in which traces of unfulfilled revolutionary potential could still be found. In the baroque, the dissolution of the analogical philosophical and cosmological systems of the Renaissance had not yet given way to a comfortably secular and empirical rationality. The baroque's reluctant mourning of the loss of transcendence, marked as it was by extremes of melancholy paralysis or spasmodic violence, kept open a space of negativity in which the overcoming of bourgeois complacency could be imagined.[7]

Far from expressing anarchic rebellion, stylistic tensions in poetry, like those in other arts, were attempts to find a new mediation between humanity and a divinity paradoxically immediately present and yet elusive in the very starkness of his transcendence. The question was whether such a mediation could be accomplished by anything other than a violent imposition of will – a theme that haunted many modern European intellectuals who had become disenchanted with parliamentary democracy as the embodiment of social reconciliation and as a vehicle for the renewal of moral values. Their ambivalence found an echo, as Malina Stefanovska shows in her essay in this volume, in the reactions of political writers like the 'baroque' cardinal de Retz to the development of absolute monarchies over atomized individual subjects, at the expense of intermediary legal and corporate bodies. The church of the baroque age, polarized between the absolutist papacy of a reinvigorated institutional Catholicism and reformed confessions that submitted to the civil order while redefining the church as an invisible community of saints, mirrored the political developments of its time and seemed to anticipate the ambiguities of its relationship to twentieth-century regimes.

For the generation that emerged after the Second World War, on the other hand, a key value of the baroque was that, unlike the Renaissance, it had put down roots in Germanic and Slavic lands as well as in those of the Latin or liberal West. Studying the baroque was a way of resisting nationalist interpretations of culture. More positively, it sought to integrate into a more inclusive European cultural history those areas of the south and east ignored by a narrative of historical progress from Renaissance to Enlightenment that recent events (including the new division of Europe by the Iron Curtain) had shown to be naïve as well as partial.[8] These considerations perhaps also help to explain why the term did not catch on in English studies, where the distinctiveness of England's national development in politics, religion, and literature did not seem to call for any challenge. Indeed, early attempts to speak of an English baroque by eliding historical and political issues and concentrating on stylistic analogies not only failed to convince, they also fed the suspicion that 'baroque' was a notion devoid of real analytical purchase. Ironically, the baroque was discredited as a manifestation of the very kind of cultural dilettantism against which its best scholarship had been directed. The widespread popularity of 'baroque' in Latin American criticism was not always a compensation. While it served to link colonial and contemporary culture across the boundary of political independence from Spain and Portugal, instead of putting national boundaries in question 'baroque' often became a tool for constructing a cultural tradition localized in an ideal 'American' or 'New World' space – a different kind of nativism.[9]

In reaction to these dangers, scholars have adopted a more pragmatic view of concepts like that of the baroque as part of provisional and avowedly partial histories or genealogies of culture. Often, these begin as counter-narratives to established histories of national, gender, or religious identities, designed to expose the limitations of the latter in accounting for the complexity of cultural phenomena. For example, the French version of 'Enlightenment' can no longer be taken as normative. It has become possible to identify Scottish, Swiss, and even English Enlightenments, not as instances of an ideal construct, but as overlapping patterns of relationships between discourses in a variety of fields.[10] What we used to call the Counter-Reformation has been re-baptized 'early modern Catholicism,'[11] in order to dispel the fog of old polemics and set religious history within a broader and more pluralistic context. Similarly, identifications of the 'baroque' with the Counter-Reformation have been criticized for assuming the relevance of confessional and political boundaries that call for re-examination.[12]

Equally important, critical appreciation of what Walter Moser has called the 'baroque resurgences' in today's culture is no longer framed merely in stylistic terms (images of metamorphosis, *trompe-l'œil* perspectives, and so forth). With the greater intersection of critical and cultural theory in recent years (Deleuze's influence has been especially important here), the more facile applications of the baroque label have given way to greater historical specificity. For example, in cultures still haunted by a legacy of authoritarianism, including French Canada and some European countries, as well as Latin America, the appropriation of 'baroque' forms functions as a way of dealing with the past without erasing it. A work such as Nicole Brossard's *Baroque d'aube* appeals to a contested 'moment' in cultural tradition precisely in order to relieve the oppressiveness of tradition in a Quebec burdened with an constricted past; it provides a sense of cultural depth and taps into inherited resources even as it focuses on the surfaces of linguistic and other kinds of ornamentation.[13] In this respect, the baroque becomes the past of the postmodern.

Other circumstances, however, have prompted a more self-consciously historical, indeed political, understanding of the baroque's contemporary resonance. The spread of a global digital culture raises questions about techniques of propaganda, persuasion, and the disciplining or transcendence of bodies in ways that echo the concerns of those who wrote on the baroque in the inter-war period.[14] In a landmark study originating in the Spain of the Franco era, José Maravall argued that the mobilization of modern scientific techniques in the service of reactionary rule was the defining dynamic of the baroque.[15] Today, we can see that his definition was a limited one, in that the ways those techniques were deployed often signalled – and reinforced – a breakdown of the traditions of authority they were supposed to buttress, but his original insight is worth recalling as we look at the past from the vantage point of the problematically 'global' culture of the twenty-first century. As the essays in this volume show, some degree of ambivalence about the tendency of the baroque helps us to appreciate the complexity of particular cultural phenomena, and the provisional nature of overarching historical narratives.

The focus of this ambivalence, we would claim, is the necessity of mediation in knowledge and power. Do the detours that characterize baroque modes of persuasion serve as obstacles to a clear and liberating vision of the nature of authority, or do they blunt the impact of unfettered will? Alongside Malina Stefanovska's study of the Cardinal de Retz we may set Ann Delehanty's essay, which ponders Racine's attempt to allegorize the absolute power of Louis XIV through the Biblical story of Esther. To what extent does this move reflect a forcible appropriation of a prestigious model, or subordinate the idea of royal will to a narrative context it does not control? Ernest Zitser's account of Peter the Great's parodic religious order offers another striking example of the complex interplay between modern will and traditional forms. Lisa Vollendorf's investigation of women's narratives under the Spanish Inquisition presents a contrasting study of the same problem from the point of view of the powerless rather than the powerful.

Yet, the issue is not limited to political power alone. It arises in poetics as well, as shown by Paolo Cherchi's analysis of the importance of *dispositio*, the area where individual poetic agency is most prominently displayed, in early modern Italian writing. The hidden patterns of Marino's *Adone* give unexpected depth to the surface structure while at the same time drawing attention to their arbitrary character. Perhaps the most successful outcome of these problematic mediations of power is less to resolve them than, as Paolo Fasoli suggests, to shift the tension from the object studied to the contemplating subject: the unity of immediate experience and mediated knowledge is re-grounded in the preverbal impressions of that subject, and the loss of that unity in the attempt to articulate it then falls on the subject him or herself. In this respect, Fasoli's paper complements Andrew Dell'Antonio's work on the emergence of the critical listener in baroque musical performances. The issue is perhaps most acute for the moral philosopher Pierre Nicole, for as John Lyons shows, the difficulty of achieving an integrated image of oneself directly affects the possibility of virtuous action.

Another way of stating the same theme in the realm of religion is to ask whether baroque strategies preserve the transcendence of divinity, or, by calling attention to the earthliness of their strategies, transform transcendence into inscrutable remoteness, and ultimately to something dispensable. This issue has attracted scholarly attention for some time in the context of religious philosophy, notably around the work of Pascal, but the Orthodox liturgical experiments analysed by Ronald Vroon and the English cosmological poetry studied by Lorna Clymer offer fresh examples of the ways this tension appears in unexpected contexts.

What may unite these different explorations is the effort to keep wonder alive in an age of rationality and predictability, so as to prevent a premature closure of the world – even the world of religious imagination – upon itself. The theme of wonder is highlighted by Peter Platt in his essay on Shakespeare, but it appears as a key theme throughout the volume, from the discussion of *meraviglia* in Italian aesthetics to the meditation on the inscrutability and sudden revelation of the organizing principles of historical or social action. The extent to which the baroque 're-enchantment of everyday life,' to borrow the title of a popular contemporary book,[16] was the last gasp of a world-view made obsolete by modernity, or a precious resource for understanding and assessing the forces at work in our postmodern (some would add postsecular)[17] age, itself remains an open question.

Notes

1 Henry A. Millon, 'Introduction,' in *The Triumph of the Baroque: Architecture in Europe, 1600–1750*, ed. Millon (New York: Rizzoli, 1999), 19. For a historical investigation informed by contemporary concerns, see Jésus Roberto Escobar, *The Playa Mayor and the Shaping of Baroque Madrid* (Cambridge: Cambridge University Press, 2003).

2 For two recent examples, see Nan Ellin, *Postmodern Urbanism* (Princeton: Princeton Architectural Press, 1999), and Angela Ndalianis, *NeoBaroque Aesthetics and Contemporary Entertainment* (Cambridge, MA: MIT Press, 2004).

3 Gilles Deleuze, *The Fold: Leibniz and the Baroque*, foreword and trans. by Tom Conley (Minneapolis: University of Minnesota Press, 1993); Anne-Laure Angoulvent, *Hobbes, ou, La crise de l'Etat baroque* (Paris: Presses universitaires de France, 1992); Saverio Ansaldi, *Spinoza et le baroque: infini, désir, multitude*

(Paris: Kimé, 2001); and John Milbank, *Theology and Social Theory* (Oxford: Blackwell, 1990).

4 For a recent reinterpretation of an English baroque, see Douglas J. Canfield, *The Baroque in English Neoclassical Literature* (Newark: University of Delaware Press, 2003).

5 Milbank, *Theology and Social Theory*, 429. See also Deleuze, *The Fold*, 127–8.

6 Claude-Gilbert Dubois, *Le baroque en Europe et en France* (Paris: Presses universitaires de France, 1995), 288.

7 Walter Benjamin, *The Origin of German Tragic Drama*, trans. by John Osborne (London: Verso, 1977).

8 Jean Rousset, the leading scholar of the generation that emerged after the Second World War and whose *La Littérature de l'âge baroque: Circé et le paon* (Paris: Corti, 1954) remains a standard reference, has written that his intention was to 'connect to Europe a culture that had lived on exchanges, even if it cost it something to admit it.' See Rousset, *L'Intérieur et l'extérieur* (Paris: José Corti, 1968), 241, and also *Dernier regard sur le baroque, suivi de, Le geste et la voix dans le roman* (Paris: Corti, 1998).

9 *Résurgences baroques*, ed. Walter Moser and Nicolas Goyer (Brussels: Ante Post, 2001).

10 See *The Enlightenment in National Context*, ed. Roy Porter and Mikulas Teich (Cambridge: Cambridge University Press, 1981); and *Reconceptualizing Nature, Science, and Aesthetics: Contribution à une nouvelle approche des Lumières helvétiques*, ed. Patrick Coleman, Anne Hofmann, and Simone Zurbuchen (Geneva: Slatkine, 1998).

11 See *Early Modern Catholicism: Essays in Honour of John W. O'Malley, S.J.*, ed. Kathleen M. Comerford and Hilmar M. Pabel (Toronto: University of Toronto Press, 2001).

12 In his path-breaking study, *Devotional Poetry in France, c. 1570–1613* (Cambridge: Cambridge University Press, 1969), Terence Cave argued that Protestant and Catholic modes were not as different as had been supposed, and recent studies of George Herbert still grapple with his 'Calvinist' and 'Catholic' tendencies. See Elizabeth Clarke, *Theory and Theology in George Herbert's Poetry: Divinitie, and Poesie, Met* (Oxford: Oxford University Press, 1997).

13 Nicole Brossard, *Baroque d'aube* (Montreal: l'Hexagone, 1995). For a study of the novel in relation to French surrealist interest in the baroque, see Katharine Conley, 'Going for Baroque in the Twentieth Century: From Desnos to Brossard,' *Québec Studies* 31 (2001): 12–23.

14 See for example the work of Timothy Murray, including *Drama Trauma: Specters of Race and Sexuality in Performance, Video, and Art* (London: Routledge, 1997).

15 José Antonio Maravall, *The Culture of the Baroque: Analysis of a Historical Structure*, trans. Terry Cochran (Minneapolis: University Minnesota Press, 1986).
16 Thomas Moore, *The Re-Enchantment of Everyday Life* (New York: HarperCollins, 1996).
17 See Philip Blond, ed., *Postsecular Philosophy: Between Philosophy and Theology* (London and New York: Routledge, 1998); Bill Martin, *Politics in the Impasse: Explorations in Post-secular Social Theory* (New York: State University of New York Press, 1996).

chapter one

'Believing and Not Believing': Shakespeare and the Archaeology of Wonder

PETER G. PLATT

Sometime in the fourth century BC, there was a marvellous birth: the philosophical concept of wonder in the West was born. The first classical reference to wonder and philosophy can be found in Plato's *Theaetetus* [155d]: Socrates tells Theaetetus, 'This sense of wonder is the mark of the philosopher. Philosophy indeed has no other origin, and he was a good genealogist who made Iris [Philosophy] the daughter of Thaumas [Wonder].'[1] Wonder, then, gives birth to philosophy. Plato's student, Aristotle, developed the concept of wonder in many texts, especially in his *Metaphysics* and *Poetics*. I would like to take as a working definition Aristotle's explanation of wonder in the *Metaphysics* restated by Thomas Aquinas in his *Summa Theologiae*: wonder 'is aroused when a man sees an effect and does not know its cause, or when he does not know or cannot understand how this cause could have that effect.'[2] Although in this paper I will discuss many sources of wonder, the so-called phenomenon of unknown cause gives us room for a wide-ranging investigation, an investigation not only of the marvels of God's works but also those of human makers, particularly artists, poets, and dramatists, all of whom can make us, as David Summers has said, 'see something we cannot understand how we can see.'[3]

The experience of wonder puts the marveller in an inbetween state, a state of unknowing on the way to finding something out. Difficult philosophical problems could inspire wonder for an early modern audience, but so could the new or rare; so could natural anomalies – Siamese twins, very small or very large human beings or animals; foreign cultures; amazingly beautiful (or small or large) works of art; or visual marvels on the stage. All of these and more were sources of wonder for the Renaissance, and I will discuss some of them below.

But wonder was not always embraced as a good. The Aristotelian tradition for the most part considered wonder as a means to an end. Wonder – and the encounter with the marvellous – stimulated inquiry but should dissipate when the problem in question was solved. In short, wonder should cease; understanding or reason should replace wonder. Or as Francis Bacon would have it, wonder was 'broken knowledge.'[4] Later in the seventeenth century, René Descartes claimed that the extreme form of wonder – which he called *étonnement* or astonishment – 'can never be otherwise than bad.'[5]

I will first provide an archaeology of wonder; that is, an exploration of the ancient history of wonder as a philosophical, rhetorical, and aesthetic concept. After this brief history – from Aristotle to the Renaissance – I will discuss an alternative tradition *within* the Renaissance that does *not* seek to make wonders cease. Renaissance Italian philosopher and literary critic Francesco Patrizi will be the spokesman for this tradition, a tradition that I hope will have something to teach us about returning wonder to our encounter with poetry and art. Instead of emphasizing the containment of wonder, this alternative approach focused on the power of wonder as an elemental factor in pushing forward the frontiers of intellectual and aesthetic experience. In this vision wonder is ongoing and its own end; what diminishes is not wonder but the desire – indeed, the capacity – to bring reason to bear upon it.

I will next examine an important Elizabethan curiosity cabinet – a place where the archaic or unusual was displayed as marvellous. I will then turn to another site of the marvellous: the Shakespearean stage. After providing a few Shakespearean touchstones of wonder, I will visit a Shakespearean *wunderkammer*, in which someone seemingly lost is unburied, resuscitated, and staged as new and wondrous. Finally, I will close by invoking Michel Foucault, who, in important remarks on curiosity, suggested what the alternative tradition of wonder did: that keeping wonder alive – in the philosopher's study, in discourse, in the encounter with the natural world – provides us with an intellectual and emotional vitality that can be lost if we seek to resolve wonder into an all-too-often precarious certainty.

An Archaeology of Wonder: Classical to Renaissance

Aristotle's treatment of wonder proved to be the one that shaped future discussions, and it is important to sketch it briefly. In Aristotle's system, a mind stimulated by wonder sought a larger rational 'design,' whether in the world at large or in a work of art, and this exercise was part of an even greater move in the mind from ignorance to knowledge. Wonder, Aristotle claimed, was the origin of our interest in anything: 'For it is owing to their wonder that men both now begin and at first began to philosophize; they wondered originally at the obvious difficulties, then advanced little by little and stated difficulties about the greater matters, e.g. about the phenomena of the moon and those of the sun and of the stars, and about the genesis of the universe.'[6] Wonder and the pursuit and acquisition of knowledge were fundamentally linked in the Aristotelian scheme, and this dynamic was often triggered by an encounter with art. Indeed, Aristotle tells us in the *Metaphysics* that he considered 'artists to be wiser than men of experience' because 'the former know the cause, but the latter do not. For men of experience know that the thing is so, but do not know why, while the others know the 'why' and the cause.'[7] By extension, the audience of the world make up the potential marvellers; the artists are the wonder-workers.

Aristotle's first invocation of wonder in the *Poetics* also links wonder to both epistemology and art – this time specifically dramatic art: 'incidents arousing pity and fear ... have the very greatest effect on the mind when they occur unexpectedly and at the same time in consequence of one another; there is more of the marvellous in them than if they happened of themselves or by mere chance.'[8] Although Aristotle's writings prominently featured wonder, they nonetheless indicated a drive to domesticate the marvellous: wondrous moments 'occur unexpectedly and at the same time in consequence of one another.' For Aristotle, there is always a cause that *somebody* knows. Just as Aristotle's philosophy required that wonder dissipate when understanding or knowledge was obtained, so his literary theory required a reason for the presence of the marvellous in drama. Wonder threatened to undo the certainty that should be the end result of tragedy, so Aristotle made certain that he reined it in. As Stephen Halliwell, an important commentator on the *Poetics*, has claimed, 'The "sense of wonder" to which [Aristotle] refers is ... not one which allows for deep or final inscrutability.'[9]

We need to be careful, however, not to distort Aristotle's view of wonder. The scheme sketched above became the dominant one in the medieval and early modern periods, but Wesley Trimpi has shown that Aristotle recognized that, while some things could be known to us through sense perceptions, others – the more marvellous, wonderful, divine – could be known only intrinsically and therefore with much less precision. A representative passage of these 'two types of intelligibility'[10] can be found in Aristotle's *Parts of Animals*: 'The scanty conceptions to which we can attain of celestial things give us, from their excellence, more pleasure than all our knowledge of the world in which we live; just as a half-glimpse of persons that we love is more delightful than an accurate view of other things, whatever their number and dimensions. On the other hand, in certitude and in completeness our knowledge of terrestrial things has the advantage.'[11] This passage complicates the Aristotelian system of wonder. Even for Aristotle, it seems, there are things that cannot be known – or can be known only dimly – and that we pursue all the more intently as a result. There is a tantalizing suggestion that Aristotle, whose system for wonder often seems so closed, could conceive of wonder as ongoing and potentially infinite.[12]

But wonder could be evoked in human beings by speech as well as by 'celestial things.' Because inevitably at least part of the power of wonder lies in its affective capabilities, we need to consider ever so briefly the figure of *admiratio* – or wonder – in the classical rhetorical tradition. For the classical writers on rhetoric allowed wonder a little more freedom than did Aristotle, and in the *Rhetoric* Aristotle himself gave wonder a power more akin to that in the *Parts of Animals* that I have just quoted than that revealed in the *Poetics*. In a passage that would become a *locus classicus*, Aristotle claimed that 'departure from the ordinary makes it [the style] look more dignified, as men have the same reaction to style as they do when comparing strangers with fellow citizens. That is why one should make one's style something out of the ordinary; men feel wonder at what is not to hand, and what rouses wonder gives pleasure.'[13] Like the wonderful 'scanty conceptions,' the stylistic 'departure from the ordinary' is seen as a marvellous and potent tool for the orator. Indeed, wonder was mentioned as a crucial component of rhetoric by countless classical rhetoricians, including the two with the greatest influence on the Renaissance: Cicero, in his *De partitione oratoria*, and Quintilian, in his *Institutio oratoria*.[14]

Christian thinkers had to negotiate with both the philosophical and the rhetorical traditions of wonder. Saint Augustine Christianized the marvellous by connecting it to miracles, a connection that is expressed etymologically in the embedding of *miror* (Latin for 'to wonder') and *admiratio* in *miraculum*.[15] Augustine defined a miracle as 'anything great and difficult or unusual that happens beyond the expectation or ability of the man who wonders at it,'[16] but he found nothing unnatural in the miraculous since God created all things in nature. Conceiving of miracles within an Aristotelian scheme, Thomas Aquinas set out to systematize the marvellous.[17] An event was a *marvel* when its cause was known by a select few; it was a *miracle* when its cause was known by no one but God. Like the classical orator, God uses wonder and the miraculous to persuade and convert; like Aristotle's artist, God alone knows 'the 'why' and the cause.'[18]

In the Renaissance, as in the medieval period, it was commonplace, when writing about wonder, to affirm Aristotelian conclusions. But sixteenth-century Italian philosopher and literary critic Francesco Patrizi was a theorist of wonder with a significantly different approach to the marvellous, and his *La deca ammirabile* (1587), part of his *Della poetica*, constituted a striking break with Aristotle.[19] Patrizi's unique place in the world of Renaissance poetics has been noted before. Indeed, literary historian Baxter Hathaway called him 'the most persistently anti-Aristotelian critic of his century.'[20] However, the radical nature of Patrizi's thought has remained underappreciated, especially, as I shall seek to indicate, in relation to his discussions of the power that wonder wields over an audience. (To be fair, this underappreciation is understandable: the bulk of Patrizi's writing on wonder was lost until Paul Oskar Kristeller discovered it in 1949.)

The only significant critical forebear who explored wonder in such sustained terms was Longinus, in *On the Sublime*. In spite of Patrizi's fame as a Platonic philosopher and professor, it becomes clear that Longinus is – in terms of wonder – his chief influence, as Patrizi's many references to *On the Sublime* (in *Della poetica* in general and *La deca ammirabile* in particular) reveal.[21] Patrizi was unusual in the Renaissance, then, not so much because he said something never said before but because he dared to promulgate a Longinian instead of an Aristotelian poetics. This itself was a significant departure, for Longinus's treatise had been virtually unknown until it was published in 1554 by Francesco Robortello, with whom Patrizi studied in the 1550s in Padua. For Longinus, like Patrizi, advocated a poetical form of fragmentary, scattered bursts that, on account of their wonderful and incredible nature, had the power to take the audience 'out of themselves.' Also crucial to Patrizi's theory of poetry was Longinus's anti-Aristotelian preference of wondrous 'transport' to rational persuasion.[22] Finally, although Longinus does not make overtly epistemological claims for the wonderful, Patrizi uses Longinus to undergird his writings on poetry, which certainly have cognitive implications: to be in wonder for Patrizi is to encounter, in Patrizi's words, what is 'sudden, new, and not before either known, thought, or believed able to exist.'

Patrizi's three most important contributions to the study of wonder are 1) his assault on versimilitude as the most important end of art; 2) his expansive list of sources of wonder; and 3) his description of how wonder works on the audience – the process of marvelling.

The poet, *il facitore del mirabile* – the maker of the marvellous[23] – had a duty to refashion reality, 'to give to a thing a form and appearance different from that which it first had, that is, a new or renewed form.'[24] This attack on the verisimilar led Patrizi to develop a poetics of *incredibility* that constituted an attempt to liberate poetry and its essential quality – wonder – from Aristotelian shackles: 'there must be incredible things if the marvellous is to be known from them, because the credible cannot bring about the marvellous ... all poetry must have as its object the incredible because this is the true foundation of the marvellous, which must in such wise be the principal object of every poem[,] that any poet who does not attend to it or use it will commit a great error in his art, such as cannot possibly be excused.'[25] Where other critics stressed the power of reason to subordinate wonder and incredibility, however, Patrizi posited a new solution that is as important as it is – perhaps necessarily – tenuous: the *potenza ammirativa*, or power of wonder.

Patrizi saw this power originating from twelve possible sources: ignorance, fable, novelty, paradox, augmentation, departure from the usual, the 'exceeding-natural,' the divine, great utility, the very exact, the unexpected, and the sudden.[26] In other words, for Patrizi, wonder could be evoked by the standard Aristotelian sources – ignorance, surprise, novelty, and the unusual – but also by the plots and subject matter of fiction (wizards, monsters, winged horses, unicorns, romance narratives); useful and instructive texts and events; religious manifestations and the supernatural; both rhetorical precision and *copia*; and the paradoxical and inexplicable. Some recent discussions of wonder have limited the sources to one or two of these, and thereby – I would argue – have circumscribed wonder too much.[27] Patrizi's ample, various list is important for understanding not only the early modern marvellous but also the twenty-first-century marvellous.

How did wonder work, though, according to Patrizi? Patrizi's most important discussion of the power of wonder occurs in Book Ten of *La deca ammirabile*, which deals primarily with how a sense of the marvellous is generated in the mind of the reader and hearer – in short, the audience:

> [wonder] will be a mediatory power between the two [operations of reason and affect], and its movement will be a third operation between those ..., darting from the middle position both upwards and downwards.
>
> ... the ... power of wonder [*potenza ammirativa*] is neither reason, nor

emotion, but separate from them both and in the business of communicating between them both; and that, placed on the boundary between the two, it is able to spread and flow, through its movement, swiftly up to the regions of reason and down to those of emotion ... the power of wonder is almost an Euripos [violent current] ..., the tide running back and forth from reason to emotion ...

... something new and sudden and unexpected which appears before us, creates a movement in our soul, almost contradictory in itself of believing and not believing. Of believing because the thing is seen to exist; and of not believing because it is sudden, new, and not before either known, thought, or believed able to exist.[28]

This theory describes a wondrous state in between reason and emotion that thrives on an absence of absolute knowledge – a state of 'believing and not believing.'[29] Instead of eradicating wonder in favour of reason and certainty, Patrizi celebrated it as a power that is fluid – a violent current that draws on both emotion and intellect. To be in wonder is not merely to be dumbfounded; it is to be on the verge of seeing something 'not before either known, thought, or believed able to exist.' In short, wonder allows us to entertain new worlds, and poetry and the arts are a vehicle for these new world encounters.

Wonder Collected

Of course, wonders came in other forms than philosophical ideas and rhetorical figures of speech, and the marvellous was collected in books of secrets, marvels, and wonders, as well as in travellers' tales from the likes of Sir Walter Ralegh and Samuel Purchas. A non-verbal, material analogue of wonder-collecting can be found in the wonder – or curiosity – cabinet, a physical expression both of the culture's obsession with collections of the marvellous and of the increased attention to scientific accuracy.[30] These were sites where one experienced, according to Adalgisa Lugli, the 'suspension of the mind between ignorance and enlightenment that marks the end of unknowing and the beginning of knowing.'[31] These cabinets also performed, in a sense, an archaeological function: objects lost or previously unknown were presented as found and displayed as marvels from another time and/or place. In fact, as Leonard Barkan has shown so brilliantly, this marvelling at the past is just what early modern 'observers of newly discovered ancient marble' did.[32]

The most important wonder cabinet in Renaissance England seems to have been that of Sir Walter Cope, who was a member of the Elizabethan Society of Antiquaries, held several positions in King James's government, and was a patron of the theatre. Cope's collection was recorded by Thomas Platter on his travels to England in 1599. It included a wild array of objects, suggesting the multiplicity and variousness inherent in the concept of the wonder cabinet, what Jean Céard has called a general '*plaisir à conter*' – a delight in telling, relating, accounting. Platter delighted in relating this partial list of the contents of Cope's cabinet: 'an African charm made of teeth ...; shoes from many strange lands ...; a string instrument with but one string...; the horn and tail of a rhinoceros ..., a large animal like an elephant ...; the bauble and bells of Henry VIII's fool ...; a unicorn's tail ...; [a] flying rhinoceros ...; heathen idols ...; a long narrow Indian canoe, with the oars and sliding planks, hung from the ceiling of this room.[33] Platter concluded his description of Cope's collection by saying, 'There are also other people in London interested in curios, but this gentleman is superior to them all for strange objects, because of the Indian voyage he carried out with such zeal.'[34] Indeed, Arthur MacGregor tells us that John Tradescant the elder 'knew Cope and probably knew his museum, which may have provided a model for Tradescant's own cabinet.'[35] This cabinet – described in Tradescant's epitaph as 'A world of wonders in one closet shut' – would form the basis of the Ashmolean Museum in Oxford.

Shakespeare and Wonder

If Walter Cope connects us – indirectly – to the wonder cabinet as natural history museum, he also connects us to a very famous acting company. Cope was the master of James Burbage's elder son, Cuthbert,[36] the man who in 1597 would take a half-interest in ownership of the Globe Theatre with his brother, Richard; the other half-interest was shared by five members of the the Lord Chamberlain's Men: Augustine Phillips, William Heminges, Thomas Pope, Will Kempe, and William Shakespeare.[37] Cope helped the Burbages arrange – and was almost certainly in attendance at – this same company's production of Shakespeare's *Love's Labour's Lost* in 1605, and plays were performed regularly at his house in Kensington.[38] It seems fitting, then, that Cope is connected both with collecting the marvellous and with facilitating the production and the witnessing of staged wonders. While the marvellous was helping redefine the known world, Cope's former servant, his brother, and their theatre company were busy reconfiguring the parameters of the Elizabethan-Jacobean stage.

Shakespeare's theatre was often a site of wonders, especially in his marvel-filled last plays. In *All's Well That Ends Well*, the old courtier Lafew advocates caution in dismissing wonders from the world: 'They say miracles are past, and we have our philosophical persons, to make modern and familiar, things supernatural and causeless. Hence is it that we make trifles of terrors, ensconcing ourselves into seeming knowledge, when we should submit ourselves to an unknown fear.'[39] Indeed, Lafew's scepticism towards the power of reason allows him to sustain the wonder necessary to believe that Helena has effected something akin to a miracle by curing the king of his mysterious fistula. There are things that occur, Lafew suggests, not dreamt of in their philosophy.

The next touchstone is two lines from the god Hymen in *As You Like It*: 'Feed yourselves with questioning; / That reason wonder may diminish' (5.4.138–9). The critical consensus has always been that these lines suggest the triumph of reason and order over wonder and confusion; the conventional reading, then, takes 'reason' as the subject of the second clause and 'wonder' as the direct object. The New Variorum *As You Like It*, citing Moberly's edition of 1872, glosses the line as follows: 'That the facts when stated may diminish wonder.'[40]

I have argued elsewhere that this reading is jarring because of the power that wonder often wields over reason in Shakespeare's drama – think of *A Midsummer Night's Dream*, as well as the late plays. Furthermore, the conventional interpretation seems reductive, seems to suppress an alternative reading that arguably lies in hiding. For clearly it is possible to take 'wonder' as the subject of the clause, the object of which would be 'reason'; this would not be the first time that Shakespeare buried his subject and inverted his syntax (see 'Sonnet 109': 'For nothing this wide universe I call'). A reading that posits the characters feeding themselves with questioning but discovering that this ingestion leads inevitably to a diminishing of reason by wonder seems much more in *As You Like It*'s marvellous spirit. Moreover, the eating metaphor becomes even more compelling: the characters feed on questions only to find their epistemological selves diminish; the more they ask, the less they understand and the more their rational stability wastes away.

With *The Winter's Tale* we see, arguably, Shakespeare's most thorough examination of the powers of the marvellous. This play illustrates and enacts the two previous touchstones: *The Winter's Tale* reveals that what appears to be certain is often only *seeming knowledge* and that wonder can diminish reason. But we are also introduced to a Walter Cope-like collector of marvels, Paulina, the waiting woman and friend of Hermione, Queen of Sicilia.

Let me set the stage for the wonders that occur in Act 5. In the early acts of the play, the King of Sicilia, Leontes, is so convinced that his wife Hermione has sexually betrayed him with his best friend Polixenes that he has done two rash things: first, he has sent away his newborn daughter – whom he is sure is a product of the adulterous union – to certain death; and second, he has consulted an oracle in order to confirm his plans to execute his wife. To Leontes's surprise, the oracle unequivocably clears Hermione and Polixenes. The king is nonetheless undeterred: 'There is no truth at all in the oracle,' he insists. 'The sessions shall proceed; this is mere falsehood' (3.2.140-1). His certainty sets in motion a deadly sequence of events. His son, Mamillius, dies, and Hermione, upon hearing the news, collapses in grief. Moments later, Paulina reports that the queen herself is dead.

Sixteen years elapse, and we see that Polixenes' son – Florizel – and Leontes' daughter – Perdita – have fallen in love in Polixenes' kingdom of Bohemia. For various reasons, they flee to Sicilia, where there is a grand reunion of Leontes, Polixenes, Perdita, and Florizel. Shakespeare has these meetings told to us in the language of wonder by courtiers, who explain that what they have seen is beyond the power of speech to describe. They also tell us that – as an act of celebration – a statue of Hermione by the famous Renaissance artist Giulio Romano will be revealed.

As Act Five, scene three opens, the guests have been on a tour of Paulina's 'gallery,' which, Leontes says, has provided them with 'much content / In many singularities' (5.3.10; 11–12). I think it is clear that they have witnessed the rarities – the 'singularities' – of a *wunderkammer*. And if this point is accepted, then Paulina plays three roles in this scene: by figuratively unearthing the 'dead' Hermione from 'her grave' (141), she is an archaeologist; by gathering and displaying curiosities, she is a collector; and by helping to bring stone to life, she is a thaumaturge or wonder-worker.

Paulina thus enables Shakespeare's stage to become a curiosity cabinet writ large, where we witness an astonishing version of the natural and artistic blending that is characteristic of the *wunderkammer*. For we – along with the other visitors – see a statue of Hermione, but one that miraculously seems to have aged. More wonderful still, Hermione, at Paulina's beckoning, steps from the pedestal into life. Many critics have seen this moment as the triumph of life and reason over art and wonder: Paulina, they argue, preserves Hermione all along. I would claim, however, that the play presents the naturalistic and the marvellous participating in a tense dynamic, a dynamic that requires not the subordination of one to the other, but rather an ongoing dialectical exchange between the two.

Examples of this sort of exchange can be found in the interplay between Paulina, Hermione, and their audience onstage. Addressing the sculpture of his dead wife, Leontes suggests he is 'more stone than it' (38). His daughter Perdita, he further observes, is 'standing like stone' (42). When Paulina addresses the statue – ''Tis time; descend; be stone no more; approach; / Strike all that look upon with marvel' (99–100) – onlookers of the spectacle are astonished – astonied – with wonder as they watch the stone become flesh. Hermione goes from stone to life, as the living audience inside and outside the play turn with astonishment to stone.

Is epistemological order restored by the play's tentative suggestion that there is some explanation for Hermione's wondrous resurrection? I am suggesting it is not. At least part of the point is that, unlike the audience even of Shakespeare's other plays of wonder – *Pericles*, *Cymbeline*, and *The Tempest* – the external witnesses of *The Winter's Tale* (you and I) are ignorant of many of the play's crucial details and share the astonishment at Hermione's being alive with most of the onstage audience. We become part of a textbook case of the marvellous: we see the statue-become-woman but are not at all sure how this can be. Ignorant of cause, we wonder – we marvel *and* inquire – how we are able to see what we see.

I would like to close with an exhortation to wonder by Michel Foucault. His archaeology of knowledges and methods and cultural practices – his epistemological digging – has been portrayed by his detractors as a project of deconstruction without reconstruction. But, as he revealed in his 1980 interview, titled upon publication 'The Masked Philosopher,' at least part of what lay behind all of that archaeology was wonder, and its cousin, curiosity.[41]

> Curiosity is a vice that has been stigmatized in turn by Christianity, by philosophy, and even by a certain conception of science. Curiosity is seen as futility. However, I like the word; it suggests something quite different to me. It evokes 'care'; it evokes the care one takes of what exists and might exist; a sharpened sense of reality, but one that is never immobilized before

it; a readiness to find what surrounds us strange and odd; a certain determination to throw off familiar ways of thought and to look at the same things in a different way; a passion for seizing what is happening now and what is disappearing; a lack of respect for the traditional hierarchies of what is important and fundamental. I dream of a new age of curiosity. (325)

As we contemplate a new millenium for the arts, I would like to join Foucault in calling for a renewed interest in the *potenza ammirativa*, or power of wonder, in poetics and art. This new age of curiosity would encourage us to sustain wonder – as aesthetic response and as inquiry – instead of working towards its disappearance. In 1588, Francesco Patrizi claimed that 'wonder follows us everywhere.' Wonder is still there today, lurking benevolently, awaiting our recognition.

Notes

I would like to thank Jennie Kassanoff and Benedict Robinson for their invaluable contributions to the shape of this essay.

1 Plato, *The Collected Dialogues of Plato*, ed. Edith Hamilton and Huntington Cairns (1961; repr., Princeton: Princeton University Press, 1973), 860.
2 Saint Thomas Aquinas, *Summa Theologiae*, ed. Thomas Gilby et al., Blackfriars Edition, 61 vols. (London: Eyre & Spottiswoode, 1964–), 20:50–1. For Aristotle, see the *Metaphysics*, IA.2.980a–983a. See also the Pseudo-Aristotelian *Mechanics*, 847a10ff, trans. Forster: 'Our wonder is excited, firstly, by phenomena which occur in accordance with nature but of which we do not know the cause, and secondly by those which are produced by art despite nature for the benefit of mankind,' in *The Complete Works of Aristotle*, ed. Jonathan Barnes, The Revised Oxford Translation, 2 vols. (1984; repr. Princeton: Princeton University Press, 1985), 2:1299.
3 David Summers, *The Judgment of Sense: Renaissance Naturalism and the Rise of Aesthetics* (1987; repr., New York: Cambridge University Press, 1994), 127.
4 Francis Bacon, *The Advancement of Learning*, Book I, in *Works of Francis Bacon*, ed. James Spedding et al., 14 vols. (London: Longman and Co., 1857–74), 3:267.
5 René Descartes, *Passions of the Soul*, 2. 73, in *The Philosophical Works of Descartes*, ed. Elizabeth S. Haldane and G.R.T. Ross, 2 vols. (1911; repr., Cambridge: Cambridge University Press, 1986), 1:364.

6 Aristotle, *Metaphysics*, Book A.2, 982b12–18, trans. W. D. Ross, in *The Works of Aristotle*, vol. 7, ed. W.D. Ross (1908; repr., Oxford: Clarendon Press, 1928). Thomas Bishop examines some of the resonances of wonder in other Platonic texts in his *Shakespeare and the Theatre of Wonder* (Cambridge: Cambridge University Press, 1996), 21–6. See also Coleridge's fascinating misreading of Plato: 'In wonder ... says Aristotle, does philosophy begin: and in astoundment ... says Plato, does all true philosophy finish.' Samuel Taylor Coleridge, *The Friend*, sec. 2, essay 11 [1818], in *Collected Works of Samuel Taylor Coleridge*, ed. B.E. Rooke (London: Routledge and Kegan Paul; Princeton: Princeton University Press, 1969), vol. 4, pt. 1, p. 519. I thank Cary Plotkin for this reference.
7 Aristotle, *Metaphysics*, IA, 981a25-30, in Barnes, ed. *Complete Works*, 2:1553.
8 Aristotle, *Poetics* 9 1452a1ff, trans. Ingram Bywater, ed. W.D. Ross (Oxford: Clarendon Press, 1924).
9 Halliwell, *Aristotle's Poetics* (London: Duckworth, 1986), 111–12.
10 *Muses of One Mind: The Literary Analysis of Experience and Its Continuity* (Princeton: Princeton University Press, 1983), 87–129, esp. 97–106 and 116–29.
11 *On the Soul*, I.1.402a, trans. Smith, in *The Complete Works*, ed. Barnes, 1:641, and *Parts of Animals*, I.5.644b, trans. Ogle, in *The Complete Works*, ed. Barnes, 1:1003–4. Wesley Trimpi also draws on the *Posterior Analytics* (1.2.71b–72a) and the *Metaphysics* (XI.7.9.1064b5–6). See his *Muses of One Mind*, 116–30.
12 Trimpi, *Muses of One Mind*, 131. See also James Biester, *Lyric Wonder: Rhetoric and Wit in English Renaissance Poetry* (Ithaca, NY: Cornell University Press, 1997), 42. For the implications of wonder and the obscure both to Renaissance Neoplatonism and to Renaissance art, emblem, and masque theory, see my *Reason Diminished: Shakespeare and the Marvelous* (Lincoln: University of Nebraska Press, 1997), 99–123.
13 *Rhetoric* 3.2, 1404b8–15, trans. Hubbard, in *Ancient Literary Criticism: The Principal Texts in New Translations*, ed. D.A. Russell and M. Winterbottom (1972; repr., Oxford: Oxford University Press, 1983), 137.
14 For accounts of wonder in, among others, Theophrastus, Hermogenes, Plotinus, Strabo, Polybius, and Plutarch, see J.V. Cunningham, *Tradition and Poetic Structure* (Denver Co: Alan Swallow, 1960), 194–6. In addition to Cunningham's, pioneering work on wonders, marvels, and monsters that has implications for the early modern period includes Rudolph Wittkower, 'Marvels of the East: A Study in the History of Monsters,' *Journal of Warburg and Courtauld Institutes* 5 (1942): 159–97; Jean Céard, *La nature et les prodiges: L'insolite au 16e siècle, en France* (Geneva: Librairie Droz, 1977); M.T. Jones-Davies, ed., *Monstres et prodiges au temps de la Renaissance* (Paris: Jean Touzot, 1980);

Katharine Park and Lorraine Daston, 'Unnatural Conceptions: The Study of Monsters in Sixteenth- and Seventeenth-Century England and France,' *Past and Present* 92 (1981): 20–54; and José Antonio Maravall, *The Culture of the Baroque: Analysis of a Structure*, trans. Terry Cochran (Minneapolis: University of Minnesota Press, 1986), esp. 207–47. Although not published in English until 1986, this book appeared in Spain in 1975 and represents reworkings of ideas Maravall had been exploring since the 1940s.

Recent studies that examine wonder's power in negotiating the boundaries of travel, literature, and knowledge include Terence Cave, *Recognitions: A Study in Poetics* (Oxford: Clarendon Press, 1988), esp. 57–63; Mary Campbell, *The Witness and the Other World: Exotic European Travel Writing, 400–1600* (Ithaca NY: Cornell University Press, 1988); Walter Stephens, *Giants in Those Days: Folklore, Ancient History, and Nationalism* (Lincoln: University of Nebraska Press, 1989); Lorraine Daston, 'Marvelous Facts and Miraculous Evidence in Early Modern Europe,' *Critical Inquiry* 18 (1991): 93–124; Stephen Greenblatt, *Marvelous Possessions* (Chicago: University of Chicago Press, 1991); Neil Kenny, *The Palace of Secrets: Béroalde de Verville and Renaissance Conceptions of Knowledge* (Oxford: Clarendon Press, 1991); Joy Kenseth, ed., *The Age of the Marvelous* (Hanover: Hood Museum of Art, Dartmouth College, 1991); James V. Mirollo, 'The Aesthetics of the Marvelous: The Wondrous Work of Art in a Wondrous World,' in Kenseth, *The Age of the Marvelous*, 61–80 and reprinted in Peter G. Platt, ed., *Wonders, Marvels, and Monsters in Early Modern Culture* (Newark: University of Delaware Press, 1999), 24–44; Paula Findlen, *Possessing Nature: Museums, Collecting, and Scientific Culture* (Berkeley and Los Angeles: University of California Press, 1994), esp. 17–150; Marie Hélène Huet, *Monstrous Imagination* (Cambridge: Harvard University Press, 1993), esp. 13–35; Thomas Bishop, *Shakespeare and the Theatre of Wonder* (Cambridge: Cambridge University Press, 1996); Jeffrey Jerome Cohen, ed., *Monster Theory: Reading Culture* (Minneapolis: University of Minnesota Press, 1996); Douglas Biow, *Mirabile Dictu: Representations of the Marvelous in Medieval and Renaissance Epic* (Ann Arbor: University of Michigan Press, 1996); Platt, *Reason Diminished*; Biester, *Lyric Wonder*; Caroline Walker Bynum, 'Wonder,' *American Historical Review* 102, no. 1 (1997): 1–26; Stuart Clark, *Thinking with Demons: The Idea of Witchcraft in Early Modern Europe* (Oxford: Oxford University Press, 1997); Katharine Park and Lorraine Daston, *Wonders and the Order of Nature, 1150–1750* (New York: Zone Books, 1998); Jeffrey Jerome Cohen, *Of Giants: Sex, Monsters, and the Middle Ages*; Mary Campbell, *Wonder and Science: Imagining Worlds in Early Modern Europe* (Ithaca, NY: Cornell University Press, 1999); Platt, ed., *Wonders, Marvels, and Monsters*; and Zakiya Hanafi, *The Monster in the Machine: Magic, Medicine, and the Marvelous in the Time of the Scientific Revolution* (Durham, NC: Duke University Press, 2000).

15 It is important to note, too, the etymological connection between wondering and beholding, between wonder and spectacle. The *Dictionariolum puerorvm* (London, 1552) defines *miror* as both 'to maruaile at' and 'to be astonied at any manner of thing.' For a fascinating linguistic analysis of sight and wonder that distinguishes types of astonishment in ancient Greek, see Raymond Adolph Prier, *Thauma Idesthai: The Phenomenology of Sight and Appearance in Archaic Greek* (Tallahassee: Florida State University Press, 1989), 68–117.

16 Augustine, *De utilitate credendi*, 16.34, trans. Cunningham, in *Tradition and Poetic Structure*, 204.

17 See Saint Thomas Aquinas, *Summa contra gentiles*, sec. 101, trans. English Dominican Fathers, 4 vols. (London: Burns, Oates & Washburn, 1928), vol. 3, pt. 2, pp. 60–1.

18 See *Summa contra gentiles*, secs. 99 and 103: vol. 3, pt. 2, pp. 57; 65–6. Following Aristotle in the *Metaphysics* and anticipating Aquinas in the *Summa* in associating wonder with a lack of knowledge about the cause behind the perceptible effect, Hugh of St Victor raised interesting issues about wonder and the artist: 'the infinite varieties of painting, weaving, carving, and founding have arisen, so that we look with wonder not at nature alone but at the artificer as well.' *The Didascalicon of Hugh of St. Victor: A Medieval Guide to the Arts*, 1.9, ed. and trans. Jerome Taylor (New York: Columbia University Press, 1968), 56. For the Latin, see *Didascalicon. De studio legendi: A Critical Text*, ed. C.H. Buttimer (Washington, DC: Catholic University of America Press, 1939), 17.

19 In the debate over Ariosto in the 1580s, Patrizi defends the poet of the marvellous against, among other writers, Tasso, Mazzoni, and Pellegrino. See Bernard Weinberg, *A History of Literary Criticism in the Italian Renaissance*, 2 vols. (Chicago: University of Chicago Press, 1961), 1:600–20 and 2:997–1000.

20 Baxter Hathaway, *Marvels and Commonplaces* (New York: Random House, 1968), 64.

21 The Longinian touchstones for Patrizi are – in addition to 1.4–15.2, 15.9, 35.5, and 36.3. All of Patrizi''s references to Longinus in the *Poetica* follow; the bracketed passages are from *La deca ammirabile*: I:44; II:64, [259, 263–5, 267, 268, 303, 304, 316, 324–6]; III:112, 258, 259, 293, 367, 387. For Longinus's influence on Patrizi, see Weinberg, 2: 784-5; Hathaway, *Marvels and Commonplaces*, 69; and both Aguzzi-Barbagli's introduction, *Della Poetica*, 2: viii, and his 'Humanism and Poetics,' in *Renaissance Humanism: Foundations, Forms, and Legacy*, ed. Albert Rabil, Jr (Philadelphia: University of Pennsylvania Press), 3:136.

22 Other sections in Longinus involving astonishment and wonder are 12.5, 15.11, and 35.4. For helpful commentary on Longinus, see *On the Sublime*, ed. D.A. Russell (1964; repr., Oxford: Clarendon Press, 1984). For an important more recent account of *On the Sublime*, see Paul Fry, *The Reach of Criticism* (New Haven, CT: Yale University Press, 1983), 47–86.

23 Patrizi, *La deca ammirabile*, in *Della Poetica*, ed. D. Aguzzi Barbagli, 3 vols. (Florence: Nella Sede Dell'istituto Palazzo Strozzi, 1969–71), 2: 284.

24 'dare ad una cosa forma diversa da quella che havea prima ed apparenza: ciò è una forma nuova, o rinnovata.' Patrizi, *La deca plastica*, in *Della Poetica*, 2:19; translated – from the MS – in Weinberg, *History of Literary Criticism*, 2:776. See also Puttenham, 'Of Ornament,' *The Arte of English Poesie*: 'arte is not only an aide and coadiutor to nature in all her actions but an alterer of them, and in some sort a surmounter of her skill, so as by meanes of it her owne effects shall appeare more beautifull or straunge and miraculous ...,' in *Elizabethan Critical Essays*, ed. G. Gregory Smith, 2 vols. (1904; repr., Oxford: Oxford University Press, 1937), 2:188.

25 '... che fa mestieri di cose incredibili se maraviglia ne dee nascere, perchè il credibile, non può operare maraviglia ... che la poesia habbia per oggetto lo incredibile, perchè questo è il vero fondamento del maraviglioso, che dee essere così principale oggetto d'ogni poesia, che qual poeta non vi mira, o non l'adopera, commette fallo grandissimo nell'arte sua, non meritevole di niuna escusazione.' Patrizi, *La deca ammirabile*, in *Della Poetica*, 2:307; translated – from the MS – in Weinberg, *History of Literary Criticism*, 2:774.

26 Patrizi, *La deca ammirabile*, VI, in *Della Poetica*, 2:305. See also Hathaway, *Marvels and Commonplaces*, 66.

27 See, for example, Philip Fisher's elegant and illuminating, if ultimately too prescriptive and constrictive, *Wonder, the Rainbow, and the Aesthetics of Rare Experiences* (Cambridge: Harvard University Press, 1998).

28 '... ella sarà una potenza mezzana tra quelle due [potenze conoscenti e potenza affettuosa], e il moto suo un terzo moto in mezzo a quelli per tutti loro, dal mezzo all'alto, e dal mezzo al basso discorrente.

   '... la ora detta potenza ammirativa nè conoscente sia, nè affettuosa, ma da ambedue separata e ad ambedue communicantesi; e che, posta di quelle in sul confino, sia atta a diffondere, e ad infondere, il moto suo tostamente allo'n sù nelle conoscenti, e allo in giù nelle affettuose ... la potenza ammirativa essere tra queste due potenze quasi uno Euripo, per lo quale la marea, dalla ragione agli affetti correndo e ricorrendo ...

   '... adunque nuova, e subita, e improvvisa, che ci si pari avanti, fa un movimento nell'anima, quasi contrario in sè medesimo, di credere e di non credere. Di credere, perchè la cosa si vede essere; e di non credere, perché ella è improvvisa, e nuova, e non più da noi stata nè conosciuta, nè pensata, nè creduta poter essere.' Patrizi, *La deca ammirabile* in *Della Poetica*, 2:361, 361–2, 365; my translation. See Weinberg, *History of Literary Criticism*, 2:774, for a paraphrase of this essential passage; he gives no reference to the location of the text in the manuscript.

29 This 'inbetweenness' evokes the figure of paradox, a figure named by Puttenham 'the Wondrer.' See 'Of Ornament,' in *Elizabethan Critical Essays*, ed. Smith, 2:170. For the complete passage, see *The Arte of English Poesie*, ed. Gladys Doidge Willcock and Alice Walker (Cambridge: Cambridge University Press, 1936), 225–6. Patrizi, too, noted the connection between wonder and paradox, translating part of Longinus, *On the Sublime*, 35.5, as '*mirabile è sempre il paradosso.*' See *La deca ammirabile*, in *Della Poetica*, 2:264. For Patrizi and doubleness, see Cesare Vasoli, 'Francesco Patrizi and the "Double Rhetoric,"' *New Literary History* 14 (1982–3): 539–51. The definitive study of Renaissance paradox remains Rosalie Colie's *Paradoxia Epidemica: The Renaissance Tradition of Paradox* (Princeton, NJ: Princeton University Press, 1966). See also the lucid discussion of wonder and paradox in Castiglione in Wayne A. Rebhorn, *Courtly Performances: Masking and Festivity in Castiglione's 'Book of the Courtier'* (Detroit: Wayne State University Press, 1978): 47–51, and my '"The Meruailouse Site": Shakespeare, Venice, and Paradoxical Stages,' *Renaissance Quarterly* 54, no. 1 (2001): 121–54.

30 Julius von Schlosser, *Die Kunst und Wunderkammern der Spätrenaissance* (Leipzig: Klinkhardt & Biermaun, 1908); Margaret T. Hodgen, *Early Anthropology in the Sixteenth and Seventeenth Centuries* (Philadelphia: University of Pennsylvania Press, 1964), 111–61; A. Regond-Bohat and A.J.M. Loechel, 'Les cabinets de curiosité au XVIe siècle,' in *La curiosité à la renaissance*, ed. Jean Céard (Paris: Société d' Édition d'Enseignement Supérieur, 1986), 65–70; and Oliver Impey and Arthur MacGregor, eds, *The Origins of Museums: The Cabinet of Curiosities in Sixteenth- and Seventeenth-Century Europe* (1985; repr., Oxford: Clarendon Press, 1986). See more recently Kenny, *The Palace of Secrets*, esp. 162–84; Kenseth, 'A World of Wonders in One Closet Shut,' in *Age of the Marvelous*, ed. Kenseth, 81–101; Adalgisa Lugli, 'Inquiry as Collection: The Athanasius Kircher Museum in Rome,' *Res* 12 (1986): 109–24; Lawrence Weschler, *Mr. Wilson's Cabinet of Wonder* (New York: Pantheon Books, 1995), esp. 75–97; and Barbara Maria Stafford and Frances Terpak, *Devices of Wonder: From the World in a Box to Images on a Screen* (Los Angeles: Getty Research Institute, 2001).

31 Lugli, 'Inquiry as Collection,' 123.

32 Leonard Barkan, *Unearthing the Past: Archaeology and Aesthetics in the Making of Renaissance Culture* (New Haven: Yale University Press, 1999); *passim*; quotation at xxv.

33 Thomas Platter, *Thomas Platter's Travels in England 1599*, trans. Clare Williams (London: Jonathan Cape, 1937), 171–3.
34 Ibid., 173.
35 Impey and MacGregor, *Origins of Museums*, 149.
36 E.K. Chambers, *The Elizabethan Stage*, 4 vols. (Oxford: Oxford University Press, 1923), 2:306, 389.
37 Andrew Gurr, *The Shakespearean Stage 1574–1642*, 2nd ed. (Cambridge: Cambridge University Press, 1980), 46.
38 Chambers, *Elizabethan Stage*, 4:139 and 1:220.
39 William Shakespeare, *All's Well That Ends Well*, 2.3.1–6. References to the texts of Shakespeare are taken from *The Riverside Shakespeare*, ed. G. Blakemore Evans (Boston: Houghton Mifflin, 1974), unless otherwise noted.
40 William Shakespeare, *As You Like It*, ed. Richard Knowles, New Variorum Edition of Shakespeare (New York: Modern Language Association of America, 1977), 295.
41 Michel Foucault, 'The Masked Philosopher,' in *Ethics: Subjectivity and Truth*, ed. Paul Rabinow (New York: New Press, 1997), 321–8.

chapter two

Philosophical Tours of the Universe in British Poetry, 1700–1729, Or, The Soaring Muse

LORNA CLYMER

> See, through this vast extended theatre
> Of skill divine, what shining marks appear!
> Creating power is all around exprest,
> The God discover'd, and his care confest.
> Nature's high birth her heavenly beauties show;
> By every feature we the parent know.
> Th' expanded sphere, amazing to the sight!
> Magnificent with stars and globes of light ...
>
> Richard Blackmore, *Creation; A Philosophical Poem*

A particular kind of verse, what I call the 'philosophical tour of the universe poem,' was exceedingly popular in England during the first half of the eighteenth century. The poems, by John Reynolds, Sir Richard Blackmore, David Mallet, Alexander Pope, Henry Baker, Elizabeth Tollet, Henry Brooke, and many others, are imaginative, expressive theodicies that appeared shortly after influential physico-theological prose tracts and treatises of the late seventeenth century, or concurrently with similar prose published after 1700. This essay investigates some of the concerns and characteristics of the philosophical tour poem in its first phase, roughly 1700–29, and interprets five related poems published during that time. After 1730, and especially after Pope's *Essay on Man* (1733–4), the philosophical tour poem develops into a distinct, second movement lasting several decades that will be the subject of another essay.

During the seventeenth century, as various 'rational' approaches to the mystery of God and his works were devised, the idea of natural revelation, supposedly available to all who observed the material world, became central to several related currents of thought. For some, natural revelation obviated scriptural revelation. For others, it was a question of emphasis.[1] Although regarding the natural world as the 'book of nature' was a concept already well established, in these decades we encounter a self-consciously 'physico-theological' movement that was defined by Samuel Johnson (in 1755) as 'divinity enforced or illustrated by natural philosophy.'[2] It began as a response to materialist explanations in natural philosophy and to the allegedly atheistic (or in any event provocatively unorthodox) trends in the philosophy of Hobbes and Spinoza, all of which seemed to pose serious challenges to religion. Its central tenet was teleological: the universe demonstrates an orderly design; this design could have been created only by an intelligent being; that being could only be God; therefore God exists, and He requires our gratitude. Perhaps needless to say, this 'argument' has not been immune to criticism and controversy. Its consistent appeal and utility throughout the eighteenth century for those committed to a theological foundation for their explanations of phenomena are nonetheless indisputable.[3]

Perhaps the earliest example is Walter Charleton's *The Darknes of Atheism Dispelled by the Light of Nature: A Physico-Theological Treatise* (1652). Others soon followed, most of which were reprinted many times, such as Thomas Burnet's influential cosmogony, *Telluris Theoria Sacra* (1681–9), translated into English as *Sacred Theory of the Earth* (1684–90), and John Ray's *The Wisdom of God Manifested in the Works of Creation* (1691). Systematic accounts of the world's order had appeared before the physico-theological movement was fully developed; for example, G. Hakewill's *An Apologie of the Power and Providence of God in the Government of the World* (1627), like Ray's, attempted systematically to account for the world's order according to providential design. Hakewill was wrestling with the problem of decay and its implications for sin, topics that Ray, in his latitudinarian and (perhaps as a result) more sanguine emphasis on the rightness of design, was equally concerned about. Other physico-theological writers similarly emphasized the beauty of design.[4]

We find a series of related, rational approaches to divinity and to the proper place of revealed religion – that is, as supported by natural religion – presented in the Boyle Lectures, delivered each year from 1691/2 to 1732 by leading ecclesiasts, according to the terms of Robert Boyle's will.[5] Each lecturer was to refute 'notorious Infidels' (a term that encompassed a variety of positions, depending on the lecturer), promote the Christian religion without descending into 'Controversies that are among Christians themselves,' and to assist and encourage the Christian religion.[6] Several lecturers found support for their divinity in a balance struck between natural and scriptural revelation, while others found it almost exclusively in natural philosophy. One lecturer, William Derham, presented and then published what became one of the most influential physico-theological treatises, *Physico-Theology: Or, A Demonstration of the Being and Attributes of God, from his Works of Creation* (1714). He immediately followed up the success of that work with *Astro-Theology* (1715), in which he applied the same methods to an exhaustive survey of astronomical phenomena. Derham's works were reprinted in many editions, and, if not original, were certainly esteemed as standard texts in this tradition.

While there are many significant differences among the various poetic examples of the philosophical tour, this kind of poem generally takes its goals from physico-theological writing in prose. Instead of a disquisition guided by an author, we generally find a first-person narrator – who may or may not present himself as a bardic figure – guiding the reader through a soaring, imaginative survey of the heavens and earth. The survey involves more than looking, however, because it is supplemented and informed by a discussion of scientific findings and, inevitably, religious purpose. There are three related goals for this tour: first, to demonstrate through a teleological argument the presence of the Creator as found in his creation, without recourse to scriptural revelation; second, to catalogue and discuss fairly new scientific information with some degree of accuracy; and third, to settle conflicts between what we would now identify as separate discourses of theology and physics.

Study of these poems can provide an index to early modern receptions of new scientific work, particularly in astronomy and atomism. More importantly, however, the poems demonstrate how 'natural philosophy' was profoundly entwined with theology, and how many varieties of natural religion – external to and within orthodox Christianity – there were at this time. Such assertions are not new. Many scholars have pointed out the evolving interrelations between science and theology in the early modern period. What tend to get overlooked in most studies, however, are possible distinctions among various works that combine science and theology. These oversights may result from an exaggerated identification of 'the' Enlightenment with an inexorable and inevitable secularization. As one philosopher recently argued, however, it would be a mistake to equate 'rationalism with the *critique* or *rejection* of religion.'[7]

For a number of reasons, in the last few decades it has become especially difficult to make productive distinctions between kinds of poetry, regardless of content, or even to read verse respectfully, without making it conform to critical standards established by the lyric or by current ideological concerns. Judicious readings of the interaction of theology and science in poetry have been particularly hard to come by. Consequently, varied and sometimes aesthetically successful poetic expressions of the physico-theological movement are typically reduced to a simple misleading category of 'scientific verse.' For many critics, poems in this category have seemed slightly ludicrous for their exhaustive (and exhausting to the modern reader) mimetic tendency and for their unapologetically didactic approach. But if we accept this dismissal, we may overlook how these poems offered to their contemporary readers much more than a rational disquisition in verse on physico-theological matters. In fact, the poems demonstrate how didactic verse was a legitimate form of public, discursive expression that offered meaningful intellectual and emotional possibilities for the reader. In these long, often expansive poems, the reader is invited to thrill to the sublimity of the universe, its vastness, its beautiful orderliness, all of which are wondrous, material proofs of God's presence.

As we will see, such expansiveness often involves an essential contraction: after imaginative, transported flights, the mortal viewer is reminded of (or even severely chastised for) his limited view from his circumscribed, assigned place in the universe.[8] By virtue of its insistence on a measured transport and a transcendence based in limitations, this early eighteenth-century 'religious sublime' is distinct from other instances of early modern sublimity, such as those defined by Edmund Burke later in the century. The poems do not usually suggest an unlimited, Longinian view, but rather assert that a pious response to views of space is mostly properly 'a sublime of limitation.' We can detect another sublime in philosophical tour of the universe poems that we should call physico-theological, a counterpart to the sublime of limitation. I will have more to say about these distinct instances of religious sublimity after an investigation of the poems themselves.

If we consider religion in the early eighteenth century, then we must consider Deism. 'Deist' tendencies in these works are hard to detect if we treat Deism as a monotheistic doctrine of a *deus absconditus*, an absent god who created and wound up his watch, the universe, and then left it to its own devices. This form of Deism was influential in Britain, but not until after the first few decades of the eighteenth century. During Deism's earlier phases of the mid-seventeenth through the early eighteenth century, however, perhaps motivated in part by a desire to preclude any further civil strife caused by doctrinal differences, a Deist would have stressed a universal creed that all men rationally – or even intuitively – believe, and that can be derived solely from observation of the natural world. The exact terms of that creed varied in the extent to which traditional Christian tenets were retained. In 1704, Samuel Clarke – another Boyle lecturer – purported to distinguish between four separate classes of Deists, only one of which corresponds to what has become our standard definition.[9] In fact, there was such variety that it became difficult to detect where Deism left off and Anglican rationalism, especially latitudinarianism, began. Although the more adamant Deists entirely rejected revelation, orthodox, rational apologists were united with Deists of all kinds in a view of revelation as less desirable or reliable than natural religion, that collection of rather vague conclusions that supposedly can be drawn from either intuition or basic observations of the world. What separated them is that '[b]elief in Divine Providence, as well as in rewards and punishments, was gradually abandoned' by Deists but remained central tenets of orthodox Christianity.[10] One class of Deism identified by Clarke is potentially quite close to the natural religion of the physico-theologians: a Divine Providence is granted, 'but only in the material, not in the moral or spiritual, order.'[11] As we will see, some authors expend their poetic energies in demonstrating the existence of God in the material world, and have little to say that is convincing about His presence in other realms. In any event, because many of the authors of philosophical tour of the universe poems 'prove' the existence of the Deity through an inventory of His Creation but without recourse to scriptural revelation, we may conclude that they were generally of the Deist party.

Regardless of the type, Deism and its affinities with natural religion and the physico-theological argument should interest us as related attempts to come to terms with a new materialism, brought on in part by developments in natural philosophy. Two important developments challenged long-standing convictions concerning God's providence: the seventeenth-century revival of atomism and the thrilling discoveries of Newton, that seemed to explain the workings of the world so definitively that God's ongoing intervention could seem distant or even superfluous. At the least, a rational Christianity grounded in a physico-theological tradition provided a buoyant means by which to assert the ways of God to man without denying the reality and excitement of an increasingly measured and often mechanized world. Some of the poems are obviously awkward in the ways they combine their philosophy with experimentation in literary forms. Such awkwardness indicates not only an unsettled state in literature, but also the poets' urgent desire to create effective literature that will allow their readers to re-envision the world.

Far from being a demonstration of the supposedly rigid rationalism of the Enlightenment, therefore, these poems create a 'space' for feeling by moving the reader imaginatively through the space of God's created universe. Mystery may have been partially lessened by scientific observation and discovery, but these poems called for a compensatory response of wonder at the world as a place of beauty and order. Responses of delight and contentment, which would culminate later in the eighteenth century as trends of religious sentimentalism, were encouraged by philosophical tours.

Death Beds and the Last Day

Two popular kinds of literature found in religious tracts and poetry were adapted to new literary and social purposes and provided tours of the universe before the 'philosophical' tour came into its own. The 'death bed vision' and scenes of the Day of Judgment both treat the world as a central concern, seek to promote a spiritual awareness and consequent detachment from worldly desires, and eschew scientific accuracy. Both kinds of poems sought to inspire awe – but typically of a terror-induced, fearful variety – in the reader in order to produce a change of perspective. Matters of the next world are asserted to be more substantial and more meaningful than those of the mortal world.

Spiritual exercise books, such as Jeremy Taylor's *The Rule and Exercise of Holy Dying* (1651), taught *ars bene moriendi*, that is, the art of dying well. Narrative is used to illustrate injunction. Typically, two scenes of death are opposed. In the first, an unbeliever is terrified by his approaching death. Torment may come in the form of vexing doubts about the afterlife; the moment of death is anguished and frantic. In the second, a believer serenely meets his end, attended by angels or saints. A quiet prayer and a barely audible, happy sigh usually close the life; the released soul is often depicted joyfully winging its way to join a heavenly host. These opposed scenes are intended to teach the reader to '*memento mori*,' to be mindful of death and to 'die' in anticipation of the actual death by means of a cultivated detachment from the world's delights.

This spiritual awareness has a social function: the individual has a responsibility to be prepared so that he can manage his death as a proof of his belief and an instruction to others. In addition, depending on the denomination of the writer, these exercise books may stress the importance of repentance throughout one's life because a last-minute declaration of sorrow for one's sins might not be acceptable to God. William Payne intended to remove the fears from 'some few' believers and the 'Presumptuous and false hopes of the far greater number of Sinners' (who are swayed by Catholic doctrines of final absolution) with *A Practical Discourse of Repentance ... and Demonstrating the Invalidity of a Death-Bed Repentance* (1708).[12]

Commonly in a death bed vision poem, the unbeliever and the believer each report their experiences. The joyous soul describes its wonder and relief at its newly liberated state, while reporting in vivid, present-tense verbs its tour through the skies populated by whirling planets, whizzing comets, and finally, heavenly hosts. There may or may not be a guide for the soul on its journey. If there is one, it is often a soul who already knows the ins and outs of spiritual existence. These poems do not teach detachment in the manner of a 'progress poem,' such as Johnson's *The Vanity of Human Wishes,* in which an array of purportedly admirable achievements is set out for the reader, only to reveal how every path of glory leads but to the grave. Instead, because there is no time to linger in the world to enumerate its falsehoods and snares, the released soul's view thoroughly reduces the world's status: the world is immediately small, and then is infinitesimal in the vast empyrean. Thus the view, both literal and metaphoric, is didactic: how can the reader take anything in the world seriously when the world itself is revealed in its proper perspective? And only death can give the soul its proper view. The reader, though not yet dead, is meant to cultivate the same perspective of detachment.

Didactic tours of the universe were also a common feature of 'last day' or 'four last things' poems, a significant kind of religious verse that dealt with the eschatological matters of death, judgment, heaven, and hell. This kind of poem was well established almost a century before the flourishing of the philosophical tour poem and remained vital throughout the first half of the eighteenth century.[13] Last day poems, more common than death bed vision poems, were written by many major and minor poets, including John Bulkeley, John Ogilvie, William Tans'ur, Joseph Trapp, Isaac Watts, and Edward Young. These poets often treated religious topics in an emotional, abrupt style indebted to the

Pindaric tradition, whether or not the poems were written in the form of an ode. The reader is asked to contemplate what will be the final, apocalyptic order of the universe, as established through its complete destruction. The narrator of these poems is usually a dazzled mortal who struggles to describe the sublimity occurring throughout the universe. Drama is suggested through standard scenes, or *topoi*: the noise of the world-sundering last trump stuns the ears of the witness; the heavens fill with stupendous choruses of angels; graves burst open, ejecting their dazed occupants skyward; body parts, such as hands or legs lost in battle and long separated from the body, shoot across the world to rejoin their resurrected whole.

> scatter'd limbs, and all
> The various bones, obsequious to the call,
> Self-mov'd advance; the neck perhaps to meet
> The distant head; the distant legs the feet.
> Dreadful to view, see through the dusky sky
> Fragments of bodies in confusion fly ...[14]

Such scenes can quickly topple over into the bathetic and often strike the modern reader as ludicrous examples of the 'exclamatory sublime,' in which seemingly excessive punctuation marks bear the burden of the unutterable, especially when God himself gives commands: 'Rend, all ye tombs; and, all ye dead arise! / ... / Earth, be dissolv'd, with all these worlds on high!'[15] Nevertheless, the poems are a good indication of how thrilling to an early modern audience religious topics were, especially those that sought to encompass the known universe and Christian tenets on its composition and destiny.[16] Although these poems may present information about how the universe works as explained by scientific inquiry (and the later the last day poem is published, the more likely it is to include detailed information drawn from astronomy or other disciplines), this information is undercut by the inevitable, terrifying destruction. Prolepsis is the primary strategy for the last day poem, whereby the reader is projected into the future to view imaginatively the inevitable conclusion to the world. Anticipation of this event is meant to change one's view of the world: it is inherently empty and headed for total destruction. As the speaker of Edward Young's *The Last Day* exults:

> In hopes of glory to be quite involv'd!
> To smile at Death! to long to be dissolv'd!

From our decays a pleasure to receive!
And kindle into transport at a grave!
What equals *this*? [17]

What, indeed.[18]

The last day poem remained an important source of religious sublimity for eighteenth-century readers. During the same period, however, a religious delight became as firmly established as the long-standing religious sublime of thrilling terror. Such delight could be found in the philosophical tour poem, which is rooted primarily in the present and cheerfully seeks to arouse the wonder we should feel when we contemplate Creation as it currently appears. By such contemplation, we are to know its Creator, not a wrathful, destructive, apocalyptic deity concerned with punishing our sinfulness, but rather, a serenely benevolent God who arranges everything to be orderly and pleasing. By omitting eschatological matters, the philosophical tour poem can promote and reward curiosity about the universe's intricate workings. The world is marvellous at this very moment; its appearance is not disagreeably illusory but has instead a pleasing aesthetic and scientific reality; and there is no need to imagine its fearsome destruction. Wonder is meant to replace awe. Consequently, the vanity of the world and last things – such as death beds, apocalyptic destruction, open graves, terrifying judgment, and fearsome hell – are disregarded. Such delight could be the outcome of an author's latitudinarianism or outright adherence to Deistic tenets. Historians and theologians have attributed the waning of apocalyptic terror and the waxing of a sentimental religious sensibility in Protestant Christianity to a variety of causes.[19] Philosophical tour of the universe poems both reflect and contribute to this change.

Death's Vision and *The Ecstacy. An Ode*

For its many poetic faults, including pedestrian rhythms and often poorly executed Pindaric sections in the manner of Cowley, John Reynolds's *Death's Vision Represented in a Philosophical, Sacred Poem* often justly deserves the rough handling it has received from commentators on early eighteenth-century poetry.[20] But, combining as it does traditions of the death bed vision and of *memento mori* with an emerging philosophical tour, this is a revealing poem for its multiple, sometimes competing, goals. *Death's Vision* is one of the earliest poems to use the adjective 'philosophical' in its title to indicate its topic and its range, while 'sacred,' of course, asserts the overt religious intent. In the early eighteenth century, 'philosophical' promises a systematic account of the world's order which will typically be supported by theology. Such an account may or may not recommend detachment from the world, regardless of its wondrous workings.

Death's Vision is more concerned with sin, decay, the actual process of death, and the release of the soul than will be the case with later poems of transport. First published in 1709, the poem had a robust publishing history, appearing in a number of variant issues and editions, through 1735.[21] Reynolds, a dissenting minister, launches his narrator by using the *topos* of the soul released by death. After first-person descriptions of the universe organized by stanzas, the soul views its decaying, discarded body, witnesses the body's funeral, and bids it adieu until resurrection will reunite them.

Despite Reynolds's reliance on the traditional 'vision' tour, he recognizes that his readers now seek something more 'rational.' As he explains in the preface: 'Tho' the Prospect, as in the State here suppos'd, may be Term'd *Death's Vision*, yet it need not thence be Concluded to be altogether Visionary; It being Rational enough to suppose, that Departed Spirits have a much Larger View of the World's Fabric and Aeconomy, than here, in Flesh, they cou'd attain to. Their Journey thro' the Aerial Regions (which way soever they Tend) one wou'd Think, must necessarily afford it them.'[22] This 'larger view' is strictly contingent upon the release of death, something that later philosophical tour of the universe poems will not require:

> Learn'd death! that in one hour informs me more
> > Than all my years on earth before;
> > Than all the academic aids could do;
> > Than chronics, books, and contemplations too!
> Death! that exalts me strait to high'st degree!
> Commenc'd a more than *Newton* in abstruse philosophie![23]

Reynolds says: 'Philosophy has sometime been call'd *meditatio mortis*, the contemplation and study of death. According to that account of it, it becomes us all to be philosophers. And death may well be studied, when it will open our eyes, and lead us into the regions of philosophy.'[24] These regions are suggested by the verse and described in the notes, which are often quite extensive. In the preface to the expanded 1725 edition, Reynolds declares that 'I was willing to have spared much of the notes that are here added; and to have trusted the reader's understanding; but I was told, // that I must assist the beginners in philosophy, and others also, in seeing some of the phaenomena, that are remarkable.'[25] His narrator often enthusiastically exclaims over the workings of the universe or asks questions that are partially answered in the notes. Both verse and notes are intended to provide the reader with a vivid, immediate feel for the phenomena described.

For example, on the subject of gravitation, which many interpreters of Newton linked to the long-standing idea of universal harmony and attraction, the narrator discovers 'the Mysterious Love ... / That Binds and Acts the Vast Corporeal Whole, / That Plays the Universal Soul.'[26] Several notes pertain to this extensive section on universal attraction, which is lengthier than can be traced in detail here. The authors referenced or quoted in the notes are – in this order – 'the Philosopher, that said the Soul was Harmony,' Acts, Samuel Parker (who made Newton's work more accessible to the lay reader), Lucretius, Abraham Cowley, Isaac Newton, and John Keill (another explicator of Newton).[27] Reynolds asserts that Cartesians and others are entirely mistaken because the 'Law of Gravitation (or Attraction, as others call it) seems a signal instance of Divine Wisdom and Power, and a Reproof to the moral World, that is not better acquainted with moral Gravitation, or Love.'[28] Elsewhere, Reynolds relies on philosophers and scientists such as Burnet, Descartes, Locke, Ray, Huygens, and on the Cambridge Platonists, such as More, whose extensive poem *A Platonick Song of the Soul* (1647) influenced Reynolds's choice of images. This range of sources, many of which we would now sort into separate disciplines, is typical of Reynolds' approach to his subject. *Death's Vision* demonstrates the interrelationship of religion and science found in natural religion and how moral implications were drawn from science.

On the one hand, Reynolds's religious views are not as cheerful as subsequent tours will be. For Reynolds, the world is alluring, making us loathe to leave, although fulfilment and knowledge await in the next world. Such is the traditional *vanitas* motif that suggests that correct perspective – found in a literal and metaphoric distance – can be achieved only after death or after its contemplation. On the other hand, pleasure in the contemplation of Creation will now have delightful, positive results: "Tis meet the Creator's works should be better known (especially by those that have pleasure therein) than they can be here. The deepest philosophers are much in the dark. The prospect will be delightful to the spectator (to the religious ones, at least;) will commend the perfections, the dominion, and grandeur of the architect and owner; and contribute much of the great ends of future retribution.'[29]

Notwithstanding the ready accessibility of Creation and its lessons, mortals are in need of correction for their lack of otherworldliness. In his preface, Reynolds criticizes the 'all-a-mode' satire that fails to reform.[30] His newly informed narrator wishes that he could interrupt the 'noise and hurry of each rav'nous town' by his preaching 'Th' eternal *news*' gained from his celestial vantage point. After momentarily imagining that his words could halt 'Dear gain and mirth,' he realizes that this thought is 'fond,' that is, silly, because

> ... this complicated throng
> Of works and laws divine,
> In which immense perfections shine,
> More loudly tells the news without a tongue![31]

The best source for the needed corrections, therefore, is the Book of Nature. It speaks most effectively, conveying directly to the viewer a revelation of God's presence, without need for scriptural revelation or a fulminating visionary. The narrator's indignation over the human world is therefore barely registered. Even this minimal level of indignation will be absent from most other philosophical tour of the universe poems, in which the didactic style will be more concerned with pointing and arguing with imaginary opponents and less with hectoring the reader. The omission of death will, of course, go a long way to lightening the view.

It is worth pausing briefly to consider a short poem that, in eleven economical stanzas uses many of the traditional elements I have described. John Hughes's *The Ecstacy. An Ode* (1720) is a deft, if formulaic, poem. He launches his first-person narrator with little ado and without a death. Apparently as the result of contemplation only, the narrator begins: 'I leave Mortality's low sphere.'[32] The narrator remains a living person, mysteriously allowed a soaring tour through 'a wide space of air,' who at first marvels at the earthly sites below him. But his distance brings the requisite detachment and provokes a standard meditation on the inevitability of ruin and the impossibility of happiness in the mortal world: 'Around the space of Earth I turn my eye; / But where's the region free from woe?'[33] The narrator then happily turns upward, going 'to realms with ever-living light,' and views the planets and the stars, which are only briefly described. In the penultimate stanza, switching to a more exclamatory style, the narrator encounters a 'pointed flame,' shooting upwards from the earth: it is Newton's soul, 'The great Columbus of the skies.'[34] The narrator implores the 'happy spirit' to 'stay, / And lead me on thro' all th' unbeaten wilds of day.' If Newton were his companion, the narrator would see more accurately, and would, among other things, 'trace each comet's wandering way,' measure the light's 'descending speed,' or 'learn how sun-born colours rise.' He would not return to earthly things, but would remain exploring wonders and 'Still the great Maker's power adore.'[35] But he is not yet 'adopted into light' as Newton is in two ways (because Newton was the explicator of light and because he is now dead). The poem closes with the narrator's hopeful longing that he will be incorporated into the heavenly fulfilment that only resurrection will bring.[36] In the advertisement to the poem, Hughes declares that he modelled his ode on Abraham Cowley's *Ecstasy*. But he claims also to have done something new, by which he has improved the 'Plan' of the poem as taken from his predecessors: 'the latter Part, which attempts a short View of the Heavens, according to the Modern Philosophy, is entirely Original, and not founded on any Thing in the Latin Author.'[37] Hughes's poem demonstrates how even an abbreviated tour – lacking the level of exhaustive detail of other similar but much longer poems – and a cameo appearance by Newton would be perceived as improving upon standard poetic elements and would cater to early eighteenth-century tastes for the modern philosophy, and for Newton's work in particular, that were just being addressed in verse.[38] The didacticism of *The Ecstasy* is the mild sort that we often find in religious lyrics: the reader is simply taken on the tour and implicitly encouraged to derive the right lessons from it.

Creation

Extensive philosophical tour of the universe poems, however, employ outright argumentation and exegesis, often to an extent that leaves the modern reader incredulous. Richard Blackmore shared Reynolds's view of 'all-a-mode' satire as ineffective and offensive. Both writers were uneasy about the necessity and difficulties of writing persuasive and popular religious verse. Blackmore was disgusted by late seventeenth-century wit in poetry and drama because he found it irreligious, immoral, pernicious, and willfully failing to provide proper models for pious, virtuous behaviour. He has no intent of balancing the traditional, Horatian goals of literature: instruction must take complete precedence over delight. As Blackmore states in the preface to his first major poem, the epic *Prince Arthur* (1695): 'To give Men right and just Conceptions of Religion and Virtue, to aid their Reason in restraining their Exorbitant Appetites and Impetuous Passions, and to bring their Lives under the Rules and Guidance of true Wisdom, and thereby to promote the publick Good of Mankind, is undoubtedly the End of all Poetry.' He acknowledges that one 'End of Poetry is to give Men Pleasure and Delight; but this is a subordinate, subaltern End, which is it self a Means to the greater, and ultimate one before mention'd.'[39] To Blackmore, the epic form initially seemed most suited to these goals. To his credit, he kept producing them, despite incurring the scorn of those in witty circles, and while maintaining his practice as a physician. *King Arthur* appeared in 1697 and *Eliza* in 1705.[40] He attempted some philosophical topics in *The Nature of Man* (1711), but he was still too concerned with attacking wit to make the poem successful as a treatise.[41] Blackmore may have thought he had found a solution to the problem of effective Christian verse when he wrote *Creation; A Philosophical Poem. Demonstrating the Existence and Providence of a God. In Seven Books* (1712). Because this poem is often only briefly cited in current criticism (especially in reference to Pope's gibes), and is rarely discussed in detail despite its importance for eighteenth-century verse, it will be worthwhile to consider it carefully.

Instead of presenting noble characters in epic conflict, or directly criticizing the immoral style of his age, Blackmore wrote an overtly philosophical poem. He intends, as he declares in his preface, to demonstrate 'the self-existence of an Eternal Mind from the created and dependent existence of the universe.'[42] In addition, he will trace the primary source of immorality, and 'confute the hypothesis of the Epicureans and the Fatalists, under whom all the patrons of impiety, ancient or modern, of whatsoever denomination, may be ranged.'[43] Blackmore gathers just about every position he objects to, including Deism, under the heading of 'Epicureanism,' which may at first seem like poor thinking. While acknowledging that the poet blurs his adversaries' positions, Hoxie Neal Fairchild speculated that because Blackmore was born around 1650, he would have interpreted 'the deism of 1712 in relation to the Epicureanism of Restoration times.' Furthermore, in the early eighteenth century, Deism could be used 'as a means of rationalizing a libertine viewpoint which in the seventeenth century would probably have been expressed in Epicurean ... terms.'[44]

Blackmore is not reluctant to admit that he has taken his ideas from prose and that the poem's argument is not meant to be original.

Because the existence of God had already been 'abundantly demonstrated, by many pious and learned authors,' the appearance of his poem might be deemed 'impertinent and unnecessary.' But given that those texts were in prose, and most of them 'in the learned languages, or at least in a scholastic manner,' they are 'ill-accommodated to great numbers not of a learned education' who will not bother to read them, finding such writing 'obscure, dry, and disagreeable.' Blackmore, therefore, taking a traditional view of the powers of poetry, has 'formed a poem on this great and important subject, that I might give it the advantages peculiar to poetry, and adapt it more to the general apprehension and capacity of mankind.'[45] In fact, he set out to challenge Lucretius, recognizing the enduring efficacy of *De Rerum Natura*: 'I persuade myself that the Epicurean philosophy had not lived so long, nor been so much esteemed, had it not been kept alive and propagated by the famous poem of Lucretius.'[46] Blackmore, therefore, believed that he countered one major source of his contemporaries' impiety in the very form in which it had been preserved. He meant *Creation* to be a Christian *On the Nature of Things*.[47]

For these reasons, the poem is unapologetic in its didacticism, but this alone did not make Blackmore one of Pope's vilified dunces. Pope and others thought that Blackmore deserved criticism for his epics, all of which sorely tried the patience of those who wanted any imitations of Milton and Classical writers more cleverly managed, and couplets more competently written than Blackmore was capable of. He was an obvious target for Pope's derision in *Peri Bathous, Or, Martinus Scriblerus His Treatise of the Art of Sinking in* Poetry (1727/8), that brilliant send-up of allegedly all too earnest and clumsy writing. Despite attacks by wits, provoked no doubt in part by Blackmore's contentious prefaces concerning the high-mindedness he wanted in poetry, the two *Arthurs* were extremely – albeit briefly – popular.[48] *Eliza* did not do well.[49] But the lasting status of *Creation* is another matter. John Dennis, who had attacked Blackmore's earlier efforts, admired it.[50] In the *Spectator* essay of 29 March 1712, Joseph Addison praised it as 'one of the most useful and noble Productions in our *English* verse.'[51] Several decades after its publication, Johnson insisted it be included in the series of English poets for which he wrote the *Lives*.[52] In fact, *Creation* is remarkably successful in its stated goals, and it is one of the great physico-theological texts of the early eighteenth century.

The modern reader will frequently wish that Blackmore had edited his poem to eliminate apparent redundancies. In some ways, however, its prolixity is exactly the point. If one is going to present 'the proof of a Deity, from the instances of design and choice, which occur in the structure and qualities of the earth and sea,' as his summary for Book I declares, then one cannot be anything but comprehensive. Furthermore, in a physico-theological text, more evidence is always better than less because we are meant to observe, closely and systematically, the many proofs that God is the creator and organizer of the universe. Blackmore knew exactly how his poem would fit in with prose texts in the same tradition. For example, in *The Wisdom of God Manifested in the Works of the Creation,* John Ray found his evidence in the following, as his title declares: '*The Heavenly Bodies, Elements, Meteors, Fossils, Vegetables, Animals (Beasts, Birds, Fishes, and Insects),*' as well '*the Body of the Earth,*' and '*the Bodies of Man, and other Animals, as also in their Generation, &c.*' We find field of inquiry piled upon field of inquiry, with seemingly endless iterations of the same teleological argument concerning design. In the enumeration of the vast but intricate workings of the universe, the soaring muse must notice this proof, and then move on to this other proof, and then to this next one. In the apparently obsessive volume of observation, we can understand that the methods of a relatively new scientific inquiry are brought to bear on St Paul's observation: 'For the invisible things of him from the creation of the world are clearly seen, being understood by the things that are made, even his eternal power and Godhead' (Romans 1:20). Addison understood *Creation*'s scope as productive. 'The Author has shown us that Design in all the Works of Nature, which necessarily lead us to the Knowledge of its first Cause. In short, he has illustrated, by numberless and incontestable Instances, that Divine Wisdom ...'[53]

Perhaps such 'numberless and incontestable Instances' are especially important if the concept of innate ideas is discarded. Blackmore declares that he wishes to refute those who believe we have 'an innate idea of a Divine Being,' and by this he loosely means a Deist position. He says he takes his lead from St Paul (and implicitly, from Locke), who finds no 'characters of the Divine Being originally engraven on the heart, but deduces the cause from the effect, and from the creation infers the Creator.'[54]

The first two books of *Creation* are traditional teleological arguments from the nature of the earth, sea, and astronomical heavens interspersed with extensive responses to possible objections. The reader's progress is varied by description, dialogue, and disquisition. A first-person speaker, at first modelled on that of *Paradise Lost,* declares that he will leave behind trivial subjects such as 'courts' or 'arms.' Instead, he 'would th' Eternal from his works assert, / And sing the wonders of creating Art.'[55] He invokes the Holy Spirit for assistance, 'That I may reach th' Almighty's sacred throne, / And make his causeless power, the cause of all things, known.'[56] It was the Holy Spirit that gave the universe its being: 'Order from thee, from thee distinction came, / And all the beauties of the wondrous frame.' Nature has not lost this order: 'Hence stampt on Nature we perfection find, / Fair as th' idea in the Eternal Mind.' Throughout his survey, the narrator uses deictics – words indicating literal pointing, such as 'See' or 'Behold' – to direct the reader in vivid, present tense to the wonders viewed. We come now to the passage that opened this essay as our epigraph. We are to 'See ... the shining marks' which remain 'amazing to the sight' because of their complex yet orderly nature.[57] Such phenomena must have an organizing principle:

> And here behold the cause, which God we name,
> The source of beings, and the mind supreme;
> Whose perfect wisdom, and whose prudent care,
> With one confederate voice unnumber'd worlds declare.[58]

Unnumbered worlds may be convinced, but not all mortals are, which necessitates much haranguing by the speaker. In between observations of natural phenomena, the narrator argues against various positions opposed to an argument by design, but especially those attributed to the atomists, 'Cartesians,' and, in subsequent books, the 'Fatalists.' The narrator addresses persons who supposedly hold these positions in short questions or statements: 'You, who the Mind and Cause Supreme deny, / Nor on his aid to form the world rely, / Must grant' the ideas the narrator has just set out. These wrong-minded people are not personified or given allegorical-style names, as is the case in other philosophical or theological texts, such as William Law's *A Serious Call to a Devout and Holy Life* (1728). Instead, we always know who they are by their obvious generic identification, such as 'the Lucretian,' or 'the whole mechanic tribe.'[59] They may be allowed lengthy passages of direct discourse, in which they present their views, only to be refuted by the narrator, often point by point. Exploring the theories of 'stupid atoms,' the narrator argues with his similarly dull adversaries: 'But let us then, ye sages, next inquire, / What cause of their cohesion can you find? What props support, what chains the fabric bind?'[60] But he eventually dismisses their views, as we know he must: 'What can insult unequal reason more, / Than this magnetic, this mysterious power' upon which the atomists rely for their first cause.[61] They are, of course, impotent adversaries: 'But hold! perhaps I rudely press too far; / You are not vers'd in reasoning so severe.'[62]

One of the most offensive results of the atomists' position is that the world must be understood as filled with stupid matter, which sorts itself out only by chance. Beauty would thereby be eliminated. 'Now view the Earth in finish'd beauty drest' urges the narrator as he issues a series of imperatives to 'observe,' 'see,' and 'Proceed yet farther, and a prospect take / Of the swift stream, and of the standing lake.'[63] To emphasize the existing beauty and order, the narrator often questions what would be the 'fatal consequences' if there were a less competent order.[64] If, for example, the sun had been placed further out in the heavens, 'How sad, how wild, how exquisite a scene of desolation, had this planet been!'[65] Such scenes rely on an apocalyptic imagination without the irrevocable upheaval of the Last Day. We can imagine the world's destruction as played out in separate spheres (e.g., the sun is placed differently and the world freezes; planets collide because their orbits are not correct; seas stagnate and marine life dies because there is no movement of the tides). This is, however, an entirely imaginary destruction because once it is asserted, it is replaced by a thrilling recognition of just how beautifully ordered the world's elements remain.

Once this world's perfection is established, however, the narrator suggests we take a larger view to see that ours is 'But one of thousands, which compose the whole, / Perhaps as glorious, and of worlds as full.'[66] This is a common strategy in the argument by design: what is one part, contiguous with many others in an ordered system, is first explored as if it were an independent phenomenon. Then, the perspective shifts to reveal a much larger and overwhelming whole, which is itself interpreted as designed properly. 'If we, with one clear comprehensive sight, / Saw all these systems, all these orbs of light,' we would be entirely convinced: 'Would not this view convincing marks impart / Of perfect prudence, and stupendous art?'[67] In an attempt to be comprehensive, no world is lowly or without wonder. We can 'farther yet pursue[,] / The wondrous world of vegetables view!'[68] We have, therefore, worlds within worlds, all indicating the same thing.

In the third, fourth, and fifth books, Blackmore continues his refutation of those who deny the existence and providence of God, including (allegedly) Hobbes and Spinoza. For one stage of his refutation, he returns in the third book to the question of appropriately arranged parts comprising a whole. But this time, the part is envisioned as part of a hierarchically arranged whole, consistent with the traditional concept of the great chain of being, upon which Pope will rely in *Essay on Man*. Our 'globe terrestrial' is of the whole a part, a 'mean one too,'

> Though 'tis not like th' ethereal worlds refin'd,
> Yet is it just, and finish'd in its kind;
> Has all perfection which the place demands,
> Where in coherence with the rest it stands.[69]

If we could see the entire universe at once, we would 'grant our globe had all the marks of art, / All the perfection due to such a part.'[70] 'It is a finish'd world, and perfect in its kind.'[71] But of course, we cannot see the entire universe at once, and can only conceptualize it or imagine it.

There are in *Creation*, then, two visual approaches to the nature of parts, horizontal and vertical. First, a part is understood as self-contained and admirably designed, and is best surveyed in a visual sweep that moves horizontally across vast distances and many instances. Second, a part is understood as contiguous with other, related parts that have been arranged vertically in a systematic distribution, according to the relative level of perfection of each. Both approaches existed long before the physico-theological movement of the early modern period. But it seems that an oscillation between these two views was especially appealing to early eighteenth-century readers, and is one reason that the philosophical universe tour was popular at a time when developments in new science were disturbing established ideas of the meaning of space. Alexander Koyré suggested that because of the so-called Newtonian revolution that established the principles of physics throughout both celestial and terrestrial worlds, the division between the two was no longer strong. The universe seemed to become 'open, indefinite, and even infinite ... united not by its immanent structure but only by the identity of its fundamental concepts and laws; a universe in which, in contradistinction to the traditional conceptions with its separation and opposition of the two worlds of becoming and being, that is, of the heavens and the earth, all its components appear as placed on the same ontological level.'[72] As a result, there is the prospect of a 'disappearance – or the violent expulsion – from scientific thought of all considerations based on value, perfection, harmony, meaning, and aim, because these concepts, from now on *merely subjective*, cannot have a place in the new ontology.'[73] This is not to suggest that early eighteenth-century readers necessarily pined for the 'old' vertical view, or that they excitedly (or reluctantly) embraced any novelty in a 'new' horizontal view. Furthermore, not everyone (certainly not Newton himself) saw Newtonian ideas as necessarily overturning established religious tenets, and some, such as Samuel Clarke, devised metaphysical systems to support religion with Newtonianism.[74] But for a few decades, these readers enjoyed a particular verse form that could present both views simultaneously, or, as in *Creation*, *seriatim*. The insistence on hierarchical relationships immediately following a sweeping tour that we find in many philosophical tour poems becomes intelligible, however, with these ideas in mind, and need not be dismissed as an author losing control of his subject. In addition, it is certain that the poets' emphasis on the beauty of the universe, a result of God's perfect providence, is one answer to an altered view of the universe's character and to an aesthetic threat posed by developments in science and philosophy, such as atomism, that Blackmore responded to with such vehemence.

With this stress on beauty and order, some explanation has to be found for the fact of death. Blackmore presents a traditional account: it is part of our mortal nature and should be understood as a release, allowing us simply to 'change our seat,' and to be admitted into 'Fair scenes of bliss, and triumphs in the skies.'[75] The event is to be accepted in a Stoic, matter-of-fact way. Remarkably, there is no discussion of sin as the cause of all our woe, of Christ's intervention, or of the Resurrection. Treatment of such topics is drastically curtailed, compared to earlier poems, such as that of Reynolds.

The sixth book is a precise exploration of 'the existence of God demonstrated from the prudence and art discovered in the several parts of the body of man.' As a physician, Blackmore knew of what he wrote. Clearly, he had been at the anatomy table or had read the books of those who had, and this book shows that he understood that medicine could not rely on untested hypotheses.[76] Certainly, the human body had been represented for centuries as a microcosm, indicative of God's astonishing designs in the universe at large. As is the case in other fields in which scientific advances provided more evidence for the teleological argument, we find that the rapidly accumulating knowledge about anatomy and medicine provided greater precision in prose or poetic considerations of God's providence. For example, John Ray devoted a substantial portion of *The Wisdom of God* to anatomical structure, both in man and in other animals. In 1692 the first Boyle lecturer, Richard Bentley, gave three of his lectures on the topic of 'A Confutation of Atheism from the Structure and Origin of Human Bodies.' Blackmore argues that our true origin could not possibly be found in some 'spontaneous production of the Earth,' as he reports Epicureans hold.[77] Our physical nature, with each part performing its appointed tasks, is so complex that only the Eternal Mind could have created us.

Some of the more explicit passages of this sixth book seem guilty of enervated epic simile, antiquated poetic diction, and inappropriate personification. For example, in describing the blood's circulation, the narrator observes that it 'Calls in the scatter'd streams, and recollects the flood' back to 'the vein, we cava name,' and then illustrates the action in a simile:

> As when the Thames advances through the plain,
> With his fresh waters to dilute the main;
> He turns and winds amidst the flowery meads,
> And now contracts, and now his waters spreads;
> . . . . .
> So the red currents, in their secret maze,
> In various rounds through dark meanders pass,
> Till all, assembled in the cava vein,
> Bring to the heart's right side their crimson train ...[78]

And the passages on digestion do not bear quotation, however brief. We do miss the point of such verse, however, if we disparage it as a feeble attempt to versify what is better left in prose. Blackmore is out to observe everything in the universe before him, no matter how external and large (celestial movements), or internal and small (intestinal movements). Everything is glorious in its successful function. There is supposedly only one conclusion: 'Who can this field of miracles survey, / And not with Galen all in rapture say, "Behold a God, adore him, and obey!"'

In the seventh and last book, Blackmore contemplates 'the instincts in brute animals, and the faculties and operations of the soul of man.'[79] He explores the nature of thought, sense impressions, human intelligence, emotions, the conscience, and the sources of our morality. He reiterates the Lockean tenet of the poem, that we have no innate ideas of God or of any other subject. 'When man with reason dignify'd is born, / No images his naked mind adorn.'[80] We can, however, use our 'abstracting faculty, the Mind,' and give birth to 'notions universal.'[81]

After a 'recapitulation of what has been treated of' in all the previous books, and one last taunt at the now supposedly 'vanquish'd Atheists,' the poem has a two-part conclusion: a short Last Day scene and an enraptured 'hymn to the Creator of the World.' Predictably, it is the unbeliever who will 'feel immortal vengeance roll / Through all his veins, and drench his inmost soul' for having persevered in his atheism, despite the volume of evidence of God's design which includes, of course, the poem. The correct response is homage and praise. Everything is either described as already praising the Creator, or is urged to do so:

> Ye fish, assume a voice; with praises fill
> The hollow rock, and loud reactive hill.
> Let lions with their roar their thanks express,
> With acclamations shake the wilderness.[82]

Thunder resounds; waves 'Strike with applause the repercussive caves'; and so forth.[83] In the final lines, the epic-style narrator returns. He declares that 'Grateful to Heaven, I'll stretch a pious wing, / And sing his praise, who gave me power to sing.' Thus, the tour ends with the sound of the narrator's voice, raised in harmony with the rest of exulting, grateful Creation.

Ultimately, the physico-theological strategy of arguing from effect to cause is less than wholly convincing. As is typical for this kind of work, both of Derham's treatises conclude with lists of 'practical inferences from the foregoing survey' that remind us of our understanding of and duty to God, but these are not rigorously demonstrated by what has come before. Similarly, despite Blackmore's energetic efforts, his poem 'presents only a religion of natural reason.' He 'does not advance far beyond the deism which he execrates.'[84] *Creation* is perhaps the last verse appearance of the traditional, extensive physico-theological argument as established by Ray and others; Derham's two immensely popular treatises would immediately follow Blackmore's poem without significantly changing the tradition.

Philosophical Tours of the 1720s

Although poets continued to use the argument by design, by and large they eschewed an exhaustive coverage of Creation. For example, in *An Essay on the Universe* (1725), Bezaleel Morrice is concerned with harmony created by 'Nature's universal Laws,' but is less inclined to enumerate them in detail as Blackmore would have done.[85] Richard Collins's *Nature Displayed* (1727) is long, bursting with observations on 'scientific curiosities,' but is largely lacking in religion, natural or otherwise.[86] John Hughes's *The Ecstacy. An Ode*, considered earlier in this essay, is illustrative of an even shorter, more selective approach. In 1720, Aaron Hill remarked in the preface to his ode *The Creation* (a paraphrase of the creation scenes from *Genesis*, not an enumeration of the workings of the universe) that for 'so masterless a Subject, as the *Creation*, of all others the most copious, and illustrious only,' it ought to be 'touch'd with most Discretion, and Choice of Circumstance' that only the Pindaric ode can supply. He places Blackmore in good company with other religious writers such as Milton and Cowley, but he finds fault with the exhaustive nature of Blackmore's poem: 'he is too minute, and particular, and rather labours to oppress us with every Image he cou'd raise, than to refresh and enliven us, with the noblest, and most differing.'[87] Blackmore may have thought that every image was necessary in order to describe the vast Creation and to counter his opponents' misunderstandings. Hill's comments anticipate those of Johnson's Imlac in *Rasselas* (1759): 'The business of a poet ... is to examine, not the individual, but the species ... he does not number the streaks of the tulip.'[88]

One poem of the late 1720s demonstrates how the philosophical tour remained important, even though it faltered as a vital poetic form until the 1730s. Experimenting to find new modes of expression, poets often combined the philosophical tour poem's elements with other kinds of poetry. David Mallet's *The Excursion. A Poem. In Two Cantos* (1728) is not successful because there are too many poetic goals in the space of one poem. Awkward verse, however, can help our understanding of the evolution of poetic kinds. An unsuccessful poem may reveal a conjunction of styles and goals that in other, more competent poems would have been merged seamlessly.

Mallet's *The Excursion* combines a physico-theological survey – albeit in a much reduced scope – with soothing descriptions of the landscape, the comforting, repetitive diurnal cycle, and stirring, sublime, natural disasters.[89] Johnson thought that the poem was a 'desultory and capricious view of such scenes of nature as his fancy led him, or his knowledge enabled him, to describe,' even though it was not 'devoid of poetic spirit.'[90] The poem suffers from too many views and viewpoints, too many types of excursiveness, and too many literal spaces in conflict with metaphoric or allegorical spaces.

For example, the narrator asks 'Imagination' to 'come invok'd, / to waft' him 'O'er EARTH's extended space: and thence, on high, / Spread to superior WORLDS thy bolder flight, / Excursive, unconfin'd.'[91] At times, the narrator is present as a meditative, withdrawn figure, quietly wandering alone at break of day. At other times, the reader's view is directed by vivid deictics that do not require the narrator: 'And see, exhaling from th'atlantic surge, / Wild world of waters, distant clouds ascend / In vapoury confluence ...'[92] Then again, personifications may do the viewing: 'IMAGINATION travels with quick eye / Unbounded o'er the globe, and wondering views / Her rowling seas and intermingled isles.'[93] After scenes of destruction caused by earthquake or volcanic eruption, the narrator jauntily closes the first canto: 'Thus roaming with adventurous wing the globe, / From scene to scene *excursive*,' he sees 'Fair *Nature*,' and 'in all wonder trace / The sovereign MAKER.'[94] This is a Creator who is both 'first, supreme, and best,' as we have found before in the physico-theological tradition, and a vengeful and reproving deity, rousing natural disasters to 'scourge the nations.'[95] This is a universe in need of correction and punishment. But in the second canto, which, according to the argument, 'contains ... a survey of the *solar system*, and of the *fixed stars*,' we have returned to an argument by design, but only for the astronomical world.[96] The earth is viewed as the 'mutable region, vext with hourly change,' while the sun shines in a 'noon without night.'[97]

The poem has several closing sections, any of which could have been the final one. As the poem is about to end with a hymn to the Creator, which would be a traditional and appropriate ending, we shift to an apostrophe to 'great Newton!' who first explained 'this spring of motion, this hid pow'r infus'd / Thro universal nature.'[98] Predictably, he is spotted as a '*pure Intelligence*,' winging his way 'Thro wondrous scenes,' now released by death and '*His* mind's clear vision from all darkness purg'd.'[99] The poem returns to the innumerable and unknown phenomena of the heavens, and wonders who could possibly name them all, much less explain them. (Blackmore's narrator was not worried by that concern and plowed ahead through his enumerations.) Only the 'First, Independent CAUSE' could devise and preserve the vast system. By contrast, all of human accomplishments are overturned by time. Now the narrator soars higher into the heavens and trembling, discovers that astronomical bodies, such as the sun, themselves can expire. Other amazing views are described. Finally, we manage to end on a view of everything ascending to 'that FIRST CAUSE,' who

Endures, and fills th'immensity of space;
That infinite Diffusion, where the mind
Conceives no limits; undistinguis'd void,
Invariable, where no land-marks are,
No paths to guide imagination's flight.[100]

It is unsettling to end on a sight of the void that prevents accurate viewing and navigation.[101] This is an obvious departure from standard philosophical tour poems that assert order and beauty. In addition, Mallet's poem suffers because in his imaginative flight he followed too many established routes in too small a space. By contrast, Blackmore's *Creation* seems positively economical: perhaps we needed the extensive enumeration after all. In the coming decades, Thomson would vary his perspectives to a sometimes astonishing degree, but *The Seasons* (1726–46), ironically, is held together by its scope (made vast in its final version of 1746) and by Thomson's adroit management of the various views.

Religious Sublimity

Instances of early eighteenth-century religious sublimity are evident in the poems discussed above. As I have suggested, we can distinguish between a physico-theological sublime and a religious sublime of limitation, both of which are grounded in natural religion. Some poems reveal one or the other, or both, as in *Creation*. The physico-theological sublime, as in *Creation*, suggests immensity and complexity that elicit transport; such transport is made manageable and sustained by an organized enumeration of detailed phenomena contained within immensity. The enumeration is often exhaustively mimetic so that immensity is revealed to contain innumerable orderly, beautiful patterns. One pattern leads to another pattern, and so on, as we traverse space horizontally, thrilling to the 'proof' of God's providence. The style of this representation of space can be understood as baroque. There are no problems, for all is arranged as it should be. Consequently, there is no terror, only praise. We do not need to wait for the resurrection to bring delight and fulfilment. Exultation is already possible and is the appropriate response from our viewing. In exultation, the reader can shake off any uneasiness caused by the dizzying multiplicity of things and their parts.

The religious sublime of limitation begins, as does the physico-theological sublime, in a description of immensity and complexity. The resulting transport is managed, however, by an assertion of hierarchical organization. All parts found within the apparent immensity have a systematic, vertical relationship to one another, and are arranged according to their proper level of perfection. Blackmore stopped there, keeping his poem firmly within the optimism asserted by the physico-theological tradition. But there can be an additional lesson preached on the basis of these hierarchies, as in Reynolds's *Death's Vision*. The mortal world is supposedly full of 'vanity,' that is, it is insignificant and downright misleading. Change is constant, and ruin is inevitable. If we do not see accurately, our downfall will be in our pride and in our confusion between this world's importance and that of the world to come. This is an old lesson given new forcefulness by new ways of describing space and, more generally, the physical principles of the universe.

As the eighteenth century unfolded, an overt Christian sublimity gradually yielded to a pantheistic natural sublimity. Mallet's scenes of destruction, caused by God's wrath but executed by natural forces such as earthquakes, anticipate the natural sublime that will be central for Burke's treatise. Immensity, a vast space that is nonetheless filled with God's designs and initially viewed through tours through space, will be refashioned into immense things, such as mountains, oceans, chasms, and so on.

Such distinctions between various kinds of sublimity must be made if we are to understand precisely the ways in which philosophical tour of the universe poems combine scientific materialism with religion, without abandoning one for the other.[102]

British philosophical tour of the universe poems reveal some of the complex responses to new ways of viewing the world during the early eighteenth century. This religious, didactic verse sought to combine science with theology, and observation about the material world with spiritual conviction. The poetics of the philosophical tour are not always aesthetically successful, but the poems' range of concerns, approaches, and sublimity are illuminating.

Notes

I sincerely thank the following: Patrick Coleman and Massimo Ciavolella for their good advice and encouragement; Richard A. Barney, Helen Deutsch, J. Paul Hunter, Paul Newberry, Peter Reill, and John Sitter for their generous suggestions; and particularly Michael Newman, who challenged and improved this work at every stage.

1 Because of the necessary scope of this essay, I have simplified the complexities of these trends. To name only a few useful studies, see Isabel Rivers, *Reason, Grace, and Sentiment: A Study of the Language of Religion and Ethics in England 1660–1780*, 2 vols. (Cambridge: Cambridge University Press, 1991, 2000); and Roger D. Lund, ed., *The Margins of Orthodoxy: Heterodox Writing and Cultural Response, 1660–1750* (Cambridge: Cambridge University Press, 1995).

2 Samuel Johnson, *Dictionary* (London, 1755), 19P2^v.

3 Robert Markley explored the contested nature of representation itself of the period and pointed out some of the inherent contradictions in the 'argument by design' that the physico-theological tradition relied upon as well. See his *Fallen Languages: Crises of Representation in Newtonian England, 1660–1740* (Ithaca, NY: Cornell University Press, 1993), esp. 120–3. For lucid (and sometimes overly tidy) introductions to the tradition, see Basil Willey's *The Seventeenth Century Background: Studies in the Thought of the Age in Relation to Poetry and Religion* (New York: Columbia University Press, 1934) and *The Eighteenth Century Background: Studies on the Idea of Nature in the Thought of the Period* (London: Chatto and Windus, 1940). See also Richard Kroll's far-reaching study of neoclassical thought: *The Material Word: Literature Culture in the Restoration and Early Eighteenth Century* (Baltimore: Johns Hopkins University Press, 1991).

4 Thomas Burnet's important *Sacred Theory of the Earth* (1681–9) merges an emerging physico-theological tradition with an earlier theology that makes more of ruin and decay as proofs of God's original design in decline. See Willey, *The Eighteenth Century Background*, especially Chapter 2. Although he overstates matters while putting his finger on a crucial difference, Willey interprets the lack of concern for the Fall in Ray and others as an index to 'the emergence from the tragic shadows of the past into the common daylight of the eighteenth century' (35). In 'Space, Deity, and the "Natural Sublime,"' *Modern Language Quarterly* 12 (1951), Ernest Tuveson declares Burnet to be the 'forerunner of the tellurist poets of the earlier eighteenth century' (34). Burnet is more accurately described as part of the evolving physico-theological tradition.

5 Shaftesbury's *Characteristics* (1711) was another important influence on early eighteenth-century formulations of natural religion.

6 Richard Bentley (the first Boyle lecturer), 'Dedicatory epistle,' in Sampson Letsome, ed., *A Defense of Natural and Revealed Religion: Being a Collection of the Sermons Preached at the Lecture founded by the Honourable Robert Boyle, Esq; (From the Year 1691 to the Year 1732.) With the Additions and Amendments of the Several*

Authors, and General Indexes. In Three Volumes (London: Printed for D. Midwinter ..., 1739); A2ʳ–A2ᵛ.

7 Frederick C. Beiser, *The Sovereignty of Reason: The Defense of Rationality in the Early English Enlightenment* (Princeton: Princeton University Press, 1996), 14, 15.

8 See David Morris, *The Religious Sublime: Christian Poetry and Critical Tradition in 18ᵗʰ-Century England* (Lexington: University of Kentucky Press, 1972), 152. Morris's study is extremely useful, but he has not explored fully the implications of the physico-theological movement or seen 'philosophical' touring as a distinct literature. For a useful anthology of primary materials that illustrate various contexts for sublimity, see *The Sublime: A Reader in British Eighteenth-Century Aesthetic Theory*, ed. Andrew Ashfield and Peter de Bolla (Cambridge: Cambridge University Press, 1996).

9 Letsome, *Defense of Natural and Revealed Religion*, 2:72–6. For a recent edition with a helpful introduction, see Clarke's *A Demonstration of the Being and Attributes of God And Other Writings*, ed. Ezio Vailati (Cambridge: Cambridge University Press, 1998).

10 'Deism,' in *The Oxford Dictionary of the Christian Church*, ed. L. Cross and E.A. Livingstone, 3rd ed. (Oxford: Oxford University Press, 1997), 465.

11 *The Oxford Dictionary of the Christian Church*, ed. Cross and Livingstone, 465.

12 (London, 1708), A3ʳ.

13 See, for example, the miscellany *The Christian Poet, Or Divine Poems on the Four Last Things* (1735).

14 Edward Young, *The Last Day*, in Chalmers, ed., *Works of the British Poets*, 13:371.

15 John Ogilvie, *The Day of Judgment. A Poem. In Two Books* (London: Printed for G. Keith, 1759), ll.327, 330.

16 One index to the popularity and ubiquity of this sort of poem is evident in the *Gentleman's Magazine*. In 1734, one of the few poetry contests in this journal proposed the topic of 'last things.' The winning entries published in July 1735 overlapped considerably, and one can understand how familiar such poems with their various *topoi* would have been to eighteenth-century readers. But see also Jonathan Swift's poem *The Last Day*, his brilliant send-up of the foolish bombast often present in such poems.

17 Chalmers, ed., *Works of the British Poets, The Works of the English Poets from Chaucer to Cowper*, 21 vol. (1810; facsimile, Hildesheim: Georg Olms, 1971); 13:371.

18 Deriving pleasure from one's decay perhaps requires a cultivated taste after the full religious force of such an enterprise is vitiated. Later in the eighteenth century, the Gothic tradition would still provide one form of pleasure

in decay, albeit luridly. By the early nineteenth century, even in a religious setting, such pleasure is somewhat indecorous. In Wordsworth's *Excursion*, his narrator reports that, during a pensive moment in a churchyard, he and his friends were 'rejoicing *secretly* in the sublime attractions of the grave' (emphasis added).

19 In theological movements original sin was never eliminated, but its importance was certainly reduced. Topics that would have been standard or even emphasized in religious verse in earlier periods, such as the Day of Judgment, by this time almost certainly seemed too gloomy. Such topics recirculate, however. John W. Draper's *The Funeral Elegy and the Rise of English Romanticism* (New York: Phaeton Press, 1967) explores how Protestant funerary and elegiac gloom of the seventeenth and eighteenth centuries contributes to the emergence of Romanticism.

20 For example, Bonamy Dobrée declares that Reynolds's poem is part of a 'spate of philosophic verse [that] burdened the bookstalls of the early to mid eighteenth century' (*English Literature in the Early Eighteenth Century, 1700–1740* [London: Oxford University Press, 1959], 499.) Dobrée recognized the poem's importance but overlooked its strong links to traditions of religious verse. Hoxie Neale Fairchild downplayed the poem's foundation in the death bed tradition because he saw the poem primarily as an anticipation of 'later phases of eighteenth-century thought'; see his *Religious Trends in English Poetry, Vol. I: Protestantism and the Cult of Sentiment* (New York: Columbia University Press, 1939), 151–3.

21 The poem was certainly successful. Foxon (R177–R184) finds eight editions. It was printed for three different booksellers in 1709, reissued in 1713 (perhaps because of the success of Blackmore's 1713 *Creation*), and reissued again in 1716. For the second, substantially revised edition published in 1725, in which ten stanzas are expanded to twenty, Reynolds renamed it *A View of Death, or, The Soul's Departure from the World. A Philosophical Sacred Poem, With a Copious Body of Explanatory Notes, and Some Additional Composures*. After his death in 1727, his publisher or editor added more notes for the third edition printed in 1734 and 1735. Regardless of reordered and expanded stanzas, *Death's Vision* remains essentially the same poem in theme and approach. In my discussion, I have quoted from different editions but relied primarily on those of 1713 and 1725.

22 Reynolds, *Death's Vision*, 1713, 10.
23 Ibid., 1714, 10.
24 Ibid., 1725, a2^r.
25 Ibid., 1725, a2^r–a2^v.
26 Ibid., 1713, 19.

27 Ibid., notes, 6–10.
28 Ibid., 9.
29 Ibid., 1725, a1^r.
30 Ibid., 1713, 1.
31 Ibid., 1725, 52–3.
32 John Hughes, *The Ecstasy. An Ode* (London: Printed and sold by J. Roberts, 1720), 1.
33 Ibid., 2.
34 Ibid., 7. In the many encomiastic odes and rapt vision poems written after Newton's death, he is often predictably imagined as a celestial spirit, hurtling through the light he so successfully described.
35 Ibid., 8.
36 Thomas Parnell's *A Night-Piece on Death* (1721) ends on the same note of anticipatory splendour.
37 Hughes, *The Ecstasy*, [A2^r].
38 Fairchild praises Hughes for his use of Newton in this poem: 'very few other poets, if any, had responded to his discoveries in so lyrical and imaginative a strain.' *Religious Trends in English Poetry*, I.252. This is not entirely true. For the widespread influence of Newton's *Opticks* on British poetry of the early and mid-eighteenth century, see Marjorie Nicolson's *Newton Demands the Muse: Newton's Opticks and the Eighteenth Century Poets* (Princeton, NJ: Princeton University Press, 1946).
39 'Preface,' *Prince Arthur* (London: Printed for Awnsham and John Churchil, 1695), A1^r.
40 The *Dictionary of National Biography* and some entries for Blackmore in the ESTC conflate the two poems, listing the second *Arthur* as a revised edition of the first. Although they share some elements, they are distinct poems.
41 His last major poetic effort, *Redemption* (1722), explores the need for scriptural revelation, and is an uninspired attack against natural religion. He has moved away from the physico-theological argument, therefore.
42 Chalmers, ed., *Works of the English Poets*, 10:332.
43 Ibid.
44 Fairchild, *Religious Trends in English Poetry*, 1:197.
45 Chalmers, ed., *Works of the English Poets*, 10:331.
46 Ibid. Lucretius's influence was felt throughout the tradition of philosophical and scientific verse. For one economical account of this influence, see T.J.B. Spencer, 'Lucretius and the Scientific Poem in English,' in *Lucretius*, ed. D.R. Dudley (New York: Basic Books, 1965), 131–64.
47 Fairchild, *Religious Trends in English Poetry*, 1:197.
48 For an account of the literary and cultural stakes involved in this quarrel, see

Richard C. Boys, *Sir Richard Blackmore and the Wits: A Study of 'Commendatory Verses on the Author of the Two Arthurs and the Satyr against Wit' (1700)* (New York: Octagon Books, 1949, 1969).

49 Despite the *Arthurs*' immediate popularity, all of Blackmore's epic verse quickly became otiose. One possible explanation for their brief vogue is found in their composite nature. At once epic, national myth, orthodox Christian verse tract, and poetic celebration of current science and philosophy, the two *Arthurs* may have seemed to satisfy multiple desires for literature at the end of the seventeenth century. After that time, it is likely that other, newer poetic expressions replaced them. In addition, after the increasingly brilliant couplet verse of Pope and others of the early eighteenth century, Blackmore's rather pedestrian couplets would have seemed clumsy by comparison. Other poetic strategies for addressing particular topics, such as nationhood, were devised as well, which would have made his epics look ponderous. Suvir Kaul's very helpful recent book *Poems of Nation, Anthems of Empire: English Verse in the Long Eighteenth Century* (Charlottesville: University Press of Virginia, 2000) traces the evolution of this particular topic in verse.

50 In his *Remarks upon Mr. Pope's Translation of Homer* (1717), Dennis declared that Blackmore's 'admirable Philosophical Poem' not only 'equall'd' Lucretius's *De Rerum Natura* in terms of the 'Beauty of its Versification,' but also that the 'Solidity and Strength of its Reasoning' was superior. *The Critical Works of John Dennis*, ed. Edward Niles Hooker, 2 vols. (Baltimore: Johns Hopkins Press, 1939–43); 2.120. Dennis took Pope to task for sending up Blackmore in *Peri Bathous*; see 2.107.

51 Joseph Addison, *The Spectator*, ed. Donald F. Bond, 5 vols. (Oxford: Clarendon Press, 1965), 3:261. See also 4:444.

52 Boys, *Sir Richard Blackmore*, 34. Johnson reported in his *Life* of Blackmore that he had had the good sense to bring the drafts of the poem throughout its composition to a circle of writers who significantly improved it (Chalmers 10:316). Other critics have not found evidence for this claim. Furthermore, Hoxie Neale Fairchild asserts that *Creation* surpasses his other poetic efforts 'Because it is the only poem in which he does what he is best fitted to do' (Fairchild, *Regligious Trends in English Poetry*, 1:196, fn. 66)

53 Addison, *The Spectator*, 3:261.

54 Chalmers, ed., *Works of the English Poets*, 10:325.

55 Ibid., 10:339.

56 Ibid.

57 Ibid.

58 Ibid., 10:340.

59 Ibid., 10:354, 355.

60 Ibid., 10:340.
61 Ibid., 10:341.
62 Ibid., 10:342.
63 Ibid., 10:342–343.
64 Ibid., 10:345.
65 Ibid., 10:346.
66 Ibid., 10:349.
67 Ibid.
68 Ibid., 10:351. As Bonamy Dobrée remarked, the poem is worthy of praise because it is 'well constructed, well argued, and though prolix and repetitive, not unreadable.' He finds that 'it is difficult to put down if only in hopes of finding passages which to us seem funny' (*English Literature in the Early Eighteenth Century*, 502).
69 Chalmers, ed., *Works of the English Poets*, 10:354.
70 Ibid., 10:354.
71 Ibid., 10:355.
72 Alexander Koyré, 'The Significance of the Newtonian Synthesis,' in *Newton: A Norton Critical Edition*, ed. I. Bernard Cohen and Richard S. Westfall (New York: W.W. Norton & Co., 1995), 61 (first delivered as a lecture in 1948; first printed in 1965).
73 Ibid. For a full-length study of the complex changes provoked by Newton's work, see Margaret Jacob, *The Newtonians and the English Revolution, 1689–1720* (Ithaca, NY: Cornell University Press, 1976).
74 See Clarke's Boyle lectures, *passim*, and Vailati's introduction to Clarke's *A Demonstration*, xxxi.
75 Chalmers, ed., *Works of the English Poets*, 10:354.
76 He had declared in the preface to *King Arthur* how central to the successful practice of medicine neutral observation was. For this, John Locke had praised him highly. In several letters exchanged during 1697 soon after *King Arthur* was published, Locke and William Molyneux of Dublin, an amateur working in philosophy and science, discussed Blackmore's works. Locke thought that Blackmore's understanding of hypotheses 'shews as great a strength and penetration of judgment, as his poetry has shew'd flights of fancy' (11 Sept. 1697). *Some Familiar Letters Between M. Locke, and Several of his Friends* (London: A. and J. Churchill, 1708), 234. It is Molyneux who thinks that his age needs more such 'philosophick' poetry such as the second epic. In reference to this exchange, John Reynolds in 1713 added a subtitle to *Death's Vision: Writ at the Request of Mr. John Lock [sic]*. This was not really true.
77 Chalmers. ed., *Works of the English Poets*, 10:369.
78 Ibid., 10:375.

79 Ibid.
80 Ibid., 10:377.
81 Ibid.
82 Ibid., 10:380.
83 Ibid.
84 Fairchild, *Religious Trends in English Poetry*, 1:200.
85 Morrice, quoted in Alan Dugald McKillop, *The Background of Thomson's Seasons* (Minneapolis: University of Minnesota Press, 1942), 34.
86 Fairchild, *Religious Trends in English Poetry*, 1:354.
87 Aaron Hill, 'Preface,' *The Creation. A Pindaric Illustration of a Poem, Originally Written by Moses* (London: Printed for T. Bickerton, 1720), xii.
88 Samuel Johnson, *Rasselas*, chap. 10.
89 Mallet and Thomson, his friend and fellow Scot, were in close contact as they worked on their poems, and Thomson suggested some of the disaster scenes would be fitting material for elevated, sublime passages. See McKillop, *Background of Thompson's Seasons*, 70.
90 'The Life of Mallet,' in Chalmers, ed., *Works of the English Poets*, 14:4.
91 *The Works of David Mallet, Esq; in Three Volumes. A New Edition corrected* (London: Printed for A. Millar and P. Vaillant, 1759), 67.
92 Ibid., 73.
93 Ibid., 83.
94 Ibid., 93.
95 Ibid.
96 Ibid., 66.
97 Ibid., 95.
98 Ibid., 101.
99 Ibid., 102.
100 Ibid., 110.
101 This is not unrelated to the close of Pope's 1743 *Dunciad*: 'Thy hand, Great Anarch! lets the curtain fall; / And Universal Darkness buries All.'
102 Ernest Tuveson described an increased 'sensitivity to bigness' in early eighteenth-century writing, which he understood as a response to new ways of seeing the universe made possible by new science and their technology, such as advances in astronomy because of improved telescopes. ('Space, Deity, and the "Natural Sublime",' 20) His discussion of new approaches to the concept of infinity and its theological implications is certainly helpful, but he overlooks how a religious sublime, based in the perception of immensity, can be curtailed in two ways, which I have described as horizontal and vertical.

chapter three

Marino and the *Meraviglia*

PAOLO CHERCHI

It is usually reported that Marino coined the sentence 'è del poeta il fin la meraviglia' ('the poet's goal is to surprise'), which appears in every manual of history of Italian literature. This sentence is constantly repeated because it seems to contain the essence of baroque literature, and it is a commonplace to associate baroque and *meraviglia*. Commonplaces usually have a kernel of truth, but they also tend to trivialize it by reducing complex phenomena to simple definitions; and in this particular case the process creates a paradox because the definition orients the research rather than resulting from it. Nobody disputes that seventeenth-century art is filled with *meraviglia*, if we take *meraviglia* to mean that shocking sense of wonderment, of surprising dazzle we experience in front of a great number of creations and techniques that stress the unusual, the irregular, the bizarre, and the witty. These were not sporadic features, but rather dominant aesthetic pursuits in baroque art: indeed, we are overwhelmed by *concetti* and *acutezze*, by *Wunderkammern*, and by all sorts of anti-mimetic principles applied in paintings, sculpture, architecture, and in books of 'painted poems,' and by many other bizarre inventions and anamorphic constructions. All of these features prove beyond doubt that the clichéd dyad baroque/*meraviglia* identifies a main trend, if not *the* main trend, in baroque art. What can be disputed is that the notion of *meraviglia* is limited to the features just mentioned, that is to say, to the most specious and obvious techniques for causing surprise and dazzle: a culture prone to attach the highest aesthetic value to surprising readers and spectators must have had a hierarchy of values, different degrees of measuring the level of surprise a creative technique could attain, a scale by which a daring metaphor could be considered more or less dazzling than a difficult acrostic, a complex *rapportatio*, or a painted poem. What I am trying to say is that the commonplace 'baroque/*meraviglia*' has perhaps impoverished both the idea of baroque and the notion of *meraviglia* by stressing what may be the less prestigious forms of *meraviglia*, and forgotten marvellous techniques that dazzle readers and spectators in a different, more subtle way. I believe it is necessary to revisit this commonplace, to explore the nuances of the concept of *meraviglia* and enrich our view of baroque creativity.

The first step in this direction is to review some basic data, starting with Marino's famous line. It is hard to take 'è del poeta il fin la meraviglia' as a manifesto, as a program of poetics, given that it is found in a satirical sonnet, and thus is very likely a negative, ironic statement. This interpretation is not certain, but at least it alerts us to the possibility that there are many degrees of *meraviglia*, some glittering and cheap, others more subtle and rare.

It is also important to remember that Marino was not solely responsible for the sentiment expressed. In Francesco Patrizi da Cherso's *Della poetica* there is a book, 'La deca ammirabile' (completed in 1587), entirely devoted to the theme of *meraviglia*, while books eight and nine of the same deca are respectively entitled 'Che il mirabile è forma e fine della poesia' (*Meraviglia* is the form and the end of poetry) and 'Come e perché la meraviglia divenne fine proprio della poesia' (How and why *meraviglia* became the proper end of poetry).[1] Every student of the notion of *meraviglia* should be familiar with Patrizi's entire deca; it offers, among other things, an excellent survey of the notion of marvel in antiquity and in the Renaissance, from Plato to Tasso, a survey which, to some extent, discredits the idea that 'marvel' is an invention of the baroque. From this survey we learn that the *meraviglioso* is a complex notion at times synonymous with 'curiosity' and 'ignorance of causes,' especially in the face of events that depart from normality, both natural and artificial. Natural causes of *meraviglia* promote philosophical and scientific inquiries; artificial marvels imply a human operation, a 'wonderful creation' aimed at arousing that sense of dazzle we call *meraviglia*. There are also degrees of *meraviglia*, depending on the event or object observed and on the age and knowledge of the observer. Any kind of marvellous requires a degree of ignorance ('omne ignotum pro magnifico est'),[2] which stimulates inquiry into what is behind a phenomenon (this curiosity, argue philosophers from Plato to Kierkegaard, promotes science and philosophical investigation): persons who know everything and persons who are extremely ignorant have no disposition to marvel. Children are more prone to wonder than anyone else because they are both very curious and very ignorant. *Meraviglia* may be a temporary feeling which fades away as soon as we come to know the causes of an event; in some cases, however, it can last for ever. Take, for example, the case of a very close friend who betrays us: his action causes *meraviglia* in us and this feeling persists even when we discover the causes of his treason.

For our purpose Patrizi's survey is useful in two ways. First, we must distinguish between natural and artificial marvel. It seems obvious that our interest lies in the latter, since it is in this sphere that we find artistic creation. Yet Patrizi's attention to natural phenomena reminds us that at the root of wonderment there is novelty, ignorance, and subsequent curiosity. Nature is indifferent to what inspires marvel, but artists must know since they rely on novelty and curiosity to dazzle their audience. Patrizi's considerations also add a historical dimension to the problem. We know that monsters and exoticism were the primary source of medieval marvel, but in the baroque period intense studies on monsters and the explosion of travel literature had eliminated, to a great extent, 'ignorance' about those subjects. Finally, Patrizi reminds us that there is a natural marvel which consists in phenomena that Vergil called 'admiranda levium spectacula rerum' (the wondrous show of a tiny world, *Geor.*, IV, 3), that is, those phenomena that occur in our daily life or that we can see at any time – the setting of the sun, the colours of a butterfly's wings – from which daily exposure has worn away any wondrous potential, but which suddenly acquire it anew if we pause to consider them. We should not forget that a great deal of baroque literature deals precisely with these hidden wonders of nature: one has only to read some pages of Bartoli's – one of the greatest baroque prose writers – *L'ozio del saggio*, in which daily observations, such as the sight of a snail carrying its house on its back, are celebrated as containing the deepest cause of *meraviglia*.

The kind of *meraviglia* which interests me here is not an obvious or conspicuous *meraviglia*, but one which readers are supposed to discover in a seemingly mediocre poem, a totally digressive canto, or a long description apparently free of surprises. It is a type of marvel usually neglected by scholars who identify *meraviglia* with glamour.

My examples will be all taken from Marino, an author considered to be one of the most influential promoters of baroque irregular poetry – although in fact he is far from being a specious and obscure poet à la Gongora, an artist who perhaps considered obscurity and specious *meraviglia* to be the recourses of mediocre poets.

The first example is a sonnet from the *Lira* (1614). Its title, 'Seno' (bosom), would seem the most interesting part of it:

O che dolce sentier tra mamma e mamma
scende in quel bianco sen, ch'Amor allatta!
Vago mio cor, qual timidetta damma,
da' begli occhi cacciato, ivi t'appiatta;

dal'ardor, che ti strugge a dramma a dramma,
schermo ti fia la bella neve intatta:
neve ch'ognor dala vivace fiamma
di duo soli è percossa e non disfatta.

Vattene pur, ma per la tua via secreta
non distender tant'oltre i passi audaci
che t'arrischi a toccar l'ultima meta;

raccogli sol, cultor felice, e taci,
in quel solco divin (se 'l vel nol vieta)
da seme di sospir messe di baci.

[Oh, what a sweet path between tit and tit descends in that white breast that love nurses. Dear heart of mine, as a rather shy doe, hunted by those beautiful eyes, hide there;
you'll be shielded by that beautiful untouched snow from that fire which consumes you little by little; a snow which is constantly hit, but not melted, by two suns.
You do go; but on that secret path of yours, do not stretch too far your so audacious steps that you dare to reach the last goal;
you, happy harvester, in that divine furrow, reap only, and hash, a crop of kisses from seeds of sighs].

Apparently this is a plain sonnet: no conceits, no puns, non-epigrammatic closure, and no new imagery. It could become more interesting if compared to the sonnet that follows immediately after and bears the same title, 'Seno.' Such comparison would bring out some playful effects due to a clear and yet irregular specularity: images and themes persist together with their variations, which are not always regular as they should be in a mirrorlike reflection. However, for the time being, let us focus on the first of the two sonnets and question whether we have overlooked something: the stature and the well-known craft of Marino make us feel uneasy for lack of a more visible manifestation. Can we at least find a sign that we are missing something? Apparently not. Yet on a second look words like 'mamma' and 'allatta,' which belong to the low style and are not typical of Marino's vocabulary, catch our attention; moreover, we notice that the majority of rhymes ('-amma,' '-atta,' '-eta'; '-aci') are in the plain or popular style. If this observation triggers some curiosity, and we begin to notice that the plain words appear almost exclusively in the second part of each of the first ten verses, then a new perspective is opened and we are able to grasp that in the middle of those ten verses, at the point where caesuras occur, we see a line that allows us to read only the first hemistiches of the sonnet making a perfect sense: 'O che dolce sentier scende in quel bianco sen. Vago mio cor, da' begli occhi cacciato, dal'ardor che ti strugge schermo ti fia la neve ch'ognor dala neve è percossa. Vattene pur, ma non distender tant'oltre che t'arrischi a toccar l'ultima meta.' This reading allows us to see the 'path' sung in the sonnet, the 'line of Venus' which should reach the 'meta.' Where is it? It is the 'triangle' contained in the last terzina made up by the words 'Sol' (v. 12), 'SOlco' and SE (v. 13), and 'SEme,' 'SOspiri,' 'mesSE' (v. 14).[3] Unexpectedly, the seemingly plain sonnet turns out to be a *carmen figuratum*, a *technopaegnion* of respectable sophistication. Our marvel is increased by the fact that its design is hidden, contrary to what happens in the traditional *carmina figurata*. Moreover, the *meraviglia* is of the most rewarding kind because it is not immediate: it requires a high degree of ingenuity on the part of the reader who becomes a kind of accomplice in putting together the cause of his own marvelling.

How often does this kind of surprise come? Every time a reader breaks into a poem and grasps Marino's hidden message. There may be many poems, among the thousands written by Marino, of the kind just seen; we cannot know precisely how many until we are sure that no hidden design remains hidden any more. We cannot help underlining that this type of *meraviglia* has an aristocratic quality superior to any exaggerated metaphor: it is a marvel for a selected few, who in turn become admirable in the eyes of those who watch them entering such marvellous constructions.

The second example[4] deals again with a case of a hidden element, but this time it is found in a frame far larger than a sonnet, in a more difficult piece to dominate, namely, in an ample section of the *Adone*, Marino's masterpiece and the longest poem of Italian literature. The episode occurs in canto seventeen and describes Venus's journey on the Mediterranean sea. She is travelling from Cyprus, where she has left Adonis, to the island of Citera to be present at a festival in her honour. During her voyage a messenger informs her that Adonis is in danger of dying because he has been wounded by a boar, and she can save him only if she gets a special herb from Proteus, who dwells in the Black Sea. Venus then takes an immense periplus, coasting many islands before arriving at the Black Sea, but Proteus has moved to Sicily, courting a nymph. Venus goes to Sicily, again coasting numerous islands and harbours. Proteus is not there either, and she decides to go to her original destination, Citera, where she finally rests. The trip turns out to be completely useless; Venus does not find Proteus and she does not obtain the herb to save Adonis. The lengthy voyage, lasting for over eighty octaves, is totally absurd from a nautical point of view, and seems to be one of Marino's typical digressions arranged to display vast learning and an arcane mythological knowledge. But, again, a reader who has learned to mistrust Marino's 'gratuitous' digressions may be curious to trace on a map Venus's wandering from an island to another. This simple exercise reveals a capital A:

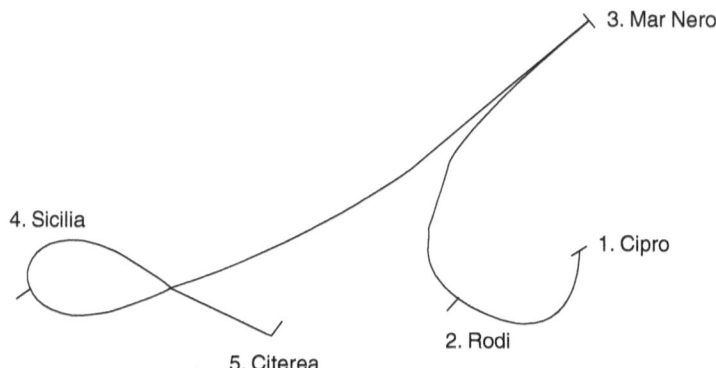

This capital A is the initial of Adonis, the far-away lover so close to death. It is almost a hidden emblem, a mental image of the hero now projected into a mythic dimension and included among the timeless riches of the seas and the lands of ancient Greece. This mental A looming over the West Mediterranean sea emblematizes Adonis's nature and role. He is, after all, the strangest of poetic heroes, rather comparable to an actor who is always present on the stage but plays no active part since he never initiates any action. This immobile and emblematic A ciphers his presence-absence as well as his inactive actions. The reader who becomes aware of the hidden message remains dazzled by Marino's craftiness in a text that plays at different and superimposed levels: on the surface he seems to be listing famous mythological islands and describing Venus's journey; on a deeper level he evokes the presence of Adonis through Venus's itinerary, using a route like a pen that designs a letter on water to mean presence but not consistency. On a still deeper level we find that the looming A alludes to the very title of the poem in a moment in which the weak story it contains is coming to an end and only an impression of it will be left.

Adone contains several episodes that cause *meraviglia* through the same technique of 'painting' an idea, a technique that has nothing in common with the emblem, the *carmen pictum*, or even with the typical *technopaignon*, genres which have ways to tell the reader how to read them. Marino's 'hidden marvels' have no way to tell the reader of their existence, and for this reason they are more precious and surprising once they are identified. If space were not an impediment, I would analyse other samples of these hidden *meraviglie* – for instance, the metamorphosis of Adonis's heart into a flower,[5] or how the wings of Time become one with the wings of desire in the episode of Piramus and Tisbe, episodes in which Marino uses different techniques for hiding *meraviglie* – to show how varied are the ways used by Marino to surprise his reader, pulling him into a deeper reading through narratives completely free from those typical rhetorical devices in which scholars place most of the baroque *meraviglia*.

Marino also makes his readers wonder through the way he uses *dispositio*, a branch of rhetoric that students of the baroque have for the most part neglected, for one main reason. Indeed, it is useful to remember that the aesthetic of the Renaissance stressed 'imitation,' a principle that covered both the *inventio* and the *elocutio*, but did not deal with the field of *dispositio*. In the second half of the Cinquecento the notion of *imitatio* underwent a crisis for reasons that do not concern us here; however, this crisis gave importance to the *dispositio*, especially through the rhetorical innovations of Petrus Ramus. The new attention to the *dispositio* promoted a series of experimentation, including a type of plagiarism which arranged stolen materials in a different and original way to create new meanings.

Marino made a stupendous use of *dispositio*, although it does not belong in the list of the means that arouse *meraviglia*, and he even based on it his aesthetic principle according to which 'in a poem words are its content and form is its meaning.' It is a complex affirmation, but it becomes a bit clearer if we think of 'painted poems' in which words have the material function of giving body to a poem, and the form in which words are disposed convey a meaning through the appearances of a painted object. To some extent the sonnet 'Seno' depends on this aesthetic idea. Giovanni Pozzi, the author of a wonderful commentary on the *Adone*,[6] has shown how the description of the palace of senses (cantos v–viii) is also a grandiose *technopaegnium* in which words play the role of material pieces in a LEGO game.

Yet Marino did not stop at this kind of *dispositio*: he used it in the modern structural sense to build meaning and create characters. One major example will suffice to make the point. Cantos II and IV contain respectively two episodes: the first retells Paris's judgment, and the second contains the story of Psyche and Cupid. Both episodes seem to be pure digressions since they are apparently extraneous to the main plot of the poem. We question the complete lack of pertinence of these two lengthy digressions, and the fact that they are so close to one another. Is it possible that a poet as calculating as Marino has gone wrong in such a naive way? Or is he telling us something? Perhaps so, but we are not yet ready to grasp what and why: the two episodes come almost at the beginning of the poems, so we must keep reading in the expectation of discovering a clue for these digressions. Our hopes are frustrated as we find even more and more digressions. But once we finish the last page of the poem and think back to its story, to its characters, to its structure, we get a sense that it is consistent in pursuing a technique of 'undoing itself' through weakening its main characters, aborting narrative episodes, and creating a sense of relativism everywhere. Now we have the clue for understanding the two episodes and we appreciate their function in the poem as a whole, in the way they relate to each other, in their respective position in a well-calculated *dispositio*. The first episode celebrates Venus as the most beautiful of the goddesses; the second shows that her beauty is inferior to that of Psyche. What is first proclaimed as an Absolute – Venus the idea itself of Beauty – is changed into a relative value once the beauty of the girl who has conquered the heart of the God of Love enters the stage. This downgrading of the Absolute is made understandable through the sequence of the two apparently unrelated episodes. Had the order or *dispositio* been inverted this sense of scaling down would have been lost. The poem as a whole shows us that Marino needs weak characters, and both Venus and Adonis are indeed very weak protagonists. The *dispositio* is a decisive element in creating this super-segmental meaning, a meaning that becomes even clearer when we realize that both stories are amply plagiarized. Marino takes them from contemporary sources, and he can do it openly because he obtains a new meaning from the stories that others have written. The sense of marvel is inescapable: Marino dazzles his reader with a technique that is not immediately visible, and which is intellectually very subtle.

The poem as a whole is the supreme marvel, even in the ups and downs of its fortune. *Adone* enjoyed great success among its contemporaries, but it later fell into disrepute, especially among the Romantics and the critics who look for 'inspiration,' 'sincerity of sentiment,' and 'moral strength' in poetry. Only recently has *Adone* come once again to be seen as a masterpiece, thanks to the studies of Giovanni Pozzi. Pozzi succeeded, through a structural analysis, in appreciating anew the plan of the work, and understood the reason for its 'antinarrative' project and its anti-mimetic principles. According to Pozzi the *Adone*'s structure forms an ellipsis which, by creating a perspective from two different points of view, imposes a sense of relativity on all aspects of life and on epistemology in particular. Pozzi shows that the two semi-elliptical parts of the *Adone* mirror each other because they contain the same sequence of the main events – the meeting of Venus and Adonis, their falling in love, the education of Adonis, and separation. I have provided a different interpretation of the work. The poem has not an elliptical structure, but a pyramidal one, and it really contains three parts, one of them the final canto dedicated to the games honouring Adonis's death. This last canto repeats the *meraviglia* of the A by essentializing in a 'gratuitous' narrative the entire poem. This process is anticipated by the second part of the work, which repeats only the structure of the first part, precisely as it happens in most of Ovidian metamorphoses, where the essential form or shape persists even though the substance changes. *Adone*, I believe, has a sort of fluid structure that ultimately allows the poem to undergo a metamorphosis, passing from the intended mythological poem to a potentially historical poem, announced in the last octaves. The fact that the main characters are weak, that the stories create 'body' but not a plot or any kind of constructive narration, is a calculated strategy that gives the poem a fluid quality which allows it to transform itself. In this metamorphic possibility lies hidden the greatest *meraviglia*: the poem that deals with a metamorphic story becomes itself the object of metamorphosis. The *Adone* is a grandiose metonymy that can be perceived only upon viewing the work as a whole. This *meraviglia* has nothing in common with the glamorous games and puns and conceits commonly found in baroque literature; it is a *meraviglioso* that proceeds in precisely the opposite way: the reader is deceived by the plain, lengthy, digressive, and essentially fluvial text that seems to run forever in a superficial way. The discovery that beneath that endless number of octaves lies a calculated anti-Tasso project, a strong cultural stand against the Italian poetry tradition, gives the poem a completely different face, and a very beautiful one at that.

Notes

1 Francesco Patrizi da Cherso, *Della Poetica*, ed. Danilo Aguzzi Barbagli, 3 vols. (Florence: Istituto Nazionale di Studi sul Rinascimento, 1969–71). The books indicated are at 2:329–44 and 345–54.
2 'Every unknown is considered great,' Tacitus, *Agricola*, 30.
3 The reading of the sonnet I have presented here is based on that done by the participants of the *Seminario di Italiano, Friburg – Una dozzina di analisi di testo all'indirizzo dei docenti del settore medio* (Zürich: Juris, 1975), 89–99; this reading was later simplified in Giovan Battista Marino, *Amori*, ed. Alessandro Martini (Milan: Rizzoli, 19??), 135–7.
4 I have discussed this example in my *La metamorfosi dell'*Adone (Ravenna: Longo, 1996), 67–9.
5 For this episode, see my 'The Metamorphoses of Adonis,' in *The Image of the Baroque*, ed. Aldo Scaglione (New York: Peter Lang, 1995), 61–72, esp. 67–72.
6 Giovan Battista Marino, *L'Adone*, ed. Giovanni Pozzi, 2 vols. (Milan: Mondadori, 1976).

chapter four

I Would Rather Drown, Than Not Find New Worlds

PAOLO FASOLI

To better clarify the topic of this paper, I would like to re-examine, briefly, the famous sentence by Giovan Battista Marino: 'I claim to know the rules much better than all the pedantic scholars put together, but the true rule, my sweet friend, is to be able to break all rules at the right time and place, adapting oneself to current customs and to prevailing taste.'[1] This quotation is from a letter that Marino sent from Naples in (late) 1624 to Girolamo Preti, a former admirer who, sensing mounting changes in literary tastes, was trying to distance himself from the poet he had once considered his master.

We might consider this letter as at a sort of epitaph (Marino would die the following year) written in a more subdued tone than the too often quoted, and too often misinterpreted, comment about 'meraviglia' in the *Fischiata 33* of the *Murtoleide*:

> The aim of the poet is to create wonder
> (of the excellent poet, not the maladroit):
> He who doesn't know how to astonish, should better groom horses.[2]

But a closer examination of these famous lines may enable us to cut through judgments and prejudices that have accreted through the ages. Whereas the anti-normative rule advocated in the letter to Preti emphasizes its own historic relativism, the *meraviglia* of the sonnet is equally unspecified or, rather, is defined only *e negativo*. Marino provides here a synthetic, highly memorable line that states only that he regarded as clumsy and ludicrous his rival Murtola's attempt to inspire wonder through a catalogue of banal objects (artichokes, cabbages) in his hexameronic poem.[3] Marino dislikes the poetic *meraviglia a minore* that Murtola, defending his *Creazione del mondo* (1608), had justified as a means of denoting more grandiosely the Providence of the Lord. Again, Marino is not offering any positive prescription on wonder, and this attitude was characteristic of a poet who preferred a performative approach to a theoretical one when questions of poetics were at issue.

But if we acknowledge that divergent strategies for eliciting the reader's astonishment, or wonder, recur through the entire range of baroque poetics, we should then explore how those poets, assigned by critical tradition to a camp opposing the *Marinismo*, have treated the issue. I shall not engage in a reconsideration of the definition 'Classicist baroque,'[4] and I do not think that this label should be regarded either as an uncritical adhesion to the programmatic declarations of a group of writers, or as an oxymoron stressing ironically the pretentiousness of that specification (although similar definitions have been the common coin of art history, as in the case of Bernini).[5] I would simply call 'Classicist Baroque' the literary production (theoretical and artistic) of certain intellectuals, from Giovanni Ciampoli to Gabriello Chiabrera, Virginio Cesarini to Ansaldo Cebà, Fulvio Testi, and Ottavio Rinuccini, whose cultural agenda, and poetic predilections (not all the same) distinguished them from the Marinist approach to language and poetry. Most of them had developed a close relationship with conservative cultural centres like the 'Barberinian Rome,' Mantua, or Florence, while occasionally seeking patronage from the same rulers who had rewarded Marino (Chiabrera and Testi courted Charles Emmanuel I of Turin, for instance).

Since this paper is more about poets' poetics than theoreticians' treatises, I will focus on the personality who best represents both aspects: in this case, Gabriello Chiabrera. I did not choose the poet from Savona simply because centuries of literary historiography have placed his name opposite Marino's on the map of seventeenth-century literary taste (or alongside it when the whole century was subjected to indiscriminate condemnation). Chiabrera was, more than any other classicist, a prolific writer who devoted his entire life to the production and the theoretical definition of poetry, and, secondarily, to the portrayal of the 'man of letters'[6] (a Daniello Bartoli on a much smaller scale, in this respect). Unlike Marino, who disseminated his reflections in scattered letters and rhymes, or represented them *en abyme*, as in the *Adone*, Chiabrera dedicated to the art of poetry a number of academic discourses, various letters, and a series of dialogues that situate him in the tradition of late-sixteenth-century theorists (with, furthermore, a snobbish attitude peculiar to the anti-pedantic, but professional, *amateur*). Also noteworthy in Chiabrera's opus is an auto-biographical text, the posthumously published *Vita* which, while restoring to the genre the composed, restrained style of humanistic auto-diegesis (a radical departure from Cellini's or even Vasari's Mannerist exaggerations), provided a portrait *posteritati* (or, in Starobinskian terms, a portrait with duration and movement) that wonderfully accomplished the purpose of image manipulation it was written for, strongly contributing to the canonization of the poet as a champion of 'measure' in the later age of *Arcadia*. It is in this excellent example of the art of dissembling, of subtle allusion (perhaps just a clever pre-emptive strike against those who might later wish to damage his reputation), that we find a famous self-quotation that Giacomo Leopardi (who was certainly inspired by the gnomic style of the *Vita* for some of his *Operette morali*) would ridicule in his *Zibaldone*: 'He joked on his poetry-writing in this way: he said that he would follow his fellow citizen Christopher Columbus, and that he wanted to find a new world, or drown.'[7]

Isolating these sentences from their context of scattered anecdotes about wine-drinking, poetic affinities, food condiments, etcetera, eliminates the nuances that come with ironical dissimulation and understatement. In any case, the longing for unchartered territories and new worlds is reiterated, in Chiabrera's works, by the obsessive reference to Columbus and Galileo, the former being praised in poems, the latter in a prose panegyric (where, according to a very anti-Galilean notion, the scientist is considered superior to the explorer for having discovered 'incorruptible' worlds).[8] It might be said that the praise of Columbus and Galileo, and of the astronomer above the explorer, was commonplace in the age of baroque. But it is Chiabrera's evocation of Columbus at every opportunity, and not only for reasons of base chauvinism, that makes this a personal obsession.

Chiabrera's peaceful demise at the age of eighty-six, in his bed and not at sea, might suggest that he did not discover new worlds. With his fulminating sarcasm, and rare gift for historiographical synthesis, Leopardi, in the aforementioned entry of the *Zibaldone*, gives us a sharp judgment: 'This motto [that he wanted to find a new world, or drown] sounds today like a fanfaronade and makes us laugh. What great boldness, what great novelty in Chiabrera's poetry! A little Pindarism, instead of the Petrarchism practiced in his day by all allegedly lyrical poets. But so it was at the time that this new thing seemed momentous, daring, and hugely effective. Today, it goes unnoticed, since even all the new things that we now find in *Faust* and *Manfred* are barely able to impress the readers. It might be useful for a Discourse on Romanticism (April 1, 1829).'[9]

As Leopardi notices, here Pindar replaces Petrarch: a change in poetic models that only the great talent for synthesis of the compiler of the *Crestomazia* could have summarized in one sentence. Not that Chiabrera had missed any opportunity to mention the great Greek heroic poet. But he never explicitly claimed to see him as an authority who might substitute for Petrarch. Let's look again at the sententious recollections of the autobiography: 'He began reading, for sheer pleasure, poetry books, and step by step, he led his mind to understand what it [poetry] really was in essence, and to study it attentively. It appeared to him that Greek writers had dealt with poetry in the best way, and he concentrated entirely on them, and he marveled at Pindar, and he dared to compose something that resembled his poetry in style.'[10] As for Petrarch, one notes that, although Chiabrera had dedicated the last of the five *Dialogues on Poetic Art* to one of the *Canzoniere*'s sonnets (but here the medieval author was a mere pretext for an academic discourse on love), the only mention of him in the *Vita* is purely incidental, and not as honourable as the inclusion in the *cursus studiorum* would have been; it appears almost in disguise, by means of a metonymy: 'To show that writing poetry was his only preoccupation, and that he spurned everything else, he had an "impresa" with a lyre and Petrarch's *motto* "I don't have anything but this one."'[11] Pindar, on the other hand, is the guardian deity of most of Chiabrera's discussions on heroic poetry, and his name, along with those of Anachreon, Sappho, and Simonides, is placed in the élite roster of canonic models. It seems that Chiabrera is actually creating a new form of radical classicism; one that deliberately leaps beyond Bembian and post-Bembian classicism, beyond the vernacular canonic model (Petrarch) as well, to draw upon a treasure of Greek poetry that the author seems to have discovered, without any form of mediation, by a caprice of taste or by sheer luck.

In 1611 Ansaldo Cebà, a Genoese aristocrat who had befriended Chiabrera and who had studied with some of his direct or indirect early mentors (Sperone Speroni, Giason de Nores), published a collection of poems that includes a sonnet dedicated to our poet. The first four lines are:

Oh gentle swan among the most illustrious
That beautiful Italy has ever had
...
You bring to Heaven the noblest voices
Crossing the Grecian way and the beautiful French path.[12]

Cebà knew more than one thing about 'Il bel cammin francese,' being himself an admirer and imitator of the poets of the *Pléiade*, and of Ronsard in particular. But what was Chiabrera's relationship to that poetic school, apart from the fact that some of the *Pléiade* poets, most notably Du Bellay, had been deeply influenced by Speroni (to the extent that portions of the *Deffence* are a close adaptation of Speroni's *Dialogo delle lingue*)? Did Chiabrera ever say, on a printed page, anything about French poetry? Yes, here and there: most remarkably, in a preface to the 1599 edition of the *Maniere dei versi toscani* (almost certainly ghostwritten by him, but cautiously signed by a friend) and in some passages of one of his *Dialogues on Poetic Art* (*Il Geri*). But these allusions are presented by the rhetoric strategies of the discourse as incidental, or as related to issues of language enrichment through the use of words imported from other languages, notably compound words modelled on ancient Greek, or as examples of versification (and of the art of writing graceful lines in the moderate and pleasurable tone of the *scherzo*). At this point it appears indubitably clear that Cebà's sonnet is an affront disguised as homage. Cebà is calling the reader's attention to Chiabrera's massive appropriation of French models. He is saying that 'The Swan' had not found any real 'Grecian way', and that his purported Hellenism was in fact second-hand and derivative. And derivative it was. It was, indeed, third-hand at times, because Chiabrera freely imitated not only translations of Anacreon and others made by Henri Estienne (it seems that Chiabrera never mastered Greek), but also the poetry of French writers, Ronsard *in primis*, who had been influenced by the texts that Estienne first published in 1554.[13] In addition, lines, themes, and even metric forms from poems by Ronsard, which had little to do with the Anacreontic style, were offered hospitality in Chiabrera's generous oeuvre, illustrating the form of relationship between texts and sources that Cesare Segre has termed 'viscosity.'[14] When Chiabrera's critical fortune was at low ebb, in the 1920s, a scholar even ventured to say that Chiabrera's *Dialoghi* on poetry depended on Du Bellay's work: which would mean that the baroque poet had chosen to imitate his own master, Speroni, through the works of an imitator.[15]

What really matters, however, is neither the size of Chiabrera's Greek-through-French imitation nor the ethics of a poet who, unlike Marino, had never taken credit for being a clever thief. What matters now is the sense of this operation as it bears upon the attempt to inspire wonder through novelty. I believe that the significance of Chiabrera's 'imitation in disguise,' and the reasons that prompted him to look beyond the Alps, exceed the simple desire to astound with new manners and new metres. I think that they have a motivation in the longing for a new, albeit unavowable, system of poetic values. Du Bellay and Ronsard had accomplished a genuine re-invention, re-foundation of poetry (of a *langue* in humanistic terms). And perhaps Chiabrera was aware of that somewhat cyclical return, in Italy as well as in France in the very late sixteenth century, to the preciosity of an earlier Petrarchism (that of the late fifteenth century in Italy, or of the first half of the sixteenth in France: with Serafino Aquilano, Tebaldeo, and Cariteo, among the Italians).[16] Perhaps Chiabrera was attracted by the way in which the *Pléiade*, studying Bembo's principles through Speroni's spectacles, turned them to their own account: a Bembo tranformed into a new, viable *auctoritas* by the eradication of his Italian legacy (a legacy that, after further manipulation and eventual implosion, will result in the poetics of *concettismo*). The *Pléiade*, perhaps, supplied Chiabrera with a model of rebirth, of starting anew from a sort of *tabula rasa*, an example that could confirm his idea of the 'youth' of poetry. The form of Petrarchism that our poet could borrow from the French poets, in a paradoxical re-routing of influences, provided an easy way to by-pass the Italian Petrarchist tradition, from Tasso to Guarini to Marino. The baroque obsession with perspective has generated here a kind of historical illusionism that conjures up the alleged retrieval of the Greek tradition with the worship of novelty. The victim is after all Petrarch himself, deprived of his canonic role as sovereign model.

Chiabrera's quest for the astonishing and for the new intersects the critical path of another Italian poet, Alessandro Tassoni, who in the early 1600s started a precocious Italian version of the *Querelle des anciens et des modernes*. But in order to do so Chiabrera had to manipulate other historical categories. And this is, I believe, the sense of his peculiar metrical taxonomy that, although borrowed largely from Trissino, manages to push the built-in limitations of the source to extreme consequences, flattening synchronically, and in a single stroke, the development of Italian poetry. Because, for Chiabrera, all types of poetic lines are the product of the combination-repetition of footlike elemental rhythmic particles, which have always existed in a sort of generative grammar (it is a mirrorlike, inverse correlative of the experimental 'barbarian' metrics that has lingered for centuries in Italian poetry from Alberti to Tolomei to Carducci).[17] This atomization of metrics paves the way, logically, to another, deeper process of segmentation. Here the motivation is open, though somehow oblique, and astonishingly 'new.' The following is a quotation from the dialogue *L'Orzalesi*: 'I heard from musicians as well as from laymen certain "manners" of verse, which caused my mind to wonder. At first, that marvel didn't prompt me to open my mind to any kind of consideration, because the world has always been replete with talented minds fond of unusual fantasies. But ... the type of lines I am now talking about, and also the way to arrange them [in stanzas and poems] seem not to be, according to what I am told, despised by those most excellent intellects.'[18]

The setting of poems to madrigalistic scores was, of course, the musicians' common practice, just as having their verse reduced to an ancillary role was the poets' routine complaint (more or less sincere, though they certainly delighted in the additional notoriety it brought them). We have to consider that, as Northrop Frye noted, 'the madrigal, where the words are tossed about from voice to voice, represents the extreme limit in the subservience of poetry.'[19] Chiabrera is the first poet who seems not only to acknowledge the unavoidable exploitation by musicians, but also to turn it into the starting point of a sort of collaboration. This is not the place to discuss the birth of melodrama and the role that Chiabrera, Rinuccini, and other baroque 'classicists' played in the pursuit of monody, together with pioneers like Peri or Caccini. And there is no space to examine all the references that our poet makes to music and composers. What matters here is to see if the marriage of verse and music did have perceptible repercussions in the writing of poetry, and how this new poetical (if not theoretical) stance is to be understood within the frame of the ineluctable search for 'new worlds.'

If a poetic text is to preserve its 'readability' in a musical performance, it must have certain characteristics that limit or abolish the need of a recursive reading. This implies that, in a performance, the meaning of the poem should be understood in a linear sequence of listening, and that the sense should build line by line, even phrase by phrase. Also, the persistence or repetition of a unit of sound or sense in a brief span of time should be secured in order to create an echo effect reaffirming an image or a concept/conceit. Can we possibly imagine a *concettista* poem – whose paralogical process compels the mind to go back and forth – to be suitable to this kind of aesthetic experience? The devolution of poetry to music is a form of consequential immunization of poetry from wit (*concetti, acutezze*). The rhetorical manipulation of essences through their appearances, the true hallmark of Marino's and Marinist poetry, has no space to breath in this 'new' form of poetry. Where is that indomitable, compulsive search for 'resemblance,' for the assimilation of the diverse into categories of opposition and symmetry, that some of the most illustrious interpreters of the baroque, from Rousset to Genette, have considered quintessential to this style, taste, culture?

It suffices to read the most typical poems included by Chiabrera in his more radically 'new' collection, *Manners of Tuscan Verses*, to see that what is excluded in terms of *dispositio* of conceits and metaphors is retrieved by completely different textual strategies. Chiabrera minces his lines in *nuclei* of sound that repeat themselves at close intervals in mostly brief lines. Figures of repetition and *geminatio* like *paronomasia*, *figura etymologica*, and *polyptoton* abound, together with other devices that almost crystallize sounds and images. The paralogical short-circuiting of the essences is pursued through the exhibition of elemental similarities. Wonder, astonishment, *stupor*, are created by inviting a 'pre-grammatical' realization of those similarities. Pleasure here is not just the convolution of *peripezie*, of the twist of the plot (narrative or purely elocutive, since in lyrical poetry *dispositio* and *elocutio*, when the latter becomes a theme by itself, interpenetrate). If the loss of relevance of the *inventio*, and a gain in weight of the *dispositio* and *elocutio* could be 'institutional' (and thus not sociological, Marxist, or purely stylistic) explanations of the birth of the baroque literature (as Guido Morpurgo Tagliabue and, more recently and along the same line, José Antonio Maravall have suggested), Chiabrera's strategies for wonder, at least as they could be detected in his 'lighter' lyrical production, seem to have been radically different. This is, I believe, Chiabrera's major departure (although very often contradicted by himself), from Marinist or even pre-Marinist, Baroque or proto-Baroque poetry. Even if we look at Chiabrera's epic poems (*Gotiade, Firenze, Amedeide*, all but the first painstakingly reviewed during his lifetime) we could see that the sometimes ostentatious adherence to Tasso's precepts tends to create an illusion of predictability that allows the poet to concentrate on the purely heroic *amplification* (with the narrative component that cedes more and more space to dialogue and oratory, with only peripheral, although trumpeted, elements bestowing an epical status on the text). It is in the heroic poems that we see how Chiabrera (even more obviously after the publication, in 1623, of Marino's *Adonis*) tries to invent his own strategy for achieving novelty. The predictability of the narrative structure is certainly a major departure from the 'wonderful' anamorphoses of the *Adonis*, from its astonishing contradiction between the epic exterior and the all-embracing interior (what Rousset, and later Deleuze, observed about Roman baroque architecture would accurately characterize the *Adonis*). In Chiabrera, the effect of surprise, or the fetishism of the 'new' as it were, takes the form of epic narration restored to its measured demeanor, with the help of a cosmetic, ultra-heroic use of *prosopopoeia*.

One of the features of this quest for the new is the inconsistency that often seems to attend the poetic practice (if not the theoretical reflection) of many writers, and of the 'classicists' in particular, arising from their unwillingness to alienate a readership that still appeared to favour the Marinists. It should not surprise us that Chiabrera and his imitators occasionally contradicted their principles to prove that they, too, could manipulate conceits. A few years ago I called attention to a series of Chiabrera's poems that had been published but not yet been studied from the point of view of poetic style.[20] It is a series of madrigals dedicated to a certain Lidia that Chiabrera undoubtedly wrote as an exercise of *aemulatio*, or, I daresay, as a parody of Marino, by way of showing that he could rival the Neapolitan in conceits and marvellous tropes. I believe this further illustrates the polymorphous, interactive nature of stupefying with the 'new,' hence my decision to pluralize Chiabrera's 'nuovo mondo'in the title of this paper.

Notes

1 'Io pretendo di saper le regole più che non sanno tutti i pedanti insieme, ma la vera regola (cor mio bello) è saper rompere le regole a tempo e luogo, accomodandosi al costume corrente, ed al gusto del secolo.' Giambattista Marino, *Lettere*, ed. M. Guglielminetti (Turin: Einaudi, 1966), 396. All translations from Italian are mine.
2 'È del poeta il fin la meraviglia / (parlo dell'eccellente, non del goffo): / chi non sa far stupir vada alla striglia.'
3 On the Marino-Murtola diatribe, see Giovanni Getto, *Opere di G.B. Marino e dei marinisti* (Turin: UTET, 1962), 248, and Marzio Pieri, *Fischiata XXXIII. Un sonetto di Giambattista Marino* (Parma: Pratiche, 1992). In order to debunk what he sees as an 'interpretive equivocation' of Marino's declaration of poetics, Guido Pedrojetta suggests a counter-intuitive reading of the famous lines, arguing that the text is wilfully ironical and parodistic ('Marino e la meraviglia,' in *Interpretazione e meraviglia*, ed. Giuseppe Galli [Pisa: Giardini, 1994], 95–105). Alessandro Martini ('La pratica mariniana,' in *Interpretazione e meraviglia*, 107–19) reassesses such interpretations, and redefines the scope of Marino's notion of *meraviglia*, noting that the poet's intention was to manifest an idea of the marvellous that would go beyond the thematic implications of heroic or hexameronic poems. See also Giovanni Pozzi, *Saggio*

sullo stile dell'oratoria sacra nel Seicento esemplificata sul p. Emmanuele Orchi (Rome: Biblioteca Seraphico-Capuccina, 1954). For a rhetorical reading of the structure of Marino's *Adonis*, see Francesco Guardiani, *La meravigliosa retorica dell'*Adone *di G. B. Marino* (Florence: Olschki, 1989). On the notion of *meraviglia* in the larger spectrum of Baroque poetics and rhetorics, see Antonio Franceschetti, 'Il concetto di meraviglia nelle poetiche della prima Arcadia,' in *Lettere italiane* 21 (1969), 62–88, and Beatrice Rima, 'La meraviglia nella retorica del seicento,' in *Interpretazione e meraviglia*, 79–93.

4 For this *vexata quaestio*, see Franco Croce, *Tre momenti del barocco letterario Italiano* (Florence: Sansoni, 1966), and 'L'intellettuale Chiabrera,' in *La scelta della misura*, ed. Fulvio Bianchi and Paolo Russo (Genoa: Costa & Nolan, 1933), 15–50. See also Stefano Bottari, ed., *Il mito del classicismo nel Seicento* (Messina and Florence: D'Anna, 1964). For monographic studies on Chiabrera, see Fulvio Bianchi, 'Gabriello Chiabrera,' in *La letteratura ligure*, vol. 1 (Genoa: Costa & Nolan, 1992), 149–215, and Pier Luigi Cerisola, *L'arte dello stile. Poesia e letterarietà in Gabriello Chiabrera* (Milan: Franco Angeli, 1990).

5 For an interesting and innovative approach, see Sandro Benedetti, 'Il falso dilemma classicismo-barocco nell'architettura di Gian Lorenzo Bernini,' in *Immagini del Barocco: Bernini e las cultura del Seicento*, ed. Marcello Fagiolo and Gianfranco Spegnesi (Rome: Istituto dell'Enciclopedia Italiana, 1982), 71–92.

6 It is inevitable to draw a comparison between this type of rhetoric, and the one that could be found in works published later in the 17th century, such as Daniello Bartoli's *La ricreazione del savio* or *Dell' uomo di lettere difeso ed emendato*. At that time Chiabrera, and even before the investiture by the *Arcadia* Academy, was still considered the standard-bearer (vis-à-vis the Marinisti) of good taste in the age of corruption of poetic styles. For Leopardi's ideas on Chiabrera, see also his letter to Pietro Giordani of 19 February 1819: 'But of the four major [lyric] poets – Chiabrera, Testi, Filicaia, Guidi – I consider the latter two to be greatly inferior to the first two; and I especially wonder how Guidi has become so famous that even nowadays his works are so frequently and diligently reprinted. And since Chiabrera with all his beautiful pieces does not have a single *Ode* that can be lauded in all of its parts – or that indeed does not deserve blame for most of its parts – I can without hesitation award Testi the palm.' [Ma fra i quattro principali che sono il Chiabrera il Testi il Filicaia il Guidi, io metto questi due molto ma molto sotto i due primi; e nominatamente del Guidi mi maraviglio come abbia potuto venire in tanta fama che anche presentemente si ristampi con diligenza e più volte. E perché il Chiabrera con molti bellissimi pezzi, non ha solamente un'Ode che si possa lodare per ogni parte,

anzi in gran parte non vada biasimata, perciò non dubito di dar la palma al Testi]. Giacomo Leopardi, *Tutte le opere*, ed. Enrico Ghidetti (Florence: Sansoni, 1966), 1068.

7 'Scherzava sul suo poetare in questa forma, dicea ch'egli seguia Christoforo Columbo suo Cittadino, e *ch'egli voleva trovare nuovo mondo o affogare*. I quote from Giovanni G. Amoretti's edition, published as an appendix to his essay, 'La vita,' in *La scelta della misura* (202). On 'La vita,' see also Marziano Guglielminetti, 'La "Vita" di Chiabrera tra biografia e autobiografia,' in *La scelta della misura*, 179–89, and Gian Piero Maragoni, 'Postille in margine all'autobiografia del Chiabrera,' in *Lingua e stile* 19 (1984): 511–17.

8 On the myths of Columbus and Galileo, see Andrea Battistini, '"Cedat Columbus" e "Vicisti Galilee:" i due esploratori a confronto nell'immaginario barocco,' *Annali d'italianistica* 10 (1992): 116–32.

9 'Questo motto pare oggi una smargiassata, e ci fa ridere. Che grande ardire, che gran novità nel poetar del Chiabrera. Un poco d'imitazione di Pindaro, in luogo dell'imitazione del Petrarca seguita allora da tutti i così detti lirici. E pur tant'è: a que' tempi questa novità pareva somma, arditissima, facea grand'effetto. Oggi par poco, e basta appena a far impressione poetica tutta la novita e l'ardire che è nel Fausto o nel Manfredo. Può servire a un Discorso sul romanticismo.' G. Leopardi, *Zibaldone di pensieri*, ed. Giuseppe Pacella (Milan: Garzanti, 1991), 251–2, entry 4479, 1 April 1829.

10 '... diedesi a leggere Libri di Poesia per solazzo, e passo passo si condusse a volere intendere ciò ch'ella si fosse, e studiarvi attorno con attenzione. Parve a lui comprendere che gli Scrittori Greci meglio l'havessero trattata e di più s'abbandonò tutto su loro, e di Pindaro si maravigliò e prese ardimento di comporre alcuna cosa a sua somiglianza.' *Vita*, 199. Notice the exquisite *hysteron proteron* that Chiabrera uses to give an aura of *sprezzatura* to his poetic apprenticeship.

11 'Per dimostrar che il Poetare era suo studio, e che d'altro egli non si prezzava, teneva dipinta come Impresa una Cetra e queste parole del Petrarca, *Non ho se non quest'una.*' *Vita*, 203.

12 'Cigno gentil fra i più famosi cigni,/che portasse d'Italia il bel paese ... tu ben nobili voci in ciel sospigni,/tra la via greca, e il bel cammin francese' (*Opere di Gabriello Chiabrera e lirici del classicismo barocco*, ed. Marcello Turchi (Turin: UTET, 1970), 741). On the controversial relationship between Cebà and Chiabrera, see Carmela Reale, '"Un'amicitia di trenta anni." Il ricordo di Ansaldo Cebà in un inedito di Gabriello Chiabrera,' *Esperienze letterarie* 12.2 (1987): 27–44. Her exquisitely researched essay seems to me to be too benevolent on the issue of Cebà's real intentions in this poem.

13 Giulia Raboni's *quellenforschung* resulted in an excellent and impeccable

apparatus. Gabriello Chiabrera, *Maniere, scherzi e Canzonette morali,* ed. Giulia Raboni (Parma: Fondazione Pietro Bembo/Ugo Guanda, 1998).

14 For the notion of 'vischiosità' see Cesare Segre, *Esperienze ariostesche* (Pisa: Nistri-Lischi, 1966), 65–6 and *Teatro e romanzo* (Turin: Einaudi, 1984), 109–10.

15 See Francesco Luigi Mannucci, *La lirica di Gabriello Chiabrera. Storia e caratteri.* (Naples, Genoa, and Città di Castello: Perella, 1925). This study is almost entirely dedicated to the uncovering of alleged sources. On French Renaissance poetics, see Kees Meerhoff, *Rhétorique et poétique au XVIe siècle en France. Du Bellay, Ramus et les autres* (Leiden: E.J. Brill, 1986).

16 For these theories of cyclical concettismo see the old studies by Alessandro D'Ancona, 'Del Secentismo nella poesia cortigiana del XV secolo,' *Nuova Antologia* 11 (1876), and Joseph Vianey, *Le pétrarchisme en France au XVI siècle* (Montpellier: Coulet, 1909).

17 Chiabrera's metric theory is expressed in various writings, the most relevant being the dialogue *Il Vecchietti* and Lorenzo Fabri's presentation of the *Maniere de' versi toscani.*

18 'Io sentiva per bocca di musici, ed anco per bocca d'altri, alcune maniere di versi, delle quali io soleva pigliar meraviglia. Ma da prima la maraviglia non mi metteva in alcun pensamento, perciocché il mondo fu sempre ripieno d'ingegni vaghi di strane fantasie; [ma io osservava che le strane fantasie poco duravano, e quelle che poco deono durare, dalle persone valorose non si prezzano] ora i versi, di che io sono per favellarvi, ed anche le maniere di metterli insieme, non sono, secondo che a me viene detto, disprezzati da quegl'illustrissimi intelletti.' *Opere di Gabriello Chiabrera e lirici del classicismo barocco,* 550. On the relationship of poetry and musical setting, see also the dialogues *Geri* and *Bamberini* and Lorenzo Fabri's preface to the *Maniere de' versi toscani.* On the issue of Chiabrera's relations with composers, and on the *persona* of Fabri, see Vassalli, 'Chiabrera, la musica e i musicisti: le rime amorose' and Raboni, 'Introduzione' in Gabriello Chiabrera, *Maniere, Scherzi e Canzonette morali.* Raboni's introduction provides the most recent and methodologically impeccable, critical assessment of some of Chiabrera's most important collections of poems.

19 Northrop Frye, 'Introduction' to *Sound and Poetry* (New York, Columbia University Press, 1963): xxiv. This reflection on the polyphonic setting of poems, although unrelated to our case, is perfectly fitting.

20 See my essay '*Non prima ebbe favella che rima.* Preliminari per un discorso su Marino e Chiabrera,' in *The Sense of Marino,* ed. Francesco Guardiani (Ottawa: Legas, 1994).

chapter five

Truth and Wonder in Naples circa 1640

JON R. SNYDER

The poet Giambattista Marino died in Naples in 1625, his fame assured both at home and abroad. Marino's influence among the city's *letterati* continued to grow throughout the first half of the seventeenth century in spite of the notoriety of his banned poem *Adone* (1623).[1] His sweeping rejection of the neoclassical rules of composition became the cornerstone of the new baroque poetry in Italy during these years, and Naples was by the 1620s a hotbed of *marinisti*. The poetics of *meraviglia* (marvel, wonder) represented a revolt not only against the established poetic decorum of the later sixteenth century, but against the notion of normative critical taste. In polemical opposition to well-entrenched Aristotelian critics in Italy, Marino argued that the ultimate judge of the success or failure of a given work was the public, whose favour the poet thus needed to cultivate. How? In a word, Marino explained, poetry was invention: for the invention of dazzling metaphors and concepts should produce *meraviglia* in the reader's mind, and this intensely pleasurable emotion should in turn make the text and the poet irresistible for the reading public. The measure of Marino's influence in the Seicento can perhaps best be grasped in Tesauro's enormous masterpiece of baroque poetic theory, *Il cannocchiale aristotelico*, which is an extended reflection on the *Adone*.[2] Marino's forceful critique of poetic mimesis in favour of freedom of invention, as formulated in his masterpiece, echoed in any case throughout the rest of the seventeenth century: 'lecita è la menzogna anco talvolta,/ quando giova a chi mente il dir bugia/ e non noce il mentire a chi l'ascolta' (*Adone* XIV, 36, 4–6).[3]

One of Marino's most important patrons in Naples, the Marchese Giovan Battista Manso, founded the Accademia degli Oziosi in 1611.[4] Marino himself was active in the Oziosi, and late in life was acclaimed *principe* of the organization by its members. This position brought with it a number of obligations, however, for the Oziosi were at the centre of literary life in the capital and constituted a rather demanding 'public.'[5] After his triumphal return to Naples from Paris, Marino complained in a letter to Antonio Bruni (May-June 1624) that 'bisogna ogni mercordì far un discorso imparato a mente per introduzione del problema, ed acciocché sia degno dell'aspettazione che si ha su di me e della gente che mi ascolta, son costretto a farvi studio particolare' (every Wednesday one must make a speech from memory to introduce the problem, and in order to be worthy of the expectations for me of those that are listening to me, I have to make a detailed study of it first).[6] Although Marino did not have long to play this role (he died the following year), recent studies have convincingly shown that the vast network of academies linking together the cultures of the peninsula from Venice to Naples formed an enduring 'republic of letters' under the Old Regime.[7] Manso's academy was a part of this cultural system until the years immediately prior to the revolt of 1647 in Naples. Having served as the academy's annually elected *principe* since 1625, the Marchese died in 1645; after his death the Accademia degli Oziosi no longer was the leading literary circle for the Neapolitan aristocracy (although it was briefly revived in the 1650s).

Some of the better-known men of letters who were members of the Oziosi, like Maiolino Bisaccioni, who took part in the failed 1635 uprising in Naples, also belonged to other famous academies in Central and Northern Italy, such as the 'Accademia degli Incogniti' in Venice (in which Marino was posthumously granted membership), whose members shared many of the same interests – if not always the same social rank – as the members of the Oziosi. Granted, academies such as the Oziosi had to compromise with the Old Regime in order to exist in the first place. Any hint of seditious talk among academicians would, at the very least, immediately have brought the wrath of the local authorities down on them.[8] The 'Laws' of the Oziosi, for instance, strictly prohibited any discussion of theology and public affairs.[9] The Italian academies of the first half of the seventeenth century nevertheless formed – in an era without newspapers, gazettes, or coffee houses – an embryonic sphere of public opinion in which at least some ideas could be circulated and contested, while generally avoiding the political and religious controversies of the era.

Among the writers in Manso's circle were Giuseppe Battista (1610–1675) and Torquato Accetto (ca. 1590–1641 or later). Although they belonged to different generations, the two men both hailed from the Apulia region of Southern Italy. The former was a convinced *marinista* and the latter was a *barocco moderato*, although both were thoroughly attuned to the literary fashions of the age in their poetry and prose. After years of study in Naples (he first took up residence there ca. 1626) that led to a *laurea* in theology, Battista joined the Oziosi around 1633.[10] A gifted orator, skilled in the academic arts of 'lezioni, risposte a quesiti, orazioni [e] composizioni,' as well as a poet, he became a leading figure in the academy's later revival.[11] Accetto – who had arrived in Naples by 1618 from Andria – participated in some of the academy's activities without apparently becoming a member. This was not at all uncommon in seventeenth-century Italian academies, and not surprising insofar as Accetto's employer, the Duke of Caraffa, was a member of the Oziosi.[12] The paths of the two writers would likely have intersected for a few years only, for there is no trace of Accetto after 1641, the year of publication in Naples of his slender treatise entitled *Della dissimulazione onesta* (*DO*). Whether Accetto died around that time, simply stopped writing, or suffered 'social death' and subsequent public oblivion (perhaps because of the nature of his writing on dissimulation), is not known to us. As Salvatore Nigro has pointed out, there are no contemporary reviews or citations of the work, and no mention of it in the voluminous correspondence of the age. It simply vanished, along with its author, under the gaze of an apparently indifferent public.[13]

I will argue here that Accetto's curious *libello* – now considered (after its rediscovery in the early twentieth century) one of the most significant works of Italian baroque prose – may well have been written in response to a debate that took place within the Accademia degli Oziosi sometime around 1640.[14] We know that such debates did take place regularly, involved any number of members at one time, and sometimes risked becoming violent public quarrels. The manuscript of the 'Laws' of the Oziosi (BNN, ms. Brancacciana V.D.14 [miscellanea manoscritti], ff. 127r–134r) is telling in this regard. After setting out the rules and procedures of the academy in elaborate detail, the manuscript suddenly changes register. Written in another hand some years later, this second part of the manuscript seems to have as its main goal the elimination of discord between the members through the careful regulation of behaviour outside the walls of the academy (publications, public altercations, etc.), which had not been foreseen at the time of the founding of the Oziosi:

E perciò quantunque a ciascuno sarà lecito di favellare di fuori degli esercitij dell'Accademia, non serà però convenevole discrovrire [sic]i difetti o gli errori de gli Accademici.
'Quindi è che fra noi non dee essere gara, ne contesa alcuna ... '[15]

[And thus however legitimate it is for members to speak on the outside of the Academy's proceedings, it is inappropriate to reveal the faults or errors of the academicians.
Hence between ourselves there is to be no competition or contention whatsoever ...]

Those who did not obey these rules forbidding members to make public the literary controversies of the academy could be expelled by the *principe*.

In the absence of other archival documents, however, I will rely here on the internal evidence of two texts, *Della dissimulazione onesta* and Battista's brief *Apologia della menzogna* (*AM*), along with what is known about the workings of the academy during this period. Although published only in 1673 in Venice, Battista's *Apologia* was written and read aloud as a part of the Oziosi's proceedings in Naples more than thirty years earlier, when European interest in simulation and dissimulation was reaching its peak.[16] As Battista noted in a letter, 'per lo spazio di questo verno porrò in assetto un fascio di Discorsi e Risposte Accademiche, funzioni da me fatte negli anni più teneri fra gli Oziosi, sotto il Principato del già Marchese Manso' (during this winter I will put in order a bundle of academic speeches and responses which I wrote in my youth among the Oziosi, whose prince was the late Marchese Manso).[17]

The debate over the 'naturality' of falsehood and deception, one of the core concerns of baroque aesthetic and social discourse, found the younger Battista and the older Accetto on opposite sides. It is impossible to say with certainty which work was composed first, although Accetto's treatise seems most likely a veiled response to Battista's text as presented to the assembled Oziosi. Whichever one came first, it is clear that this was a clash of sharply contrasting critical as well as poetic canons, exemplary of the tension running through the whole of Neapolitan literary culture in the *primo Seicento*.[18] Through an analysis of their respective treatments of the same theme, we can detect two distinctly different early modern critical positions concerning the evolving relationship between the writer, language, and the public.

Accetto composed some encomiastic verses to accompany the publication of Manso's *Poesie nomiche* in Venice in 1635, and published three editions of his own *Rime* in Naples (1621, 1626, and 1638). Thanks to these publications, which display an aversion to the poetic pyrotechnics of the Marinists, he was undoubtedly an established, if minor, local poet by the end of the 1630s. We know from one of Manso's biographers that, soon after joining the Oziosi, Battista sparked a heated controversy among its members concerning the desirability of experimental baroque poetics over the older Petrarchan/Ciceronian school.[19] Battista began to publish his *Poesie meliche* in Naples only in the 1650s, although he had first considered doing so in 1639. The final version of this work appeared in Venice in 1664, not without notice. An anonymous Venetian wit roused the long-dead libertine Ferrante Pallavicino (another member of the Accademia degli Incogniti), who had been tortured and executed by the Pope's agents in Lyons in 1644, from his unquiet grave to survey the state of contemporary literature. 'Giuseppe Battista ha stampato un volumetto di rime, ma non c'è gran cosa' (Giuseppe Battista has printed a little volume of verse, but there isn't much to it) was the dismissive comment uttered by his ghost in *L'anima di Ferrante Pallavicino, Vigilia Seconda* (1665).[20] The intense poetic and economic competition for worldly success and acclaim, exemplified by Marino himself, could not have left Battista and Accetto untouched. If they intially found themselves at odds in Naples over rival canons of poetry and poetics, this clash seems to have led to a further exchange between the two men – who perhaps vied for the patronage of the elderly Manso – in the form of these two brief 'academic' texts.

In spite of the exalted social position of its founder, backer, and *principe*, Manso, the Accademia degli Oziosi was subject to the far-reaching control of political and ecclesiastical authorities in Naples. After the revolt of 1548, for instance, nearly all of the Neapolitan academies – at the time centres of humanism that favoured scientific, philosophical, and political discussions – were closed by these same authorities.[21] Thanks to the phenomenal popularity of academies in the *secondo Cinquecento* across Italy, the institution was soon restored in Naples to a position of cultural and social prestige. Nevertheless, in the seventeenth century the royal and ecclesiastical magistrates maintained the right to censure all texts before they were read to any academic assembly.[22] This censorship, although often quite lax by later standards, was sufficient to prevent the academies from forming the nucleus of a genuine political alternative to the deeply unpopular Viceregal regime.

Battista's apology for falsehood was perhaps formulated in response to a preselected *questione* posed to the members of the Oziosi (the weekly *problema* mentioned by Marino in his abovementioned letter to Antonio Bruni), or it may have been a theme of his own choosing, to which another member might have been expected to respond.[23] Moreover, the text may well have been vetted in advance and approved by the censors before its delivery to the assembled membership, just as Accetto's treatise received a regular *imprimatur* from the same censors before publication. Whatever the case, the *Apologia della menzogna* displays a taste for figures of paradox and hyperbole of the sort favoured by the *marinisti*, who saw them as a means to generate a sense of wonder in the mind of the reading public.[24] Battista begins his text with the timeworn adage 'la verità è madre dell'odio' (truth is the mother of hatred), whose corollary, he argues paradoxically, is that 'genitrice dell'affetto sarà la menzogna' (falsehood is the mother of affection) (*AM* 65). This same trope appears in his sonnet entitled 'Per donna bugiarda,' composed in this same period but published only much later: '... se la veritade odio produce,/dritto è che la bugia produca amore' (if truth is the mother of hatred, then it must follow that falsehood is the mother of love).[25] And this love is necessary to whoever wishes to sway an audience through the power of words, as the new poetics demands: 'a persuadere, Oziosi, necessaria è predicata l'arte di cattar benevolenza' (in order to persuade, Oziosi, the art of capturing [others'] benevolence is needed) (*AM* 65). Therefore Battista's own public, he notes wryly, cannot help but be persuaded by his discourse, because what he is writing is an apology for falsehood. The argument is syllogistic: the public is swayed through words that attract its *benevolenza*; the highest form of benevolence – *amore* – is produced by falsehood; therefore falsehood will be the best *arte* through which to speak to the public. Rhetoric as persuasion is, in other words, the art of lying.

Battista confirms later on in the text of the *Apologia* that, indeed, 'l'affetto degli uomini si acquista col mentire' (the affection of men is acquired through lying) (*AM* 80). Here, however, he turns – in typically baroque fashion – to psychology rather than logic in support of his argument. Flattery conquers even the most austere of hearts, Battista claims, whereas those who speak frankly and truthfully are condemned as arrogant ('chi vuol dire la verità è censurato per uomo superbo di genio e libero di lingua' [whoever wishes to speak the truth is criticized as arrogant in character and free with his tongue] [*AM* 79]). Who can resist the power of adulation? Who can resist hearing what one would really like to hear, rather than what one does not want to hear? If flattery gives one power over one's listeners or readers, Battista notes, telling the truth is quite another thing. He observes that 'offende ciò che non vuole intendersi, e diletta quel che d'ascoltar si brama' (what one does not want to understand offends, and one what longs to hear delights) (*AM* 80). Thus the truth may even prove dangerous to s/he who speaks it, for it can cut those listening to the quick, provoking a violent and unpredictable reaction in them. He draws from the repertory of classicism to reinforce his critique of truth-telling: Alexander thrust a javelin through the heart of Clitus for speaking the truth about the king's debauchery, and Cambyses slew Prexaspes for criticizing his drunkenness. By the same token, however, falsehood penetrates with ease through the ear, 'e ci contentiamo di quelle insidie che si fanno all'udito' (and we are accepting of those deceits that are produced through hearing [them]) (*AM* 80). This weakness in human nature, however, is not to be viewed in a morally negative perspective in terms of Marinist poetics. Humanity's receptivity to falsehood offers a great advantage, Battista explains, to those who need to persuade others, and hope to do so by exploiting what is known of the human mind and heart. The sudden happiness that a listener or reader feels at the fulfilment of a secret and unspoken desire to hear what one would really like to hear, rather than the harsh truth, is nothing other than an homage to the power of falsehood, with which Battista identifies rhetoric itself.

In much of the *Apologia*, however, Battista favours a metaphysical rather than psychological mode of inquiry into the nature of things themselves and our perception of them. Like Marino in the *Adone*, he shifts restlessly from one scene or theme to the next without concern for the causal logic that connects them, rummaging through the classics ('razzolando con ronciglio')[26] for authorities to support his arguments. Like Marino, Battista seeks to generate a sense of marvel in his listeners (or readers) via the 'shock of the new' that arises from the unexpected conceptual juxtapositions and extreme rhetorical figures that fill the text of his apology. Thus all earthly appearances suddenly become one with *la menzogna* itself, bracketing the question of intention (was it the speaker's intent to deceive?) that had determined Western thinking about falsehood since the Greeks. All things 'disdain' (*sdegnano*) falsehood, Battista observes, yet falsehood is found in all things (*AM* 65). What is prime matter if not, as Augustine argues, that which is neither colour nor figure nor body nor spirit, yet which is not nothing at all? Such matter is, Battista infers, 'un'ombra del nulla, e pur si truova in tutti gli enti' (a shadow of nothing, and yet it is found in all entities)

(*AM* 66). It is a shadowy essence at once everywhere and nowhere; the sky, fire, air, water, and earth are nothing without it, and yet it is none of these. It is the elusive Proteus of the universe ('Proteo dell'universo' [*AM* 66]), which can be anything at all and yet transform itself into anything else. Battista concludes that, in fact, the nature of matter is whatever we think it to be: 'ella altro esser non abbia se non quello che le comunica l'umano intendimento' (it has no being other than that which human understanding communicates to it) (*AM* 67). Its appearance is simply a projection of the mind, while it wanders 'vagabonda' (*AM* 68) through the universe, guaranteeing at once both unity and variety to the things in it. Thus this first principle is itself an illusion and a lie ('oh quante bugie!' [*AM* 68]), upon whose deceptive foundation things themselves are constructed.

Battista asks his listeners, if they are still unpersuaded by his argument, to consider the nature of the heavens, one of the pressing issues of the new seventeenth-century science. For whatever one thinks of the heavens in scientific terms, he points out, there still remains doubt and uncertainty: 'dubbio sempre rimarrebbe e lontano pur troppo dalla certezza' (doubt would always remain, unfortunately far removed from certainty) (*AM* 68). Battista uses the rhetorical method of the contemporary *cultura classicista* to produce a catalogue of contradictory claims about the heavens from antiquity: Pythagoras says they are made of fire; Empedocles says they are like crystal; Thales says they are made of earth; the Egyptians think that there are eight heavens, but Ptolemy argues for nine of them; some say the heavens are spherical, while others think them oval; the sun has spots invisible to the naked eye and yet is 'schiett[o]'; the moon lies about itself continuously through its phases; the heavens seem stable, 'e pur si muovono' (*AM* 68–9).[27] The same chaos of conflicting thoughts and perceptions exists for the Milky Way, which could be anything from a dense cluster of stars ('le parti più dense del cielo stesso') to Juno's spilled breast-milk (*AM* 69–70). After this impressive display of erudition, Battista rhetorically asks his fellow academicians, while sidestepping any allusion to the difference between intent to deceive and illusion in general: 'oh dove, Signori, troverete il vero, quando per un sentiero di purità s'incespica in tante bugie?' (where, sirs, will you find the true, when one may stumble over so many lies [even] on such a path of purity?) (*AM* 70). He produces another catalogue for theories of the rainbow, which, like a prism, 'niun colore possiede, e ne vanta mille' (has no colour and yet boasts of a thousand) (*AM* 71). The rainbow is sheer appearance without substance, and all the metaphors produced by the philosophers and poets (including a couple by Battista himself) in order to designate it are mere simulacra of a simulacrum, shadows of what is already only a shadow.

And so it goes in the *Apologia*. Even the body itself is only a thick tissue of deceit. Understanding, will, memory, and the senses are all prisoners of error and falsehood. Battista uses the example of the eye – that crucial portal of baroque experience – to demonstrate his point, which any listener or reader versed in the illusionistic culture of the age would surely have grasped effortlessly. Politics and morality are removed from the laws of physics, he notes, and yet they too are subject to the rule of universal falsehood. The courts are full of 'cicalecci bugiardi,' and even the greatest poets are known to have lied about their political paymasters: Quintilian calls Domitian a great poet and Virgil calls Caesar a god (*AM* 75). The wise Seneca, popular among the Oziosi, instead writes: 'ti mostrerò qual è la povertà che affligge i potenti, che cosa manca a quelli che possiedono tutto: manca loro chi dica la verità' (I will show you the poverty that afflicts the powerful, [and] what those who have everything are lacking – namely someone who would speak the truth to them) (*AM* 75).[28] Spies are everywhere, Battista laments, as they were in the age of Tiberius and Domitian, and they invent falsehoods for personal gain or vendetta: 'quanti rapportatori inventano menzogne, perché invidiano gli Amani, odiano i Danieli, amano le Susanne?' (how many informers invent lies because they envy the Hamans, hate the Daniels, or love the Susannas?) (*AM* 76). The legal system is no different, and neither is the church, where many may wear the lamb's skin to disguise the fox beneath (*AM* 76). The professions of the liberal arts are equally contaminated by falsehood, whether in philosophy, rhetoric, painting, history or poetry. To deny the power of the lie to poetry in particular would mean to destroy it: 'chi tor vuole alla poesia le menzogne, la vuol distrutta' (whoever wishes to deny poetry the use of falsehoods seeks to destroy it) (*AM* 77). Moreover, philosophers from Heliodorus to Plato affirm the importance of lying at an opportune moment, as if it were the most natural thing in the world.

Battista ultimately concludes that everything in the world is a lie because everything is linked to, and conditioned by, appearances. Whatever something seems to be to our sight or to our touch, it is in truth something else again (although he does not say how that could possibly be known to us with any certainty): 'tutte le cose che chiude il mondo sono bugiarde apparenze. Altramente sono, altramente si veggono' (all things contained within the world are lying appearances. They are seen in one way, yet they are otherwise) (*AM* 80). Thus he brings to an end his hyperbolic *Apologia della menzogna* by reiterating the well-established baroque *topos* of the fragile and unstable nature of human knowledge of the universe. Calling on his audience to reject any truth-claims for the illusory, shifting world of appearances that the eye perceives, Battista affirms with a final paradoxical flourish that there is nothing natural except the absence of truth and/or the presence of error. Although we cannot say with certainty whether or not this imaginative discourse had its desired effect of producing a sense of wonder in the minds of those who first listened to it, there can be little doubt about the terms in which Battista would have defined its success.

The *Apologia della menzogna* attempts to collapse all categories of existence and knowledge into one single overarching conceit (*concetto*), in order to make its intended public – the members of the Accademia degli Oziosi – marvel at Battista's own virtuoso display of *ingegno* in spinning this glittering web of words, and, eventually, fall under his sway. If the public is bedazzled, delighted, and swayed by such extravagant bravura, which unnaturally welds together radically dissimilar objects with skilful artifice, this in turn provides confirmation that Battista's rhetoric of lying has indeed had its desired effect. Success with the public determines fashion in art, according to the poetics of Marinism embraced by Battista; 'wonder' and 'marvel' are thus the true index of the text's rhetorical and aesthetic efficacy, not a set of Aristotelian rules and norms. The *Apologia della Menzogna* concludes with the following paradox: the more lies one tells, the more success one has as an artist (thanks to falsehood's special persuasiveness), and thus the more power one obtains over others. This would seem to be the only 'truth' that cannot be subsumed by the universal nature of falsehood and the ephemeral rule of fashion.

Perhaps there were other direct interventions in this debate at the Accademia degli Oziosi, but they are not known to us. Few papers from the proceedings of the academy have survived in their original form, and most of these are sonnets.[29] At least one member of the audience, however, must not have been overly impressed with Battista's oration. For the examination of the subject's moral and ethical stance in regard to falsehood – When is it morally legitimate to utter a lie knowingly, and to what end? If we must live in a world of falsehood, how should we conduct ourselves? – that Battista sidesteps is at the very heart of Torquato Accetto's *Della dissimulazione onesta*. In the preface, Accetto states that he has been at work revising the first version of the treatise for at least a year (thus dating the completion of this first version to 1640). He adds that many in Naples are aware, moreover, that his earlier version has been radically reduced in size in order to form the present volume: 'ha un anno ch'era questo trattato tre volte piú di quanto ora si vede, e ciò è noto a molti; e s'io avessi voluto piú differire il darlo alla stampa, sarebbe stata via di ridurlo in nulla' (a year ago this treatise was three times larger than it is now, and many know this; and if I had wanted to defer further its publication, this would have been a way to reduce it to nothing) (*DO* 5–6).[30] This would seem to suggest, in light of what has been said above, that the work was known to the members of the academy, or at least to the members of Accetto's circle inside and outside the Oziosi. The final version of his treatise is written in a tersely laconic style that takes to an extreme the literary revival of Tacitean prose; its expressive logic relies on highly condensed epigrams, maxims, allusions, truncated citations, ellipses, and paradoxes. Rather than proceed by amplification, as Battista does, Accetto chooses to proceed by subtraction.[31] Indeed, he explains wryly, he would have done away with words altogether if it were possible: 'se in questa materia avessi potuto metter nelle carte i semplici cenni, volentieri per mezzo di quelli mi averei fatto intendere, per far meno anche di poche parole' (if in treating this subject I could have but put simple signs on paper, I would have willingly made myself understood through them, in order to do away with even just a few words) (*DO* 5). In a typical paradox, he thus suggests that one source of marvel and wonder for readers of his treatise will consist in the artifice of its extreme poverty of means. The choice of the laconic style, Accetto remarks, was made in order to suit the taste of the public, in accordance with Marino's poetic precepts. Nevertheless – in one of the greatest understatements in the history of Italian literature, given the resounding silence that surrounded his book for three centuries – he claims to be fully aware that he has not succeeded. 'Dopo ogni sforzo *di ben servir al gusto pubblico,* io conosco di non aver questo, né altro valore, e solo ho speranza che sarà gradita la volontà' (after [making] every effort *to serve well the public's taste,* I know that I do not have either this or any other value, and I only hope that my intent will be appreciated) (*DO* 7; emphasis added).

The first three chapters of the work are devoted to refuting bluntly the naturalizing rhetoric of Battista's *Apologia della menzogna.* Accetto notes that what is called for nowadays, given the social and economic conflicts in the Kingdom of Naples, is prudence, because there are many obstacles in the way of those who are trying to live with dignity in difficult circumstances: 'da quanto va succedendo si può veder ogni giorno il vantaggio di proceder a passi tardi e lenti, quando la via è piena d'intoppi. Da questa considerazione mi mossi a trattar di tal suggetto' (from what is happening one can see every day the advantage of proceeding with late and slow steps, when the way is fraught with obstacles. It was this consideration that led me to treat such a subject) (*DO* 5). This honest dissimulation is not to be confused with hypocrisy or amorality – the charges levelled at the sort of prudence practised by courtiers and ministers of state – for 'non è vera prudenza quella che non è innocente' (it is not real prudence if it is not innocent [*DO* 4]). Accetto is careful to point out his own edifying intent in discussing honest dissimulation, noting that 'mi sono guardato da ogni senso di mal costume' (I stayed away from any manner of bad behaviour [*DO* 5]) in composing his treatise. This does not mean that this sort of prudence is naturally preferable to candour, sincerity, and frankness. If dissimulation begins with human history, when Adam first covered himself with a fig leaf in the Garden, nonetheless its use is to be avoided whenever possible. The problem, Accetto argues, is that – in the corrupt contemporary world of absolutism and neofeudalism – it is impossible for the subject (*l'uomo medio*) to avoid employing the artifice of dissimulation in order to survive, much less prosper: sincerity and candour would lead directly to disaster. The only solution is to continue to love the truth in secret while reducing, through honest dissimulation, the risks that this love of truth entails ('amando come sempre la verità, procurerò nel rimanente de' miei giorni di vagheggiarla con minor pericolo' (loving, as always, the truth, I will undertake in my remaining days to cherish it with less danger to me [*DO* 10]).

There is no justification of any sort, however, for lying. Accetto seems to have his sights fixed firmly on Battista (and Marino) at the beginning of the first chapter of *Della dissimulazione onesta*, when he remarks that 'nel bel sereno della vita non si dee dar luogo all'importuna nebbia della menzogna, la qual in ogni modo convien che resti esclusa' (the broad daylight of life must not give rise to the troublesome fog of the lie, which in any case should remain excluded [from it]) (*DO* 9). Beauty and goodness are to be found only in truth; lying is an aberrant and unnatural act. Moreover, beauty and truth are in things themselves, and cannot be invented by art. Accetto's two Neoplatonic propositions are thus intended to demolish the rhetorical edifice upon which the *Apologia della menzogna* is built. Although the masses find happiness through the pleasures of the senses, and the politicians find it through honour and skill, intellectuals must find happiness in the contemplation of the truth inherent in Being and inseparable from God himself.[32] This leaves little room for the kind of illusionistic universe described by Battista. Although we must all occasionally step aside from the truth, this must be done without lapsing into falsehood, Accetto insists repeatedly ('si consideri il lume della verità, per prendere licenza di andare poi un poco da parte, senza lasciar l'onestà del mezzo' [one should keep the light of truth in mind in subsequently taking leave to distance oneself a bit [from it], but without leaving the honesty of the means] [*DO* 11]). In the golden age of humanity, lovers spoke to lovers, and friends to friends, with transparent and open hearts and minds. They did not need to call on witnesses to prove what had been said between them, unlike the present time, and they loved the truth not for reasons of self-interest, but in and for itself.

If this golden age of truth in human affairs has sadly been lost forever, Accetto insists, lying is nonetheless still morally repugnant. Borrowing a metaphor from the new science, he points out that falsehood is like the vacuum that nature abhors, only in this case it constitutes the moral vacuum of speech and thought: 'non tanto la natura fugge il vacuo, quanto il costume dee fuggir il falso, ch'è il vacuo della favella e del pensiero' (Nature does not so much abhor a vacuum as our behaviour must abhor the false, which is the vacuum of speech and thought) (*DO* 15). Behind this moral emptiness lies the question of intent that Battista avoids in his apology for lying. For the mind cannot lie to itself, and therefore a defective moral conscience – or moral vacuum – must always play a key role in the decision to lie knowingly to others: 'non si può fare inganno a se medesimo, presupposto che la mente non possa mentire con intelligenza di mentire a se stessa, perché sarebbe vedere e non vedere' (one cannot deceive oneself, if it is presupposed that the mind cannot lie to itself with the knowledge that it is lying, because that would be like seeing and not seeing) (*DO* 16–17). To resort to falsehood means to harm oneself and, potentially, to harm others as well. If the truth cannot be spoken because of circumstances, Accetto explains, there is another solution that avoids the moral error of falsehood: namely, the artifice of honest dissimulation.

Accetto defines honest dissimulation as "l viver cauto ... con la purità dell'animo' (living cautiously ... with purity of mind) (*DO* 4). It is a morally acceptable alternative to lying or simulation, although it is an equally unnatural act, as we shall see; but it is 'honest' precisely because it does not employ lies. Contemporary historians such as Zagorin and Villari portray early modern dissimulation as a practice of resistance to the oppressive social, cultural, and religious norms of the Counter-Reformation. Many early modern intellectuals suggest the same thing. Virgilio Malvezzi, one of the greatest of baroque stylists, writes that 'non è bene sempre dire tutto quello che si ha nel cuore, ancorché fosse bene quello che si ha nel cuore: si deve por freno talvolta al parlar libero, quando è già corrotto il viver libero' (it is not always a good idea to say everything that one has in one's heart, even though what one has in one's heart is good: at times one has to restrain oneself from speaking freely, when the free life is already corrupt).[33] This practice of dissimulation, which works through silence, reticence, withdrawal, and ambiguity, is nonetheless dialectically linked to the baroque culture of display. Honest dissimulation is understood by Accetto as freedom from the obligation to display or perform one's emotions and thoughts – but without breaking entirely with the regime of visibility, which would threaten one's social rank, prestige, and secure place in the social order. One is still apparently present and visibly part of the civil conversation, while attempting to maintain a 'zero degree' of communicability whose purpose is to safeguard one's truths (to say nothing at all would be to call attention to the fact that one has something to hide).

Honest dissimulation is designed to enable the components of individual interior experience – heart and mind – to allow themselves to be discovered only to the subject, without risking loss of face, prestige, or power, on the one hand, and without violating the moral integrity of the subject, on the other. This is not just a question of avoiding the pressure to conform to the norm, or of making a show of adapting to the norm while retaining one's moral conscience intact. Rather, interiority is taken here to be the site of full self-coincidence, split off from the classical notion of 'con-science' (as a knowing 'with others'). As Accetto observes in *Della dissimulazione onesta*: 'Tanto è nostro quanto è in noi medesimi' (what is ours is what is found in us [33]).[34] Thus honest dissimulation allows natural mental and emotional representations to emerge, through a chiaroscuro play of shadow and light, into a secret inner space where they may be screened by the subject unwilling to articulate them openly or lie about them, yet unable to repress them completely.[35]

Such an approach may function successfully only through the establishment of a relationship to oneself as well as to others: in dissimulating with others, one has to be extremely careful not to dissimulate with oneself. Following the tenets of neostoicism, there is no place in Accetto's theory of dissimulation for an 'unconscious' that might work against the

dissimulator's intentions, or for a potentially disruptive impersonal entity such as Fortune. Nor can the elusive workings of language, with its slippery metaphors and figures of speech, be held responsible for undermining the dissimulator's efforts. Shining a glaring light into the most remote recesses of the mind and heart ('quanto è in noi medesimi'), s/he is fully responsible for exercising prudence at all times and in all places, and for extinguishing expressions of spontaneity and sincerity through the proper use of the will. The foundational moment of honest dissimulation is, in short, the achievement of full self-consciousness or self-transparency. The Socratic *nosce te ipsum*, or 'know thyself,' required for such a plenitude of consciousness is warmly seconded by Gracián in his *Oráculo manual y arte de prudencia*, composed only a few years later: 'Comprehensión de sí: en el genio, en el ingenio, en dictámenes, en afectos. Non puede uno ser señor de sí si primero no se comprehende. Hay espejos del rostro, no los hay del ánimo: séalo la discreta reflexión sobre sí' (Know yourself: your character, intellect, judgment, and emotions. You cannot master yourself if you do not understand yourself. There are mirrors for the face, but the only mirror for the spirit is wise self-reflection).[36]

Accetto instead offers his readers a particularly vivid baroque image. Dissimulation, he notes, is like a set of lines exiting from the breast and tracing an outline around those listening or looking on, so that they are caught up in the web of representation spun by the dissimulator, who alone knows the meaning of his or her own heart and alone can see outside the contours of the web that s/he has spun: 'dal centro del petto son tirate le linee della dissimulazione alla circonferenza di quelli che ci stanno intorno' (the lines of dissimulation are drawn from the centre of the breast to the circumference of those who are around us [*DO* 17]). These lines are cast like beams of light that blind others to the truth, but do not envelop the dissimulator's own mind and heart, precisely because one cannot – and should not – fool oneself. Thus, in attempting to define a relationship to herself or himself, the honest dissimulator seeks to establish her or his own subjective position in ethical terms.

If limited only to this, however, the project of honest dissimulation would be just a footnote to prior attempts in Western philosophy and moral thought to attain full and complete self-knowledge. Accetto notes along these lines that 'prima dunque ciascun dee procurar non solo di aver nuova di sé e delle cose sue, ma piena notizia, ed abitar non nella superficie dell'opinione, che spesse volte è fallace, ma nel profondo de' suoi pensieri, ed aver la misura del suo talento e la vera diffinizione di

ciò ch'egli vale' (therefore first of all one ought to try not only to get some news of oneself and one's concerns, but a complete report, and dwell not only on the surface of opinion, which is often mistaken, but in the depth of one's thoughts, and take the measure of one's talent and the true definition of what one is worth [*DO* 37]). What distinguishes honest dissimulation from the Socratic-Platonic and Augustinian philosophies is its attempt to transform that hard-won 'news' about the self into a secret – that is, into something not only dissimilar from others, but unknowable for others.

For the nature of this secret defines the very (limited) possibility of psychic freedom for the Old Regime subject. By keeping one's 'news' secret from others, honest dissimulation makes it hypothetically possible to maintain one's position in absolutist society and at the same time avoid a complete neutralization of one's mental and emotional experience. To paraphrase Gracián, to master the art of secrecy means to have no master other than that art itself. The honest dissimulator seeks to experience a kind of solipsistic liberation from the pressures of the other, while producing a morally and ethically tolerable experience devoid of falsehood. Others cannot see through the blank wall of honest dissimulation; there is no need to mislead them with lies, but only to block out their gaze. Through diligent exercise of the carefully honed techniques of honest dissimulation – reticence, silence, equivocation, and indirection – the subject may move freely within the limits of his or her own mental and emotional sphere, although denied the possibility of a sincere exchange of minds with other subjects.

Accetto notes with no small amount of irony that 'si ammira, come grandezza degli uomini di alto stato, lo starsi ne' termini de' palagi, ed ivi nelle camere segrete, cinte di ferro e di uomini a guardia delle loro persone e de' loro interessi; e nondimeno è chiaro che, senza tanta spesa, può ogni uomo, ancorch'esposto alla vista di tutti, nasconder i suoi affari nella vasta ed insieme segreta casa del suo cuore' (one admires, as the grandeur of men of high rank, their remaining within the walls of the palace, and in the secret rooms therein, encircled with iron and men guarding their persons and interests; nevertheless it is clear that, without such expense, every man can, although exposed to everyone's gaze, hide his affairs in the vast and secret house of his heart [*DO* 59–60]). Thus honest dissimulation plays a formative role in the appropriation of a space – secularized and psychologized – for the disciplined inner life of the early modern subject, who has to know when to express its secrets or, as far as possible, keep them silent.

Accetto concludes that 'è maggior diletto vincer se stesso, in aspettar che passi la procella degli affettii, e per non deliberare nella confusione della propria tempesta' (it is of greater delight to triumph over oneself, while waiting for the storm of the passions to pass, and in order not to deliberate in the confusion of one's own tempest [*DO* 46]). To win a victory over oneself constitutes, for Accetto, the 'most glorious victory that anyone can achieve' and the very meaning of honest dissimulation.[37] For this in turn ought to lead to the greatest of earthly delights, namely happiness itself. Such a state, for Accetto's neostoicism, could be nothing other than 'la quiete interna, ch'è bene inestimabile ed appartiene all'innocenzia' (inner peace, which is a good of incalculable value and belongs to innocence [*DO* 58]).[38] No social, political, or religious institution can restore to us this 'tranquillità del vivere' or tranquillity of living; harmony of desires and passions can be achieved only by the solitary *homo secessus* who practises honest dissimulation (*DO* 59). We are left to wonder at the radical gesture that *Della dissimulazione onesta* makes: not only does it endorse the very opposite of the kind of elite competitive sociality that defined the Accademia degli Oziosi, but it marks Accetto's farewell to the writing of poetry, the most socially prestigious of the arts. He defines success, paradoxically, as the complete absence of public recognition and acclaim – and this is in fact the reception that his treatise was to receive in the *Seicento* and beyond. In refuting Battista's *Apologia della menzogna* and its hyperbolic rhetoric of the marvellous, in short, Accetto's own work managed to prove its point by erasing itself from history, just as the most successful dissimulators have always done.[39]

Notes

1 Monica Miato, *L'Accademia degli Incogniti di Giovan Francesco Loredan, Venezia (1630–1661)*, Accademia Toscana di Scienze e Lettere 'La Colombaria' Studi 172 (Florence: Olschki, 1998), 121–30, recounts an episode in which a bookseller in Venice, Giacomo Batti, was prosecuted in 1648 for selling a copy of the *Adone*.

2 Emanuele Tesauro, *Il cannocchiale aristotelico*, ed. August Buck, Ars poetica 5 (Bad Homburg v.d.H., Berlin, and Zürich: Verlag Gehlen, 1968), anastatic reprint of the 1670 Turin edition.

3 'A lie is also sometimes licit, ... When it benefits the person telling the lie, ... And lying does not harm those who hear it.' For an excellent bibliography of

Marino's works in print, see Francesco Giambonini, *Bibliografia delle opere a stampa di Giambattista Marino* (Florence: Olschki, 2000).

4 Girolamo De Miranda, *Una quiete operosa: forma e pratiche dell'Accademia napoletana degli Oziosi, 1611–1645* (Naples: Fridericiana Editrice Universitaria, 2000), has an excellent chapter on the historiography of the Oziosi (see 19–47). See also V.I. Comparato, 'Società civile e società letteraria nel primo Seicento: l'Accademia degli Oziosi,' *Quaderni storici* 2 (1973): 359–81.

5 See the laws of the Oziosi, found in the following manuscript in the Biblioteca Nazionale di Napoli: 'Regole dell'Accademia degli Oziosi,' BNN, ms. Brancacciana V.D.14 (miscellanea manoscritti), ff. 127r–134r. This text, first reprinted in C. Padiglione, *Le leggi dell'Accademia degli Oziosi in Napoli ritrovate nella Biblioteca Brancacciana* (Napoli: F. Giannini, 1878), is now in De Miranda, *Una quiete operosa*, 327–43.

6 G.B. Marino, *Epistolario*, ed. A. Borselli and F. Nicolini (Bari: Laterza, 1911), Letter CCXXVI, 2:49, now in de Miranda, *Una quiete operosa*, 359–61 (the passage in question is found on 360–361). For a better sense of the range of arguments dealt with in the weekly meetings of the Ozioso or other academies in Naples in this era, see Francesco De' Pietri, *I problemi accademici* (Naples: Savio, 1642).

7 I refer the reader to De Miranda's excellent brief survey in *Una quiete operosa*, 3–16.

8 Comparato, 'Società civile,' 361–3, lists the academies in Naples that were suppressed over the course of the sixteenth century by the authorities, who suspected that members of the nobility were gathering together in order to plot against them.

9 'Leggi,' 131r: 'La Materia delle lettioni dovrà essere 'ntorno alla poetica, alla Ritorica, alle discipline Matematiche, et a tutte le parti della filosofia, et intorno alla Spianatione delli Autori, che hanno delle sopradette materie scritto: vietando che non si debba leggere, alcuna materia di Teologia, o della Sacra Scrittura, delle quali riverenda dobbiamo attenerci: e medesimamente niuna delle cose appartenenti al publico governo, i quali si deve lasciare alla cura de' Principi ...' (The subject of the lectures ought to concern poetics, rhetoric, the mathematical disciplines, all the parts of philosophy, and the interpretation of authors who have written about these subjects. It is forbidden to study anything having to do with theology or Holy Scripture, from which, out of reverence, we must abstain. Likewise nothing concerning public governance [may be mentioned], as this must be left to the responsibility of princes who rule).

10 For bio-bibliographical data concerning Battista, see Gino Rizzo's introduction to Giuseppe Battista, *Opere*, ed. Gino Rizzo (Galatina: Congedo Editore,

1991), 11–83; and E.N. Girardi, 'Giuseppe Battista,' *Dizionario biografico degli italiani* (Rome: Istituto della Enciclopedia Italiana, 1965), 7: 259–61.
11 Rizzo, introduction, *Opere*, 16.
12 De Miranda, *Una quiete operosa*, 237n.
13 Salvatore S. Nigro, 'Usi della pazienza,' in Torquato Accetto, *Della dissimulazione onesta*, ed. Salvatore S. Nigro (Turin: Einaudi, 1997), xxxi: '... del trattatello non rimase memoria alcuna. Né fra i contemporanei, né dopo ... l'opera finì per smorire, senza consenso e senza dissenso.'
14 I am indebted here and throughout to Salvatore Silvano Nigro, who was the first to propose this link between the two texts: see his 'Usi della pazienza,' in *Della dissimulazione onesta*, xix–xxii, and his 'Dar passione agli invisibili,' in *Elogio della menzogna* (Palermo: Sellerio, 1990), 20–2. De Miranda concurs with Nigro here ('è chiaramente questo il *trait d'union* tra Accetto e Battista'), *Una quiete operosa*, 238n.
15 'Leggi,' 133r.
16 Mario Sechi, 'Arretratezza meridionale e tramonto della poesia nell'ideologia letteraria di Giuseppe Battista,' *La rassegna della letteratura italiana*, vol. 75, serie 7 (1971), 141n, notes that Manso 'lo introdusse nell'accademia degli Oziosi (1640 circa),' and that 'al periodo giovanile [di G.B.] vanno ascritti i primi due tomi delle *Poesie meliche* (Venezia, 1653), gli *Epigrammata* (Napoli, 1648), molte delle *Lettere* (Venezia, 1677), quasi tutti i discorsi delle *Giornate accademiche* (Venezia, 1673) e la *Poetica* (Venezia, 1676).' For more on the European dimension of the debate on (dis)simulation, see Jon R. Snyder, *Dissimulation and the Culture of Secrecy in Early Modern Europe* (Berkeley and Los Angeles: University of California Press, forthcoming).
17 See Rizzo, Introduction, *Opere*, 78–9.
18 Rizzo, notes that 'le lezioni del Battista, se pur tenute per assecondare le sollecitazioni del Manso e di altri Oziosi, affrontano e sviluppano temi pressanti e urgenti della sua ideologia ... si tratta di argomenti tutt'altro che futili, se si tien conto che l'apologia della menzogna rinvia ad una presa d'atto di fondamentali presupposti della gnoseologia secentesca (finzione-dissimulazione-maschera-incertezza del reale fenomenico, ecc.) (Introduction, *Opere*, 48).'
19 Sechi, 'Arretratezza,' 141n: 'soltanto all'arrivo di Battista ... vi si sarebbe aperta una impegnata discussione tra petrarchisti-ciceroniani e fautori della nuova scuola.'
20 As cited by Nigro, 'Usi della pazienza,' xix.
21 Comparato, 'L'Accademia degli Oziosi,' 361–3, provides a list of these. See also C. Minieri-Riccio, 'Cenno storico delle Accademie fiorite nella Città di Napoli' and 'Notizia delle Accademie istituite nelle provincie Napolitane,'

Archivio storico per le Provincie napoletane, 1877–78–79–80, as cited by Sechi, 'Arretratezza,' 138n.
22 Ibid., 141n.
23 Here is what Jean-Jacques Bouchard, *Journal. II. Voyage dans le Royaume de Naples*, ed. Emanuele Kanceff (Turin: Giappichelli, 1977), 198–9, now in De Miranda, *Una quiete operosa*, 364, recalled of the academy's procedures: 'l'ordre de l'academie est tel: l'on fait premierement un discours, soit en prose ou en vers, soit en italien ou latin. Puis chasqu'un qui veut discourt sur un probleme que l'on s'est proposé en l'academie precedente. Après le secretaire lit les vers que les academiques luy ont donez pour estre lus en l'academie, sans nomer l'auteur, lesquels vers il libre à chasqu'un de controller, et va on porter au secretaire sa censure; laquelle il lit par après en l'academie. A laquelle censure il est libre de respondre à l'auteur, ou à quelqu'un de ses amis; et sur cette censure et response intervient par après le jugement des censeurs ... et si l'oeuvre est approuvé, il est escrit *nel libro della vita*, qui est entre les mains du prince, où se mettent tous les ouvrages des academiques qui ont esté appreuvez, et le prince en fait imprimer ce que bon luy semble, et quand il luy plaist' (The order of the academy is thus. Someone first makes a speech in either prose or verse, in either Latin or Italian. Then any who wish to may speak about a problem raised at the previous meeting of the academy. Afterward the secretary reads aloud – without naming the authors – the verses given to him by members to be read at the academy. The secretary then leaves it to the members to control [censor] the verses, and each brings his censure to the secretary, who afterward reads it to the academy. The author or one of his friends is free to reply to this censure ; and afterward the censors pass judgment on the censure and the response to it. And if the work is approved, it is written down in the 'book of life' that the prince keeps, in which are recorded all the works by members of the academy that have been approved, and the prince has printed whatever seems good to him, and when it pleases him to do so).
24 Rizzo adds (citing Amedeo Quondam's *La parola nel labirinto*): 'è noto che nelle Accademie secentesche le lezioni e le risposte erano un qualificante impegno volto 'non alla discussione o alla ricerca di carattere scientifico-tecnico, ma all'esclusivo conseguimento d'un effetto di stupefatta ammirazione in primo luogo per *l'abilità* della trattazione'" (Introduction,*Opere*, 46).
25 Giuseppe Battista, 'Per donna bugiarda,' in *Poesie meliche*, Parte III (Venezia 1659): 116, as cited in Nigro, 'Usi della pazienza,' xix. See also the collected verse in Giuseppe Battista, *Opere*, ed. Gino Rizzo (Galatina: Congedo, 1991).
26 G.B. Marino, Letter to Claudio Achillini, January 1620, *Lettere*, ed. M. Guglielminetti (Turin: Einaudi, 1966), 249.
27 Both this phrase and the reference to sun spots seem to allude clearly to

Galileo, whose science had been condemned by the Church only a few years previously.

28 This passage is taken from the *De Beneficiis*, VI.30.3.
29 See Biblioteca Nazionale di Napoli codices XIII.C.82 (academic poems dedicated to Manso) and XIII.B.77 (poems and 'censure') for surviving records of the activity of the Oziosi.
30 Accetto adds: 'perché lo scriver della dissimulazione ha ricercato ch'io dissimulassi, e però si scemasse molto di quanto da principio ne scrissi' (because writing about dissimulation has required me to dissimulate, and yet what I first wrote about it has been greatly reduced) (*DO* 7). All translations into English are mine.
31 Nigro, in *Della dissimulazione onesta*, note to p. 5.
32 The passage, which is too long to cite in the body of the essay, is found on p. 11 of the *DO* (chapter 2).
33 Virgilio Malvezzi, *Il Tarquinio superbo* [1634], in *Opere historiche e politiche* (Geneva: Pietro Chouët, 1656), 40.
34 Accetto speaks of Job's 'conscienzia' on p. 62.
35 Remo Bodei, *La geometria delle passioni. Paura, speranza, felicità: filosofia e uso politico*, 3rd ed. (Milan: Feltrinelli, 1992), 144.
36 Baltasar Gracián, *Oráculo manual y arte de prudencia*, in *Obras completas*, ed. Arturo del Hoyo (Madrid: Aguilar, 1960), 176 (aph. 89); *The Art of Worldly Wisdom: A Pocket Oracle*, trans. Christopher Maurer (New York: Doubleday, 1992), 50–1.
37 Indeed, as Accetto explains to his readers (*DO* 33), 'onesta ed util è la dissimulazione, e di piú, ripiena di piacere; perché se la vittoria è sempre soave ... è chiaro che 'l vincer per sola forza d'ingegno succede con maggior allegrezza, e molto piú nel vincer se stesso, ch'è la piú gloriosa vittoria che possa riportarsi. Quest'avviene nel dissimulare ...' (dissimulation is honest, useful and, furthermore, full of pleasure; for if victory is always sweet ... it is clear that victory through the sole strength of intelligence occurs with greater happiness, and much more so in triumphing over oneself, which is the most glorious victory that anyone can achieve.)
38 Elsewhere in the same text Accetto describes this as 'un'altezza d'animo, ed una quiete, che conduce al piacer ed alla gloria immortale' (a loftiness of mind and a calm that lead to pleasure and to immortal glory) (*DO* 60).
39 'Se alcuno portasse la maschera ogni giorno, sarebbe piú noto di ogni altro, per la curiosità di tutti; ma degli eccellenti dissimulatori, che sono stati e sono, non si ha notizia alcuna' (if one were to wear a mask every day, he would be noticed more than anyone else, because of everyone's curiosity [about him]; but we have no news of those excellent dissimulators who have been, and who are) (*DO* 22).

chapter six

'Particolar gusto e diletto alle orecchie': Listening in the Early *Seicento*

ANDREW DELL'ANTONIO

On the heels of heated controversies over new musical styles, early seventeenth-century Italian presses produced a flurry of essays on music by (and for) non-musicians, constituting the most extensive amount of commentary on music to that point by poets, philosophers, and other intellectuals. In a parallel development, musical prints of the time were frequently prefaced by 'notes to the reader' concerning the expressive qualities of the music contained in the collection. Such commentary does not draw on the established rhetorical and pedagogical tradition of sixteenth-century theoretical treatises; rather, it takes its examples from contemporary performance practice. Most importantly, the pervasive emphasis on the sense of hearing found in these essays reveals an awareness that discussion of music can, and perhaps should, be approached from the listener's (rather than the theorist's) perspective; that the focus of discourse surrounding music should be the 'particular savour and delight for the ears' that provides the title for this essay.

Along with the decline in the amateur music-making that largely characterized the courtly aesthetics of the Italian high Renaissance, and the increasing polarization of the roles of musical performer and audience through the emancipation of virtuoso performers, the 'new music' of the early seventeenth century created a perceived need for the 'informed amateur' to exercise critical judgment on this newly public cultural practice. A number of scholars have remarked on the defining role played by professional performers in the development of the new music, not only in the creation of new sonic ideals but also in the construction of a market for such ideals.[1] Others have explored the systems of patronage that enabled the success of the new music, especially in

Counter-Reformation Rome.[2] This essay will explore a somewhat different facet of the phenomenon, focusing on the increasing importance of the role of the listener in descriptions of the new music; I will argue that this re-configuring of the listener's role was the first step in the development of a new understanding of musical meaning.

First, let me review some of the evidence for the self-conscious shift from amateur to professional performance ideals in early seventeenth-century Italy, for this contemporaneous awareness of a new separation between the roles of performer and listener was accompanied by an increasing realization that the listener should have an active role in the negotiation of musical meaning. Lorenzo Bianconi has remarked on the gradual but systematic shift in Italian printing practice from collections of multi-part madrigals to collections for one or two voices and BC in the first two decades of the seventeenth century.[3] This shift seems to reflect a significant drop-off in the practice that had provided the ideal for musical activity in the Italian courts of the later *Cinquecento*: *cantare al libro*, convivial singing. This trend appears to be confirmed by the contemporanous account of Vincenzo Giustiniani. Better known to art historians for his early patronage of Caravaggio and his outstanding collection of visual artwork, Giustiniani was also an active musical connoisseur. Writing retrospectively in the second quarter of the seventeenth century, Giustiniani remarks on the rapid change in fashion during his own lifetime:

> Nel presente corso dell'età nostra, la musica non è molto in uso, in Roma non essendo essercitata da gentil huomini, nè si suole cantare a più voci al libro, come per gl'anni a dietro, non ostante che sia grandissime occasioni d'unire e di trattenere le conversationi. È ben la musica ridotta in un insolita e quasi nuova perfettione, venendo esercitata da gran numero de'buoni [30] musici, che disciplinati dalli suddetti buoni maestri porgono col canto loro artificioso e soave molto diletto a chi li sente.[4]

> [During the present course of our age, music is not much in use, in Rome gentlemen no longer practice it, nor is it the custom to sing in several parts *al libro*, as in years past, despite the fact that there are many occasions to get together and hold conversations. Music has been reduced to an unusual and almost new perfection, as it is performed by a great number of good musicians, which, trained by the abovementioned good teachers, bring great delight to those who hear them with their sweet and well-crafted song.]

The change in fashion described by Giustiniani went hand-in-hand with the development of the various strands of the new music in the early *Seicento*, and especially with the diffusion of the Florentine-Roman style that G.B. Doni later characterized as 'monody.'

Giustiniani implies that the new music was considered the domain of specialized performers. Lodovico Casali, in his 'Invitation to the Greatness and Marvels of Music,' is more explicit in that regard:

> E questo è il frutto della moderna Musica concertata; fatta non per tutti, mà per puochi. Anzi che aggiungo, mentre la Concertata Musica non sarà accompagnata da Cantori, di Scienza pari, mai potrà haver garbo; perche uno, che vero Musico, ò Cantore, con un'altro, che comintia di solfeggiare, male saranno accoppiati; che dove si gustarà dal perfetto Cantore soavità, e dolcezza, dal altro imperfetto, si perderà il gusto, scemandosi il valor della Musica, con puoca reputatione de buoni Musici. Onde la vera melodia, deve esser di egual perfettione: massime nel Concerto moderno.[5]

> [This is the result of the new concerted music: it is for the few, not the many. I should add that, if concerted music is not accompanied by singers of equal ability [*scienza*], it will never be pleasant; because it will not do to pair a real musician, or singer, with another who has just begun to solmize. For while we will taste/enjoy [*gustare*] sweetness and delight from the perfect singer, our taste will be soured by the other, imperfect one; the value of music will decrease, to the disadvantage of good musicians. Hence true melody must be of equal perfection, especially in modern concerted music.]

The ability of practitioners of the new music to engage the listener – simultaneously delighting the senses and moving the emotions – was understood by contemporaries as defining the 'newness' of that music. As early as 1592 Lodovico Zacconi emphasized the sonic effect of music on the listener:

> che ben si vede l'harmonia, che esce dalle modulationi, et cantilene: non esser altro, che un dolce, et soave aere dolcemente percosso, il quale per le percussioni delle ordinate, e ben disposte voci, lo percuotano con dolcezza tale, che il senso dell'udito nostro si compiace tanto, e tanto si diletta: che mentre l'ode, si intento l'ascolta, che toglie agli altri sensi non solo di sentire, ma anche di ricordarsi d'alcun male ...[6]

[we can see that harmony, which arises from music-making and song, is nothing but a sweet and pleasant breeze sweetly moved, which is so sweetly set into motion by the movement of ordered and well-disposed voices, that our sense of hearing is so pleased, and so delighted; that while hearing it, [the sense of hearing] listens so carefully, that it removes from all the other senses not only the ability to feel, but even to remember any pain ...]

A quarter-century later, Casali also praised the effects that music can have on a listener:

Venendo il Canto, e il Suono da un'intimo pensiero della mente, e da un impeto della fantasia, e da uno affettuoso diletto del cuore, e percotendo insieme con l'aere, già dirotto, e stemperato, spirito di che ode, il quale, è un nodo dell'Anima, e del Corpo, facilmente viene à muovere la fantasia, e diletta il cuore, e penetra fin dentro all'ultime parti della mente: onde penetrato, opera il suo effetto secondo la dispositione, e complessione di chi gusta, e gode l'armonia della Musica.[7]

[Since song, and sound come from an intimate thought of the mind, and from an impetus of fantasy, and from an emotional delight of the heart; and strike together with the air the broken, untempered spirit of the listener, which connects the soul and the body; easily [song and sound] move [the listener's] fantasy, and delight the heart, and penetrate to the deepest parts of the mind; and having penetrated it, [sound/music] works its effect according to the disposition, and nature of the one who savours, and delights in the Music's harmony.]

Vincenzo Giustiniani himself defines the new style (which he calls *cantare con gratia*) in terms of its ability to affect the listener:

Il cantare con gratia non è altro se non una lunga osservatione delli modi e regole di cantare, che sogliono arrecare particolar gusto e diletto alle orecchie delle persone di giuditio per l'ordinario.[8]

[Singing with grace is nothing but a long practice with the ways and rules of singing, which provide particular savour and delight for the ears of those people who have generally good judgment.]

This is by no means the first time that Italian commentators had remarked on the extraordinary effect music could have on a listener; fifteenth- and sixteenth-century humanists frequently drew on accounts from classical antiquity to describe the wondrous effects of music, and indeed the perceived lack of such effects in contemporary styles was at the root of the campaign for various facets of the new music. What appears striking, however, is that the listener's delight or *gusto* become the primary focus of discussion concerning the new styles, eclipsing counterpoint and other structural elements that had to that point been considered intrinsic to the musical work. This focus on reception in discourse surrounding music has strong resonances with the commentary on the visual arts by Gabriele Paleotti and his followers. Paleotti's 1582 treatise on images ('Discorso sopra le immagini') is primarily concerned with the effect of art on the spectator, especially in the context of post-Tridentine devotion. Art historian Anton Boschloo suggests that 'specific attention to the *affetti* and their effect on the spectator was not new. The novelty lies in [Paleotti's] insistence on the importance of the spectator, and on the fact that the painter, in order to convince and persuade, must adapt his work to [the spectator].'[9] In both the visual and musical spheres, the importance of the interpreter appears to have been overtaking that of the artist in the production of meaning.[10]

We have seen that Vincenzo Giustiniani's definition of *cantare con gratia* is dependent on the listener's response. Giustiniani goes further, however, in specifying that music creates its effects in 'persone di giuditio': those who have good judgment. Such judgment is increasingly described as a consequence of training and good taste, the results of a 'specialization' of sorts on the part of the listener. In 1629 Lodovico Casali described those who enjoy music in the new style as having 'a well-trained intellect,' using the newly fashionable musical term *concertato*:

> Onde ben posso dire, che chi abbraccia, e gusta li dolcissimi concenti della Musical armonia, habbia l'intelletto ben concertato, e chi quella abborrisce, e disprezza, mostra per lo contrario esser d'intelletto ottuso, rozzo, e poco civile; e proverbialmente si dice, che chi poco, ò nulla la Musica stima in questo mondo, nel altro non possa haver ricetto in Paradiso; dove non altro, che Musiche, e Angelici concenti si gustano.[11]

> [Thus I can justly say, that those who embrace and savour the sweet consonances of musical harmony have a well-trained [concertato] intellect; and those who abhor and despise it, show themselves to be of obtuse, rough,

and uncivil intellect; and there is a proverb that says that those who hold music in little or no esteem in this world cannot be received into paradise, where nothing is savored except for music and angelic harmonies.]

Several introductions to musical prints of this time refer to the contents of the collection as having been designed 'to meet the taste [*gusto*] of the most learned ears,' or so that they can be enjoyed by 'the most delicate ears.'[12] The verb *gustare* (to taste, or to savour), with its implications of refined understanding, was repeatedly employed by early-seventeenth-century commentators to describe their experience of music in the new style.[13] Frequently the concept of *gusto* was linked to the superior discernment of princes; an extraordinary example is an aria musicale from Frescobaldi's *Primo Libro* of 1630 that addresses Ferdinando II Medici as a listener. After asking Ferdinando to 'listen to the pleasing sound' ('ascolta il suon gradito'), the text of the *aria* continues:

...
Mentre accordi a te stesso
Si ben gli affetti alla ragion appresso,
O beata armonia d'un cuor soave
Che tempra in questa vita
Col dolce dell'età del senno il grave;
Ma forse hor la mia lingua è troppo ardita:
Taccio, & à dir sol prendo
Quel, che da saggio intende,
Che chi quaggiù de'canti il suono apprezza
All'armonia del ciel l'anima avvezza.[14]

[...
While you concord so well
affects and reason within yourself,
blessed harmony of a sweet heart
which tempers, in this life,
the gravity of reason with the sweetness of youth;
But perhaps my tongue is too daring;
I will be quiet; and say only
that which the wise man knows,
that he who appreciates the sound of song
prepares his soul for heavenly harmony.]

Here as elsewhere, the appreciation of sounds on earth reflects the listener's appreciation of heavenly harmony. I shall return to this point at the close of this essay.

In describing the new practices of cataloguing that characterize the vogue for museums and *gabinetti di meraviglie* in early *Seicento* Italy, Paula Findlen observes that the process of collecting and classifying wonders of nature in this period was a marker of privilege and aesthetic/cultural sophistication. Findlen describes the shift during this period from inventories, which 'record the contents of a museum ... [quantifying] its reality, listing the objects without attaching analytical meaning to them,' to catalogues, which 'purport to interpret ... More than an unadorned list, the catalogue provided a self-conscious presentation of a collection.'[15] Crucial to this distinction is the interpretative presence of the cultured collector, who has 'earned the right to collect and classify the world' by virtue of his experience and *gusto*.[16] Curiosity was considered a natural reflection of the cultivated individual's *gusto*, and most importantly for this study, was closely tied to aesthetic experience rather than utilitarian practice.[17] Finally, the knowledge gained through the judicious application of *gusto* was described pragmatically rather than theoretically, as a combination of wonder (*meraviglia*) at new marvels and incorporation of those marvels into a consistent framework that reflected the sophisticated individual's depth of knowledge. Again Findlen: "Wonder' encompassed the emotions that confrontation with the unexpected aroused; 'experience' defined the knowledge gained from the repetition of such encounters.'[18] In other words, the cultivated individual achieved a 'professional' knowledge through the careful balance of receptivity to the marvellous and repeated, careful parsing and categorizations of items – or events. Findlen concludes that the increased focus on displaying knowledge and self-knowledge created an 'aestheticization of knowledge,' which in turn led to a tendency to 'aestheticize the self.'[19] One could reverse Findlen's conclusion and observe that the merger of knowledge and aesthetic experience also has a crucial bearing on the notion of experiencing a work of art (whether visual, literary, or musical); receptivity to the artwork becomes a form of knowledge, and thus a marker of sophistication. Just as the cultivated collector/ interpreter acquires knowledge over the wonders he collects, so the cultivated listener acquires knowledge – and oversight – over the musical wonders that he experiences. Just as the collector's role is inherently greater than that of the collected object, so the listener's role is more crucial than that of the creator of the sounds. The view of a musical experience as an objectified aesthetic 'work' can be seen as arising from this cultural context.

Tim Carter, in his recent essay on the print distribution of the new music, focuses on the language and terminology employed by performer-composers such as Caccini and Puliaschi in their lengthy introductions describing their new style of singing. As Carter points out, the descriptive language of these introductions is simultaneously clarifying and mystifying. On the one hand, the introductions make 'an apparent attempt to make the new and the strange seem both feasible for and approachable by the consumers at which these prints were aimed.'[20] However, while instruction in musical technique is the ostensible subject of these introductions, the implicit focus on the professional nature of the craft, and the repeated warnings that not all can aspire to the professional singer's mastery, seem to indicate that these explanations are more for the preparation of listeners than for the technical instruction of amateur performers. The *virtuosi* who touted their craft through these introductions would have been likely to derive more prestige and financial gain from the increased estimation of their art by the powerful and influential than from the acquisition of students. Thus 'approachable' means something very different for the amateur consumer of the new music than it did for musical amateurs of previous generations; the approach is meant to be through listening, rather than performing.[21]

And even 'approachable' is a relative term, since, as Carter observes, 'for all the explication and clarification, this music becomes in many senses harder, not easier to perform ... singers, instrumentalists, and composers [are] obscure where they might have been clear, almost willfully refusing to reveal the secrets of their art and distracting our attention elsewhere ... [*intendenti* and *studiosi* – nay, even performers – are told something, but never enough].'[22]

Singer/composers' descriptions tend to be cryptic, always referring the reader to their own performances for a complete understanding of the art. This is certainly intended, as Carter points out, to maintain trade secrets on which the singer/composers relied for their livelihood. It also, however, has the effect of raising the listening experience to a higher level of understanding than any rational explanation could provide. The ineffable expressive quality of musical expression can only be understood by an act of listening; the listener therefore has a crucial role to play in the signifying economy of the new music. Increasing focus on the achievements of virtuoso performers in the closing decades of the sixteenth century wrested the discourse on music away from the domain of counterpoint (where contrapuntal unfolding was equated with 'the music itself') and towards the less developed terminology of vocal technique and musical affect/effects. Such a rhetorical move allowed for a broadening of the definition of the musical work, and this in turn led to a different set of parameters by which the musical work could appropriately be assessed: if the old style could be judged only by the trained musician, and ultimately parsed through the written musical text, the new style could be judged only by the well-disposed listener, using as a criterion the expressive sonic impact of the musical experience.

The *gusto* or good taste of the professionalized listener would thus be paramount in the successful evaluation of the new music; and *gusto* was defined as inherently opaque and inexpressible by contemporaries of the new style. Historian of culture Antonio Maravall remarks that in the *Seicento* 'the cultivated, learned individual is said to have taste, which implies that this individual accepts an entire system of norms that, *although not possessed by rational means*, are adhered to on deeper levels.'[23] Well-honed *gusto* was considered crucial to the listener's experience of the new music, and descriptions of the precise nature of that *gusto* are as fully opaque as the descriptions of professional singing techniques.[24] Such opacity is by no means unique to early *Seicento* commentary on music; as Philip Sohm has pointed out, despite the evident 'growth of an articulate visual literacy' in seventeenth-century Italy, the terminology used by the newly visually literate intelligentsia can strike contemporary readers as extraordinarily vague.[25]

But to regret that seventeenth-century authors are not more articulate or precise regarding the nature of the listening experience would be to miss the point: *gusto* is an inherently opaque quality, one that can only be understood through careful aesthetic training and refined upbringing. It is a marker not only of class but also of spiritual complexity, an ability to understand the ineffable state that music can arouse as an evocation of the spiritual transport of heaven. It is to this construction of the listening process as a transcendent experience that I now turn in closing.

Alongside explicit references to the *gusto* or *diletto* of the listener as the ultimate purpose of the works in the collection, seventeenth-century writers commonly refer to the importance of conveying *affetto* through the music. The uses of the term *affetto* in conjunction with music during this period are multifaceted, and a more systematic unpacking of the term's meanings and implications must await another occasion. It is fairly clear, however, that the term *affetto* was extraordinarily pregnant in

Counter-Reformation rhetoric; far from being an exclusively musical term, it was integral to the descriptive world of the visual and literary arts in the early *Seicento*, and seems to have been a lynchpin concept in the rhetorical triad of *docere, delectare, movere* – to teach, to delight, to move – that informed the cultural efforts of the Church of Rome in the early seventeenth century.[26]

The power of music to transmit *affetto* was especially crucial to the spiritual mission of the Counter-Reformation. Specifically, the ability of the listener to gain a transcendent state through music was understood as a direct analogue to the spiritual ecstasy of the soul in paradise. Church doctrine made this point explicitly, and the metaphor of spiritual rapture was evoked in so many contemporaneous accounts of sacred music that it was clearly a rhetorical commonplace.[27] The idea of rapture through music was of course not a novelty in the seventeenth century; that image does, however, seem to have been deployed more systematically in this period, at all levels of church-sponsored artistic expression, than it ever had been before. One quick example must suffice. The cult of St Francis enjoyed a resurgence through the wave of post-Tridentine mysticism at the close of the sixteenth century; a favourite depiction of the saint in the first decades of the 1600s was in the middle of ecstatic transport ostensibly caused by an angel playing a violin. The viewer was clearly meant to identify not with the divine musician but with the recipient of the heavenly music's power; and the iconographical use of a very real contemporary instrument – one that was gaining a reputation as the most expressive of instruments – could well have been meant to evoke specific sonic memories of the experience of musical *affetto*.

To be sure, music was deployed during the Counter-Reformation for straightforwardly pragmatic reasons as well: skilled singers and musicians enhanced the sensual appeal of religious services, and a number of contemporaries testify to their choice of church service by the criteria of the quality of the singing and performing ensembles featured at that church.[28] But seventeenth-century accounts often go further, drawing an explicit link between the listener's proper understanding of the musical *affetto* and an understanding (or at least a taste) of the spiritual beauty of paradise. Thus Girolamo Diruta, in his *Transilvano*, claims that

> [Il] suono [dell'organo] che arriva all'orecchie come parole che significano gl'affetti del cuore, rappresenta l'interna dispositione dello spirito ... La soavità de'concenti ben proportionati, arrivando all'orecchie de gli ascoltanti, penetra ne' secreti pensieri, & nelle celate passioni di quelle, la

> onde debitamente è posto come in proprio luogo nel Tempio di Dio, accioche con esso s'invitino, & quasi sforzino i devoti & fedeli spiriti ad udire le lodi, & gli honori, che con gli suoni & con le voci, bene accompagnate si danno all'altissima Maestà di Dio ...[29]

> [The sound [of the organ] that arrives to the ears as if words that signify the affect of the heart, represents the internal disposition of the spirit ... The sweetness of well-proportioned music, arriving to the ears of the listeners, penetrates their secret thoughts and hidden passions; thus [music] is placed in its proper location in the temple of God, so that with it devoted and faithful spirits can be invited, and almost forced, to hear the praises and honors that are given, with well-organized sounds and voices, to the highest majesty of God ...]

Indeed, the listener was characterized as being able to praise God through the listening practice itself:

> Quegli, che ascoltano, ancorchè non possano ò con la voce ò con l'istromento dar lode a Dio, possono nondimeno con l'affetto, e col cuore cantare, e salmeggiare, come n'esorta l'Apostolo ...[30]

> [Those who listen, even though they cannot praise God with their voice or their instrument, can nonetheless sing and psalmodize with their emotions [*affetto*] and their heart, as the Apostle exhorts us to do ...]

The role of the listener, in this context, can be seen as more crucial than that of the performer. While the performer praises God through *musica instrumentalis* (the physical manifestation of sound), the listener can praise God directly through *musica humana* – his heart and emotions. The professional performer may specialize in creating beautiful and moving sounds, but the professional listener is the one who specializes in establishing a connection with divine bliss through refined savouring of those sounds. The division between performer and listener is not just one of class, but one of spiritual intensity; the more sublime role (and the more prized by Counter-Reformation standards) is clearly that of the listener.

Baroque society, Gino Stefani suggests, 'by legitimizing religion through art, simultaneously and more deeply legitimized the autonomy of music through religious means.'[31] I would add that chroniclers of the Counter-Reformation also legitimized and elevated the role of the musical listener, making that role crucial to the power of music. Further, the emphasis placed on the focus and preparation necessary on the 'professional' listener's part underscores the importance for the listener to be an active participant in the process of musical meaning-creation, rather than just a passive recipient. Thus the notion of active listening, still a common concern in Western musical training, has clear historical roots in this spiritual/edifying/moral conceptualization of music.

The Counter-Reformation's concern with the effects (ecstatic or otherwise) that music can create in enhancing the worshipper's connection with the divine is based on a model of consuming music primarily through listening, as opposed to through amateur performance. In seventeenth-century Italy, transcendence still had a specific function connected to Christian worship, and music was but one means employed by the Counter-Reformation church to convey its message of spiritual connection through connoisseurship. The spiritual message of the Church of Rome, conveyed through artistic intensity, demanded a properly well-disposed recipient; the trained elite amateur of the arts – literary, visual, or musical – was thus a crucial construction of the Counter-Reformation. But of course this trust in the transcendence of musical experience – and its unique ability to transport a suitably refined listener – survived the gradual secularization of European society in the eighteenth century, and lies at the heart of musico-aesthetic formulations about the autonomy of musical experience in the nineteenth century. Thus, I would contend that the present study of listening practices in the seventeenth century is not merely an excursion into an emergent model of musical reception from almost four centuries ago. Coming out of a crucial moment of negotiation regarding the nature of musical meaning, and who should have authority over that meaning – the composer, the performer, or the listener – Counter-Reformation intellectuals forged a prevalent role for the last member of this triad. I would suggest that understanding the historical circumstances of this privileging of the listener's role can have strong repercussions on our own early-twenty-first-century arguments concerning the autonomous and transcendent nature of 'the music itself' and the primacy of a trained, sophisticated listener.

Notes

1 See Tim Carter, 'Printing the "New Music,"' in *Music and the Cultures of Print*, ed. Kate van Orden, 3–37 (New York: Garland, 2000).

2 See, inter alia, John Walter Hill, *Roman Monody, Cantata and Opera from the Circles around Cardinal Montalto* (Oxford: Oxford University Press, 1997); and Robert Holzer, '"Sono d'altro garbo ... le canzonette che si cantano oggi": Pietro Della Valle on Music and Modernity in the Seventeenth Century,' *Studi Musicali* 21 (1992): 255–306.

3 Lorenzo Bianconi, *Music in the Seventeenth Century*, trans. David Bryant (Cambridge: Cambridge University Press, 1987), 1–3.

4 Vincenzo Giustiniani, 'Discorso sopra la musica de' suoi tempi,' ca. 1628, ed. Salvatore Bongi, Lucca: Giusti, 1878), 29–30. Further, Giustiniani remarks that 'Per i tempi passati era molto in uso il trattenersi con un conserto di Viole o di Flauti ... [he speaks of problems with keeping them in tune, then continues] e poi anche l'esperienza ha fatto conoscere che tale trattenimento, con l'uniformità del suono e delle consonanze, veniva assai presto a noia, e più tosto incitava a dormire che a passare il tempo et il caldo pomeridiano' (34). Bongi comments that this *discorso* is part of a collection of eight essays on various topics; at one point ca. 1640 it passed into possession of Nicolao Orsucci. As of 1878, it was in a miscellany in the library of the Lucca Archivio di Stato, marked O.49 in the Orsucci collection. I have not yet been able to consult the original.

5 Lodovico Casali, *Generale Invito Alle Grandezze, E Maraviglie Della Musica* (Modena: Gadaldino, 1629), 184–85.

6 Lodovico Zacconi, *Prattica di Musica ... divisa in quattro libri* (Venice: Polo, 1592), 6.

7 Casali, *Generale Invito*, 151.

8 Giustiniani, 'Discorso sopra la musica,' 24.

9 'Una particolare attenzione per gli affetti e per il loro effetto sullo spettatore non era una novità. Di nuovo c'è l'insistenza sull'importanza dello spettatore e sul fatto che il pittore, al fine di convincerlo e persuaderlo, debba adattare a lui la sua opera.' Anton Boschloo, 'Annibale Carracci: Rappresentazioni Della Pietà,' in *Docere Delectare Movere: Affetti, Devozione E Retorica Nel Linguaggio Artistico Del Primo Barocco Romano*, ed. Sible De Blaauw, Pieter-Matthijs Gijsbers, Sebastian Schütze, and Bert Treffers (Rome: De Luca, 1998), 48.

10 Iacopo Peri's introduction to the early printed music drama *Euridice* features a strong emphasis on the sense of hearing, with a series of verbs connected to '*udire*'; likewise Marco da Gagliano's introduction to the nearly contemporaneous drama *Dafne* focuses on the pleasure/surprise of the listeners. And André Maugars, a French musician who had close contacts with the Italian 'new music,' remarked 'C'est sans doute dans ces sorties agréables [i.e., licences with rules of harmony, etc.], ou consiste tout le secret de l'Art; la Musique ayant ses figures aussi bien que la Rhétorique, qui ne tendent

toutes qu'a charmer et tromper insensiblement l'Auditeur.' André Maugars, 'Response faite à un curieux sur le sentiment de la Musique d'Italie, escrite à Rome le premier octobre 1639,' no printer name, date, or place; printed probably in Paris ca. 1640; reproduced in Er. Thoinan, *Maugars: Célèbre joueur de Viole ...* (Paris: Claudin, 1865), 26.

11 Casali, *Generale Invito Alle Grandezze ...,*' 192.
12 A foreword to a collections of motets by Alessandro Grandi observes that these works are being printed so they can be enjoyed 'da gli orecchi piu dilicati' (*Celesti Fiori del Sig. Alessandro Grandi, Libro Quinto* ... Venice: Gardano, 1620). Another printer, Magni, remarks that composer Rigatti has writen music 'to meet the taste/savor of the most learned ears': 'Goderà presto la luce, e l'aura del mondo un'altra degnissima fatica del Sig. Rigati, nell'armonia della quale hà egli impiegato, per essere di sante compositioni, come buono ecclesiastico, a ragione tutto lo spirito per dar nella novità, e per incontrare il gusto dell'orecchie piu dotte ...' (a new and most worthy effort by Signor Rigati will soon enjoy the light and the air of the world; in the harmony of which (since they are holy compositions, and he is a good man of the cloth) he rightly employed all his spirit to provide novelty, and to meet the taste/savor of the most learned ears ...) (Giovanni Antonio Rigatti, *Primo parto de motetti* ... Venice: Magni, 1640).
13 Adriano Banchieri, for example, repeatedly uses this verb to describe the listening experience in his correspondence; see his *Lettere Armoniche* (Bologna: Mascheroni, 1628), *passim.*
14 Frescobaldi, *Primo libro di arie musicali* (Florence: Landini, 1630).
15 Paula Findlen, *Possessing Nature: Museums, Collecting, and Scientific Culture in Early Modern Italy* (Berkeley: University of California Press, 1994), 36.
16 Ibid., 15.
17 'Rather than singing the praises of curiosity as a utilitarian practice, seventeenth-century collectors made curiosity a virtue unto itself.' Ibid., 43.
18 Ibid., 54–5.
19 Ibid., 294 ff.
20 Carter, 'Printing the 'New Music',' 10.
21 Carter suggests that 'the more one works with these songbooks the more one realizes that they are not so much neutral transmitters of information from composer to performer as iconic representations of specific or generalized performance acts that need to be handled as carefully as any other iconographical evidence from this period' ('Printing the 'New Music',' 28). Indeed, the introductions' focus on singing technique and the visual depiction of vocal fireworks in the musical notation appear to be attempts to evoke the sonic effects of *meraviglia* experienced by the listener in the new

style. As Carter himself has implied, this reflects a significantly different function for the printed work, one that is more descriptive than prescriptive. The inherent difficulty in the descriptive evocation of sonic effect may be one of the reasons (along with economic issues that Bianconi [*Music in the Seventeenth Century*, 10 ff.], among others, has outlined) for the declining print-runs of monodic works after the sixteen-teens.

22 Carter, 'Printing the 'New Music',' 23.
23 José Antonio Maravall, *The Culture of the Baroque*, trans. Terry Cochran (Minneapolis: University of Minnesota Press, 1986), 101; emphasis added.
24 A full discussion of this topic must await another occasion; for preliminary thoughts, see the appendix to my *Syntax, Form, and Genre in Sonatas and Canzonas, 1621–1635* (Lucca: Libreria Musicale Italiana, 1997).
25 Philip Sohm, 'Gendered Style In Italian Art Criticism from Michelangelo to Malvasia,' *Renaissance Quarterly* 48, no. 4 (Winter 1995), 792.
26 See, for example, the variety of approaches to the notion of *affetto* discussed in the collection *Docere Delectare Movere*, ed. De Blaauw et al.
27 See the extensive examples cited by Gino Stefani, *Musica e religione nell'Italia barocca* (Palermo: Flaccovio, 1975), especially 190 ff.
28 Again Giustiniani: 'Et à questo proposito dirò che uno da me ben conosciuto fece elettione di frequentare una congregatione, anteponendola a molte altre, forse migliori, per l'occasione che il capo e Rettore di quella haveva bella voce nel fare i sermoni e cantava bene le litania, con gratia e voce sonora e grata' (And on this matter I can say that someone I know very well chose to attend a congregation, prioritizing it over many others which may have been better, because the leader and rector of that group had a beautiful voice in sermonizing and sang well the litanies, with *grazia* and a sonorous and lovely voice) ('Discorso sopra la musica ...', 27). Another perspective from Zacconi: 'Le genti si parton dalle piazze, et dalle loro case per girsene al sacro Tempo, invitato da i concerti spirituali per mezzo delle Musiche disposti, e però oltra gli effetti universali, che sono hormai da tutto il Mondo conosciuti, che sono quelli di rallegrare i spirti nostri afflitti, et lassi, di racconsolarci l'animo, di sollazzarci, di renderci dispositi,e di trattenerci con diletto, c'incita, et ci spinge anco alle devotioni, et a i tributi divini; perche mentre nelle Chiese si loda Iddio con canto dolce, et soave, le genti vi corrano, e correndovi acquistano mercede, essendo che non vi corrano mai indarno, ne mai se ne partano senza qualche acquisto ...' (People leave the public squares and their homes to go to the holy Temple, lured by the spiritual *concerti* arranged through music; thus beyond the universal effects known by now to all the world – those of cheering our sad and afflicted spirits, consoling our soul, pleasing us, disposing us, and entertaining us with

delight – [music] also incites us and pushes us to devotion and tributes to the divine; because while God is praised in the churches with sweet and pleasant sounds, people run there, and having run there they acquire mercy, since they never run there in vain, and never leave without some benefit ...) (Zacconi, *Prattica di Musica*, 6). A number of other contemporary commentators make very similar remarks.

29 Girolamo Diruta, *Il Transilvano dialogo sopra il vero modo di sonar organi* ... (Venice: Vincenti, 1625), 3. Gino Stefani further quotes a theologian from the mid-1600s: 'Ben giustificata è quindi l'ingegnosità della devozione, che con meraviglia e applauso di tutti opera l'incantesimo, la metamorfosi per cui l'ascoltatore, godendo musica terrestre, gusterà le delizie del paradiso.' Stefani, *Musica e religione nell'Italia barocca*, 195.

30 Gratioso Uberti, *Contrasto Musico opera dilettevole* (Rome, 1630; repr. Lucca, 1992); a similar phrase, 'licet omnes fideles laudes Deo voce non canant, possunt tamen corde, et affectu cantare,' appears in a theological treatise by Carlo Pellegrini, *Museum Historico-Legale bipartitum* ... (Rome, 1665), 48 (cited in Stefani, *Musica e religione nell'Italia barocca*, 221 n.113).

31 'Rendendo accettabile e cioè legittimando la religione mediante l'arte, la società barocca ha simultaneamente, ma più profondamente, legittimato mediante la religione l'autonomia della musica.' Stefani, *Musica e religione nell'Italia barocca*, 231.

chapter seven

From Liturgy to Literature: Prayer and Play in the Early Russian Baroque

RONALD VROON

Any attempt to assess the role of the baroque in Russia must take into consideration that it was imported by a culture that had experienced no Renaissance. It was therefore perceived by both its proponents and opponents as a challenge, not to the 'new humanism,' but to the fundamentally medieval world-view still prevailing in seventeenth-century Russia. In that sense the baroque in Russia is typologically equivalent to the Renaissance in Western Europe, associated not only with radically new forms of humanistic thought, but with new artistic strategies and devices as well. The popularization of perspective in painting, polyphony in music, and versification in the verbal arts may all be traced to the influence of the baroque.[1]

A recent study by Vladimir Martynov entitled *Song, Play and Prayer in the System of Russian Liturgical Chant* provides an interesting model derived from the musical sphere for conceptualizing the tensions that emerged when the new artistic forms associated with the baroque were superimposed on the texts, broadly conceived, of medieval Russian culture – in this case those associated with corporate worship.[2] Martynov notes that medieval discourse about music reveals a very clear distinction between successions of tones associated with the performance of liturgical texts (the monophonic chant sung without accompaniment in the Orthodox tradition) and successions of tones in all other contexts. The former is designated 'song' (*penie*), and the latter is referred to as 'music' (*musikia, muzyka*). The verbs used to describe these two forms of expression are also different. One always 'sings' (*pet'*) a liturgical text, but one 'plays' (*igrat'*) every other sort of music, be it vocal or instrumental. Liturgical chant is organized in such a way that the movement from tone to tone according to a highly complex series of melodic formulae is designed to parallel, as it were, the speech of the soul as it is engaged in the act of prayer. This is an ascetic act, one that involves the conquering of passions and communion with God. Music, on the other hand, is designed to arouse emotions, either by drawing attention to itself through the delights of artifice or by inducing various emotional states through the manipulation of a virtually infinite range of sound patterns and combinations.[3] Prayer and play cannot mix. Music, as a form of play, has no place in worship, and prayer should not be subject to the rules of play.

In the seventeenth century this distinction began to break down. Alien musical practices initially restricted to the far Western reaches of the Empire, those bordering on the Catholic West, infiltrated Russia. She found herself unable to resist the seductive beauty of polyphony, which gradually made its way into religious and secular life. As Johann von Gardner has noted, 'as a result of the introduction of polyphonic choral singing in the Western European style during the mid-seventeenth century ... the distinction between liturgical singing and secular choral/vocal music became less and less clear. The criterion for what was 'churchly' or 'unchurchly' came to be extremely subjective and open to endless argumentation.'[4] This confusion occurred at precisely the time that the Russian Orthodox Church was undergoing its first and only major schism, which pitted the practitioners of ancient Orthodox piety against reformers who wished to bring contemporary Orthodoxy in line – liturgically and ritually – with the sister churches of Constantinople, Jerusalem, Alexandria, and Antioch. And this was the period when the baroque was introduced into Russian court culture and spread throughout society's upper echelons.

Martynov's analysis of the tension between prayer and play in the nonverbal sphere can be applied to the same phenomenon in the literary arena. Russia's most important baroque poets – and we will be focusing here on the two most important and prolific writers, Simeon of Polotsk and Karion Istomin – were both monks and priests. As such they were deeply immersed in the ecclesiastical culture that had sustained a monolithic system of prayer and chant and the medieval Weltanschauung it instantiated, and that correspondingly resisted the 'degradation' of chant into music, of prayer into play, and more generally, of liturgy into literature. Why this happened is a question that has been dealt with in many studies of Russia's historical transition from a medieval to a modern world outlook.[5] How this happened on the concrete level of the text is still something of a mystery, certain aspects of which I wish to explore here.

We begin with a simple fact: both Simeon and Karion had been raised in a religious tradition that regarded the liturgical word as fundamentally inviolate. Indeed, over the course of the 1650s and 1660s attempts undertaken by the hierarchy to rid the Orthodox church books and rituals of ostensibly unsanctioned accretions had encountered significant resistance and led to a major schism in the Church. The very idea that one might, of one's own volition, modernize or otherwise 'improve' sacred texts by rendering them in poetic form was essentially alien to Orthodox East Slavic consciousness. On the other hand, both Simeon and Karion had been exposed to the poetic experiments of their Catholic confreres in the West and were clearly intrigued by these new and wonderful forms of artifice. How was the competition between liturgy and literature, broadly conceived, to play itself out in the Russian baroque, given the fact that its major practitioners were clerics raised in a milieu that absolutized the language of liturgical discourse? Here two distinct processes can be traced, the first involving the adaptation of liturgical discourse to non-liturgical use, and the second the attempt to deploy the resources of the baroque to liturgical ends.

The first of these processes might best be exemplified in the area of the panegyric, perhaps the most important mode of discourse both in the liturgy and in the writing of the major Russian baroque poets. We are speaking here of texts written to be performed, or modelled on works composed with performance in mind. They are associated with a specific addresser (the worshipper, the poet himself as a historical figure or the person he purports to impersonate), a specific addressee (Christ, the Theotokos, a saint, the tsar, or some other royal personage) and a specific occasion: a fast or feast day, name day, important state occasion, or a milestone in the life of the person being honoured. In the case of liturgical compositions we are referring specifically to various hymns composed for the moveable portions of divine worship and often organized into large, well-defined sequences; in the case of non-liturgical discourse, to religious and secular orations, dialogues, threnodies, and the like. The interfacing of the liturgical and non-liturgical is most apparent in multipartite panegyrics, which were among the most popular in the Russian baroque.

The single most important collection of such panegyrics, and one whose contents are typical for the genre, is Simeon's *Rifmologion* (*Rhyme-Book*), a large manuscript collection containing syllabic verse in praise of various august personages and in commemoration of major feasts in the liturgical calendar. Aside from the fact that the language of the poems, a modified Church Slavonic, is the same stylized, archaic language used in liturgical compositions, two factors in particular betray the overriding influence of liturgical forms on the texts themselves. The first of these is alluded to in the lengthy descriptive title of the work, which I cite here only in part: *Rhyme-Book, or Book of Verses, Containing Verses Composed in Equal Measured Lines and Rhyme, Suitable for Various Needs. To the Glory and Honor of God, One in the Trinity, the Immaculate Mother of God and the Saints Well-Pleasing to the Lord. For the Benefit of Young and Old, for the Comfort and Consolation of both Clerics and Laymen of Various Ranks, Expressing Thanksgiving, Praise, Greetings, Etc. ...*[6] The coinage Simeon uses to identify the genre of the collection, *stikhoslov* (book of verse), is modelled on the standard word for the Orthodox Horologion or Book of Hours (*chasoslov*), underscoring the paraliturgical cast of the contents. That the book has been designated as 'suitable for various needs' suggests a very practical function, which is born out by the contents: these are texts to be read aloud at various ceremonial functions associated with the major feast days of the Church. A given panegyric may be accompanied by 'stage directions' in the title or subtitle indicating that a poem is to be recited, say, by one or more 'youths' (i.e., members of a boys' choir) on the occasion of St Peter and Paul's feast day, by servants of the tsar addressing their sovereign at Christmastide, by the tsarevich to the tsar or the tsarina at Easter, and so on. Particularly telling is the fact that lines and entire blocks of texts may be repeated in various compositions. Their 'movability' is a clear clue to the model for the whole poetic enterprise: the so-called General Menaion, an Orthodox liturgical service book containing 'generic' hymns to various classes of saints that may be used in cases where a specific service in honour of a particular saint is lacking. The *Rifmologion* has a comparable function as a paraliturgical service book for various ceremonials patterned after divine worship but set apart from it. In this connection it is noteworthy that some of the poems are even identified as having been performed in churches, probably before or after important religious services.[7]

What sort of formal guidelines might have been operative for poets like Simeon in composing his panegyrics? V. Grebeniuk has noted the similarity between certain dramatic works in the collection and the theatrical productions organized as rhetorical exercises in the schools of the Rzecz pospolita – Jesuit institutions whose curricula and practices were well known to Simeon because of his personal background (he was born and raised in the borderlands between Orthodox Belorussia and Catholic Poland) and because of his studies at the Mohyla Academy in

Kiev, one of the most important cultural transit points between East and West.[8] To this we should add that the declamations in the *Rifmologion* – and these constitute the majority of the texts – are also modelled after Jesuit school exercises, in this case oratorical recitals on themes assigned to students by their teachers.[9] For example, an instructor (invariably a monk or priest) would have his students compose short declamations on the lives of ancient orators, mythic themes, or words in praise of a visiting dignitary. Indeed, records have been preserved of just such a recital by students of the school where Simeon taught as a young monk, an event occasioned by a visit to the town by Tsar Aleksei Mikhailovich.[10] But the details of the program reveal a critically important innovation: rather than relying on the naïve and possibly faulty compositions of his adolescent charges, Simeon himself composed several poems, borrowed a few others from an already published panegyric, and assigned them to his students to read in the tsar's presence.[11] The complex of poems that emerged would prove to be prototypical of later compositions by both Simeon and other baroque poets, both in terms of its multi-partite cast and a thematic unity built around the specific performative moment of panegyric recitation.

Yet the model of the schoolroom exercise is not, in and of itself, sufficient to explain the structure of such compositions, if only because there were practically no belletristic sources that could be consulted as guidelines to the overall structure of such complex works. But there was a very substantial literary corpus with which poets were intimately familiar: the service books of the Church. Among the various genres contained in these compilations specific types of panegyrics can be singled out as particularly important literary models, the most important of which is the *kanon*. The *kanon* is a complex cycle of hymns consisting of eight or nine similarly structured odes. Each opens with a hymn called a *hiermos* based on an Old Testament canticle (the song of Moses after crossing the Red Sea [Exodus 15:1–19], Hannah's song of praise following the birth of her son Samuel [I Sam. 2:1–10], and others]) except for the last, which is based on the text of the Magnificat and Benedictus (Luke 1:46–57, 68–79). The *hiermos* is followed by two or more hymns called *troparia* dedicated to the particular saint or event in the church calendar that is being celebrated. The *kanon* was of such significance as a literary model that it was identified by Karion Istomin with the very act of versifying.[12]

We do not know for certain whether or not Simeon decided to arrange for a dramatic multipartite recitation because his school boys were already familiar with this sort of rhetorical exercise or because there was a clear parallel here to the liturgical model of the *kanon*, but in any case the overlapping of the two forms was not lost on the poet, and in his subsequent panegyrics he was heavily influenced by the form of the liturgical *kanon* itself. The first step in the process of transferring the liturgical panegyric to the secular stage involved mixing purely liturgical hymns with those of the author's own creation. As a clear illustration we might consider, for example, Simon's 'Rhymed Verses on the Nativity of Christ, Recited in the Church of St. Mary of Egypt to the Glory of Christ Our God,' a panegyric written for eight pairs of youths modelled after the *Kanon* for the Nativity of Christ. It consists of eight sections, each beginning with the *hiermos* drawn directly from the *kanon* followed by two poems of Simon's own composition, which take the place of the prescribed *troparia*. When the entire piece was performed, a choir probably sang the *hiermos*, and each pair of youths recited the two pseudo-*troparia* that Simeon had written, proceeding in this fashion through all eight odes. A comparison of the first ode with its liturgical prototype gives a good idea of how the latter impinges on the former. The original *Kanon* for the Nativity of Christ opens as follows:

> *Hiermos*: Christ is born, give ye glory. Christ comes from heaven, meet ye Him. Christ is on earth, be ye exalted. O all the earth, sing unto the Lord, and sing praises in gladness, O ye people, for He has been glorified.
>
> [*Troparion* 1]: Man fell from the divine and better life: though made in the image of God, through transgression he became wholly subject to corruption and decay. But now the wise Creator fashions him anew: for he has been glorified.[13]

During an actual worship service the *hiermos* is sung, and the *troparia* (of which we have cited only one of three) are chanted. In Simeon's paraliturgical composition. the above *hiermos* would initially have also been sung (as the poem's rubrics in the manuscript indicate) followed by two poems in syllabic verse, the first of which reads:

Christ is born, praise Him all ye people.
   God is incarnate, bow down before Him.
The true God has descended to earth,
   The immaculate Virgin has given birth to Him.
He has come to renew our corrupt race,
   And to direct the image of God in humankind,

> Which was blackened by the darkness of sin,
>   And was born devoid of God's likeness.
> For that which the Lord Himself has deigned to create
>   He wishes to rectify in His wisdom,
> That we once again achieve God's likeness,
>   Freed from death, holy and saintly.
> God's image, darkened by sin within us,
>   And thereby being placed in the shadow of death,
> Henceforth, if it is rectified,
>   Is set by God in heavenly light.
> No longer is our destined place in hell,
>   But in the joyous heavenly city.
> For this reason, all you people, celebrate today,
>   Radiantly rejoice with pure minds,
> Give praise to God, who today is born,
>   Placed for our sakes in a manger;
> Acknowledge Him as God and King.[14]

What Simeon has done in his own poem is to repeat in poetic form the contents of the *hiermos* and then to expand the liturgical *troparion* into a much lengthier panegyric with denser theological content. The core structure, however, is manifestly liturgical.

The devolution of panegyric cycles away from their liturgical prototypes is marked by the creation of entirely original complexes, both religious and secular in content, based on liturgical models. Simeon's 'Verses on the Nativity of Christ' typifies the way a feast-day panegyric sequence imitates a full liturgical sequence without actually incorporating liturgical texts. It consists of twelve poems varying in length from fourteen to eighteen eleven-syllable lines.[15] Each poem, like the *hiermos* of a *kanon*, evokes an image from the Old Testament and links it to some aspect of the incarnation story. In the fourth poem, for example, Moses leading the children of Israel out of Egypt is likened to Christ, whose birth has similarly freed men from bondage to sin, a conceit suggested by the first *hiermos* of the *kanon*. The fifth poem is similarly derivative in elaborating the 'sea of life' metaphor (borrowed from *hiermos* of the sixth canticle, which in turn is linked to the story of Jonah), but introduces an original note by comparing Christ to the sun as it emerges from behind the clouds to dry up the waters of the flood, thereby rescuing the ark of the Church. The sixth poem develops an original conceit, but one also based on an Old Testament vehicle: Christ here is born in the ark of the Church, and his incarnation is likened to the dove that returns to Noah with an olive branch, signifying that the waters of sin are receding. In short, Simeon follows the liturgical prototype by constructing a sequence of poems based on a series of motifs that typologically link Old and New Testament.

Reading the sequence as a kind of paraliturgical text takes on particular significance when one reaches the last two poems, which have nothing to do with the Nativity per se: the eleventh is a prayer to Christ on behalf of Tsar Aleksei, his wife Maria, and their son, the twelfth on behalf of Patriarch Nikon and Bishop Kalist. Their presence in a sequence that has already announced, as it were, its liturgical foundations, serves to elevate these secular figures to the level of the principle objects of veneration: God the Father, Christ, and the Virgin Mary. This strategic move on Simeon's part is reinforced by a play on words that stresses the homonymy of the divine and earthly. God and Aleksei are both tsars: 'O *King* (*Tsar*) of all ages, Creator of the whole world, grant *our King* (*Tsar*) long life'; the Tsaritza and the Virgin bear the same name: 'We fall down before the feet of the most pure Virgin, *Mary the Queen* (*Tsaritza*); may she grant you, *Mary*, long life; grant that she may prosper, grant her to reign everywhere with the Tsar'; Nikon, Kalist, and Christ are all identified as hierarchs and pastors: 'O newborn *Hierarch* (i.e., *Christ*),/ Nikon has been appointed by Thee for us;/ O supreme *Pastor*, preserve him in honor and health/ for many years, that he may send up glory to Thee; and preserve Kalist, the *pastor* beneath him, and be merciful.'[16]

On the basis of this and numerous other texts we may conclude that liturgical discourse had a decisive role to play in the shaping of the corpus of Russian baroque texts. But does the opposite also hold true? Were any attempts made to deploy the arsenal of baroque literary devices to the liturgical field, and if so, how successful were they?

Among the first texts of the East Slavic baroque subject to this sort of experimentation were the Psalms. Although metrical versions of the Psalms were commonplace in Western and Central Europe, they had never been poetically paraphrased on Russian soil until Simeon undertook this task in 1678, inspired by the sixteenth-century Polish metrical translations of Jan Kochanowski. How Simeon came upon the idea is telling in itself: he was in the process of organizing a large body of his own poems into an alphabetically ordered collection and came eventually to the Greco-Slavonic letter Psi. Under this rubric he set a number of the so-called penitential psalms into syllabic verse, then decided that it might be appropriate to proceed with the versification of the entire Psalter.[17] These new versions were not specifically composed as replacements for the readings from the Psalms in the liturgy – indeed, Simeon makes it clear in his introduction that he, following Kochanowski's example, wanted to create texts that could be set to music and rendered both more popular and memorable in this fashion.[18] But against the background of the recent church schism this initiative was radical indeed. Simeon probably additionally shocked his audience by publishing the Psalms in a specifically liturgical form, that is, in *kathismata*, blocks of several psalms constituting the principle unit of reading in a worship setting. Moreover he appended to the Psalms versified versions of the nine Old Testament canticles that serve as the prototypes for the odes of the *kanon*, and added to the ninth a versified rendition of the non-biblical refrain addressed to the Theotokos, 'More honorable than the cherubim ...' one of the prayers most frequently repeated in Orthodox worship, both public and private, and prescribed to be sung precisely at this point in the reading of a *kanon* at matins. Simeon admitted that he had to alter the wording of these sacred texts to make them fit his metrical matrices, but defended himself by arguing that the words he chose, where they differed from the Church Slavic original, conveyed and explained the sense of the latter. This view ran counter to the notion that the sacred word should not be tampered with because any change in wording could affect the sense, and therefore the underlying dogmas, that they conveyed.[19]

The idea that sacred texts could be altered in this way, even if the new metrical versions could not be adopted for liturgical use, represented the beginnings of a shift in consciousness that would ultimately challenge the notion that the sacred and secular word were of an ontologically different order. It opened the door to the possibility that when new sacred texts had to be composed, they might, like Simeon's Psalms, exploit the resources introduced by the baroque.

The need for new liturgical texts, it should be pointed out, arose periodically in conjunction with the canonization of new saints and the updating of services in honour of other saints who, for political or social reasons, had assumed greater prominence in the collective consciousness of the Church. In the Orthodox tradition the composition of a new service was a major undertaking, involving the composition of scores of new hymns to be sung at various points in vespers and matins, including new *kanons* of the sort described above. These services – and their *kanons* in particular – represent a fascinating locus for examining the impact of baroque poetics on the consciousness of churchmen commissioned to enlarge the corpus of the service books.

In its original Greek form the opening *hiermos* of each ode of the *kanon* sets a specific metrical pattern that is rigorously followed by each succeeding *troparion*. When the Greek service books were translated into Church Slavonic, however, these metrical properties were almost alway lost, and thus the text became essentially prosaic, with line breaks realized only within the musical setting in which the texts were chanted. Writers like Simeon and Karion were perfectly aware of the prosodic properties of the Greek *kanons*, and one would think that, faced with the prospect of writing new *kanons* and related hymns, and thus unconstrained by the demands of fidelity to an existing text, they could experiment with new metrical forms, reintroducing the elements of poetic artifice that had been abandoned in translated works.

Karion was called upon to compose several new services – to St Donatus (1704), St Hypatius (1707), and St Daniil of Moscow (1711), among others – and his approach to the composition of these texts provides an interesting example of how baroque play impinges on prayer. Most obvious is the conservatism of the author's approach to the problem of composition. Although adept at syllabic versification, Karion almost always resists the temptation to compose any of his hymns in regular syllabic lines; nor does he make the hymns structurally isomorphic, as they were in the original Greek. In short, the fundamental prosaic structure of previously translated *kanons*, rather than the poetic structure of the Greek originals, remains his model. But certain forms of 'poeticization' creep in in ways that, to the discerning eye and ear, would promote that sense of wonder and play that we commonly associate with the East Slavic baroque.

The first of these is the use of acrostics, one of the favourite devices of baroque poets. Karion incorporates them in several of his *kanons*. For example, in his Service to St Hypatius he introduces the acrostic: 'BOGA TsSARIa PETI ChUDOPODATELIa NESE KARION' ('To hymn God the King, Miracle-Giver, Karion brings [this offering]'), which extends across the entire *kanon*, and in the service to St Daniil incorporates his signature, 'KARION NIShchi MONAKh IEREI' ('The Lowly Monk Karion, a Priest') across the first four and last odes of the *kanon*.[20]

Another form of poetic play involves the use of anaphora, sometimes combined with repeated codas, across several adjacent hymns. The effect becomes even more striking when the repeated opening and closing phrases of several hymns read in sequence is accompanied by echoing syntactic patterns in the middle sections. Here is a typical example, a series of three hymns sung successively towards the end of the Matins service (the verses at Lauds); each troparion has been broken up below into three sections to underscore the parallel syntactic and thematic development of the three hymns:

I

[1] *With what praises*
 shall we extol you, *hierarch* renowned in virtues
 and wonderworking physician, most blessed *Hypatius?*
[2] *For with the heavenly healing of [God]-pleasing* prayer
 you miraculously healed many who were ill,
 for with *God-given love* for mankind
 you are ready to call on all who call upon you,
[3] so pray to *God who loves mankind*
 that He may grant us great mercy.

II

[1] *With what* goodly-sounding *adornments*
 shall we praise the comely beauty of the *hierarchical* admonitions
 of this staunch pillar of the Church,
 worthy of astonishment, *Hypatius* of Gangra, first-seated,
 a luminary illuminating the universe?
[2] *For with his God-imitating life* he has amazed
 The ends of all the earth.
[3] *Christ our God* glorifies him everywhere,
 Granting us great mercy.

III

[1] *With what* wordly *eloquence* of our lips
 shall we honor this enlightener, our God-bearing *father Hypatius?*
[2] Stoic sufferer for Christ,
 Godly preacher of the pious faith,
 who dispersed the darkness of heresy,
 gloriously worked wonders,
 received the final reward in Heaven,
[3] and from there, to those who call on him,

grants requests to our benefit from *Christ God,*
who has great mercy.

Here, in contrast to the acrostic, the tripartite syntactic structure of each hymn, the anaphorically organized openings and the parallel codas, would have been immediately discernable to worshippers at the moment of recitation.

It should be noted that these and comparable forms of poeticization have a substantial history within the tradition of Orthodox liturgical composition. The art of acrostics was frequently practised by the Greeks, and indeed, Russian translators of early services frequently reported in the rubrics of service books how the original Greek acrostics should read, even though they were not reproduced in the Church Slavic translation. In their own original services, written to commemorate Russian saints, they not infrequently employed acrostics and other 'baroque' forms of encipherment as well.[21] Similarly, the use of anaphora and refrains was encountered sufficiently often in the Greek tradition to influence the practice of Russian composers.[22] What suggests a specifically baroque influence here is, more than anything else, the determination to resurrect these ancient traditions and, perhaps even more important, the hypertrophy of such devices. Thus, for example, in the service for St Daniil, Karion not only spreads the acrostic of his name and station (monk and priest) across the opening and closing odes, but in the fifth, seventh and eighth odes the five constituent hymns begin with the same word ('*Svet*' [light], '*ogon*' [fire], and '*angel*' [angel] respectively) and conclude with the same phrase or motif.[23] He takes advantage of these repetitions to engage in sophisticated games of symbolic equivocation, as in the seventh ode, whose subtext is the Old Testament canticle of the three youths in the fiery furnace: the prayer of the youths quenches the *fire* of the *furnace* (the *hiermos*), Daniil quenches the *fire* of youthful passions with the *flame* of divine love (*troparion* #1), the *fire* of faith burns eternally in his heart, and with it he bedews the *furnace* of worldly misfortunes (*tropiarion* #2), he pours the water of prayers pleasing to God on the fury of the *fire* of enemies visible and invisible (*troparion* #3), and the Virgin Mary bears within her womb Christ the Divine *Fire*, to whom we pray to extinguish the *flames* of our sins with the waters of Divine grace (the *theotokion*). Such anaphorization reaches its apex in the service to St Donatus.[24] The *kanon* for matins consists of eight odes, each with four or five hymns: the opening *hiermos* followed by three or four *troparia*. In every ode the *hiermos* sets the basic verbal pattern, and each *troparion* thereafter rigorously follows this structure, repeating the same opening and closing phrases. It is here, more than anywhere else, that Karion manages to resurrect the deep poetic structure of the original Greek texts, and the impetus for doing so must certainly derive from the 'will to play' that the baroque introduced.

The unwritten rule proscribing the metricization of liturgical texts was violated only rarely. One such case involves the ancient *Akathistos* hymn to the Theotokos, which church rubrics prescribe to be read once a year during the fifth week of Lent. Simeon translated this text into Polish verse, but it was not published until the twentieth century.[25] The manuscript of Karion's service to St Hypatius contains a cycle of rhymed and metricized hymns dedicated to the saint and patterned after the *Akathistos*,[26] and his service to St John the Warrior concludes with an extra-liturgical, postscriptive poem in praise of the saint,[27] but such texts have never been reproduced in official service books. The Church, resistant to any changes in the wording of the unmoveable portions of the liturgy, extended its resistance to the area of original liturgical composition, where the adoption of literary devices new to the baroque, in particular the use of syllabic verse, was limited to extra-liturgical performance – a profound irony, considering that the original Greek odes and other complexes of hymns embodied prosodic structures of the greatest sophistication, and thus the use of syllabic verse might legitimately have been welcomed as a return to the ancient traditions of the mother Church. But since this particular tradition had never taken root in the Russian Church, it was perceived as an unacceptable innovation associated with Western heterodoxy and secularization.

Here a comparison of the inroads made by the new musical culture with those of the new verbal culture may be instructive. Although the Church was resistant to changes in the structure of liturgical chant, it ultimately proved powerless to withstand the adoption of polyphony, in part because the breakdown in the monolithic cast of liturgical chant prior to the advent of the baroque had paved the way for polyphony's introduction, but perhaps most importantly because no explicit *semantic* barriers stood in the way of its adoption, and the native church possessed neither the theological sophistication nor the metalanguage to explain why polyphony was *inherently* un-Orthodox. As a consequence Russian Orthodox church *chant* reverted to *music*, that is, it adopted all the features of seventeenth and early eighteenth-century baroque choral compositions, with the attendant degradation – from a spiritual perspective – of prayer into play. Choirs grew increasingly prominent, increasingly professional, and increasingly distant from the congregation. What happens seems to instantiate Paul Hindemith's claim that 'with harmony it seems to go as with the tree of the knowledge of good and evil: once you have tasted its fruits, you have lost your innocent approach to the facts of life.'[28]

The texts used in worship, however, remained unchanged, undergirding the stability of the Church's dogmas and guaranteeing their continuity across the great cultural divide of the Petrine reforms and beyond. The style in which new texts were composed also remained static. To this day services honouring newly canonized saints, among them twentieth-century martyrs, are composed in Church Slavic rather than Russian, and versification in the strict sense of the word, whether in the syllabic form adopted by the baroque poets or the syllabotonic form of their successors, is regarded as a form of verbal play incompatible with the spirit of corporate worship.

Notes

1 Concerning the literary area, the one with which we are primary concerned in this study, Mikhail Gasparov writes, 'It was the Baroque that captured the expressive force of rhythm and rhyme, that isolated and canonized these devices and made them the distinctive features distinguishing verse from prose.' See his *Ocherk istorii russkogo stikha: Metrika. Ritmika. Rifma. Strofika* (*An Outline of the History of Russian Verse: Metrics, Rhythm, Rhyme, Strophics*) (Moscow: 'Nauka,' 1984), 20.
2 Vladimir Martynov, *Penie, igra i molitva v russkoi bogosluzhebnoi sisteme* (Moscow: Izd. 'Filologiia,' 1997). See also his more recent study that takes the graphic arts into account as well: *Kultura, ikonosfera i bogosluzhebnoe penie moskovskoi Rusi* (*Culture, the Iconosphere and Liturgical Chant in Muscovite Rus'*) (Moscow: Progress – Traditsiia, Russkii put',' 2000).
3 Martynov, *Penie*, 5–31.
4 Johann von Gardner, *Russian Church Singing*, trans. Vladimir Morosan, v. 1 (Crestwood, NY: St Vladimir's Seminary Press, 1980), 111.
5 For a broad overview of the critical literature and a new synthesis, see L.A. Chernaia, *Russkaia kul'tura perekhodnogo perioda ot srednevekov'ia k novomu vremeni* (*Russian Culture in Transition from the Middle Ages to the Modern Period*) (Moscow: 'Iazyki russkoi kul'tury,' 1999).
6 The full text of the *Rifmologion*, consisting of poems composed over the course of more than two decades and compiled in 1678, has never been published in full, though an edition under the editorship of Anthony Hippisley and Lidiia Sazonova is currently under preparation. The fullest description

of the contents is found in V.P. Grebeniuk, '"Rifmologion" Simeona Polotskogo (Istoriia sozdaniia, struktura, idei)' (Simeon of Polotsk's Rifmologion (History of Composition, Structure, Ideas), in *Simeon Polotskii i ego knigoizdatel'skaia deiatel'nost'* (*Simeon of Polotsk and His Book-Publishing Activities*), ed. A.N. Robinson (Moscow: Izd. 'Nauka,' 1982), 259–308.

7 Lidiia Sazonova claims that poems addressed to the tsar were actually integrated into the Christmas vigil service, but the evidence for this is not compelling. It is clear, however, that such verses were integrated into the broader ritual framework of the court that included both divine worship and nonliturgical performances. See Sazonova's monograph, *Poeziia russkogo barokko: vtoraia polovina XVII–nachalo XVIII v.* (*The Poetry of the Russian Baroque: The Second Half of the Seventeenth to the Beginning of the Eighteenth Century*) (Moscow: 'Nauka,' 1991), 118–19.

8 Grebeniuk, '"Rifmologian,"' 260.

9 See Anthony Hippisley, *The Poetic Style of Simeon Polotsky*, Birmingham Slavonic Monographs, 16 (Birmingham: Dept. of Russian Language and Literature, 1985), 17.

10 See Ierofei Tatarskii, *Simeon Polotskii (ego zhizn' i deiatel'nost'): Opyt issledovaniia iz istorii prosveshcheniia i vnutrennoi tserkovnoi zhizni vo vtoruiu polovinu XVII veka* (*Simeon of Polotsk (His Life and Work): An Essay on the History of the Enlightenment and Church Life in the Second Half of the Seventeenth Century*) (Moscow: M.G. Volchangov, 1886), 47–51.

11 The original autograph has been preserved (see Gosudarstvennyi istoricheskii Muzei, Sinod. sobr., No. 731, fols. 288-92). The poems are reproduced in A.F. Korshunaŭ, ed. and comp., *Xrestamatyia pa starazhytnai belaruskai litaratury* (*Anthology of Old Belorussian Literature*) (Minsk: Dziarzhaŭae Vuchebna-pedahahichnae vydavetstva Ministerstva asvety BSSR, 1959), 346–52. Simeon drew the poems, as well as a prose introduction, from a panegyric written in honour of Archbishop Mikhail Ragoza, Metropolitan of Kiev.

12 He defines poetics as 'the making of verses, the composition of the *hiermoi* of *kanons* ...'; cited in S.N. Brailovskii, *Odin is pestrykh XVII-go veka* (*One of the 'Motleys' of the Seventeenth Century*), Zapiski Imp. Akademii nauk, v. 5, no. 5 (St Petersburg, 1902), 464–5.

13 In the manuscript the text of the hymn is not reproduced; the rubrics indicate, 'First sing *hiermos* 1: "Christ is born ..." Then recite the following verses' (see Gosudarstvennyi istoricheskii Musei, Sinod. sobr., No. 287, fol. 1). The present translation of the *hiermos* and first *troparion* is taken from *The Festal Menaion*, trans. Mother Mary and Archimandrite Kallistos Ware (London: Faber and Faber, 1969), 269.

14 Only brief excerpts of the whole poem have appeared in print, and these

faultily transcribed: see Simeon Polotskii, *Virshi* [*Verses*], ed. V.K. Bylinin and L.U. Zvonareva (Minsk: 'Mastatskaia literature,' 1990), 236–8. The citation here is from a photocopy of the original manuscript (see note 14 above).
15 Simeon Polotskii, *Virshi*, 45–50.
16 Ibid., 49–50.
17 See O. A. Derzhavina, 'Simeon Polotskii v rabote nad "Psaltyr'iu rifmotvornoi"' (Simeon of Polotsk at Work on his Metrical Psalter), in *Simeon Polotskii i ego knigoizdatel'skaia deiatel'nost'* (*Simeon of Polotsk and His Book-Publishing Activities*), 117. The full collection of psalms under the title *The Psalter of the King and Prophet David ...* appeared in Moscow in 1680.
18 It should be pointed out that the music Simeon has in mind was polyphonic, and it is no coincidence that all his Psalms were set to music shortly after his death by V.P. Titov, one of Russia's early baroque composers.
19 Such was the attitude of the Old Believers, those who opposed the liturgical reforms of the late seventeenth century and ultimately severed relations with the established church.
20 See the service for St Daniil of Moscow on 4 March and for St Hypatius on 31 March in *Mineia: Mart* (*Monthly Menaion: March*) (Moscow: Izd. Moskovskoi patriarkhii, 1984), Part 1: 114–20 and Part 3: 358–64.
21 Numerous examples are cited in F.G. Spasskii, *Russkoe liturgicheskoe tvorchestvo* (*Russian Liturgical Composition*) (Paris: YMCA Press, 1951). A special excursus (274-84) is devoted to cryptographic devices in liturgical compositions.
22 Cf. the examination of particular device in more ancient liturgical texts in V.K. Bylinin, 'Poetika russkikh troparei XI veka' (The Poetics of Russian Troparia of the Eleventh Century), in *Literaturnoe proizvedenie i literaturnyi protsess v aspekte istoricheskoi poetiki* (*The Literary Work and the Literary Process From the Perspective of Historical Poetics*), ed. M.N. Darvin, F.Z. Kanunova et al. (Kemerovo: Kemerovskii gos. universitet, 1988), 40–8.
23 *Mineia: Mart*, Part 1: 114–20.
24 *Mineia: Aprel'* (*Monthly Menaion: April*), Part 2 (Moscow, 1984), 303–11.
25 Simeon, *Virshi*, 136–42.
26 See Brailovskii, *Odin is pestrykh XVII-go veka*, xxvii. Regrettably Brailovskii's description is too laconic to determine how complete the *akathistos* is: he cites only the opening hymn (*kontakion*), which begins with two rhymed couplet written in twelve-syllable lines.
27 Karion Istomin, *Mesiatsa iulia v 30 den': Pamiat' sviatago Ioanna voina i chudotvortsa ...* (*July 30: Commemoration of St John the Warrior and Miracle-worker*) (Moscow: [Pechatnyi dvor], 1695), fol. 67v.
28 Paul Hindemith, *A Composer's World* (Garden City, NY: Doubleday and Co., 1961), 62.

chapter eight

Reconciling Divine and Political Authority in Racine's *Esther*

ANN DELEHANTY

> I shall find antiquity a rewarding study, if only because, while I am absorbed in it, I shall be able to turn my eyes from the troubles which for so long have tormented the modern world, and to write without any of that over-anxious consideration which may well plague a writer on contemporary life, even if it does not lead him to conceal the truth.
>
> Livy, *Early History of Rome*, 1:1

Racine's biblical tragedy, *Esther*, opens with a panegyric prologue incanted by the character Piety in which Piety proclaims the virtues of the king, whom we can presume to be Louis XIV. Within this prologue, Piety utters a prayer for history:

> Grand Dieu, que cet ouvrage ait place en ta mémoire!
> Que tous les soins [que le roi] prend pour soutenir ta gloire
> Soient gravés de ta main au livre où sont écrits
> Les noms prédestinés des rois que tu chéris! (Prologue, 15–19)[1]

> [Great God, may this work have a place in your memory!
> May all the cares [that the king] takes to maintain your glory
> Be inscribed by your hand in the book where
> The predestined names of your beloved kings are written!]

Not only does Piety hope that Louis XIV is predestined for eternal glory, she also hopes that God himself will write (or, rather, will have already written, looked at from the divine perspective) the history of Louis's reign. She thus identifies the ultimate historian, God himself, and the only authoritative historical account, the book of God's memory. Despite this reverent prologue, in the body of the play three of the main characters put forth radically different interpretations of history, not all of which maintain the primacy of divine authority in determining history's meaning. Moreover, we know that outside the boundaries of this play, Racine himself, as the king's historiographer (*historiographe du roi*), willingly served as a substitute for God's authority – recounting the events of Louis's reign in such a way as to justify Louis's glory both as monarch and as incarnate representative of the divine on earth. Because the eternal history book that Piety mentions is accessible only to God, human beings repeatedly take on the task of representing history from their limited perspective and claiming their own authority in the articulation of its meaning.

The potentially tragic discrepancies between the divine and the human interpretation of history constitute one of the central conflicts of *Esther*, the first of Racine's two biblical tragedies, which he wrote at the very end of his career in the late seventeenth century. Esther's confidante, Elise, asks the central question about history that the play poses: 'Est-ce Dieu, sont-ce les hommes, / Dont les oeuvres vont éclater ?' ('Is it of God, or is it of men that the works [of history] will tell?') (II.ix.715–16). Since the line of David is at risk of being prematurely terminated in the play – King Assuérus has been tricked by an evil adviser, Aman, into ordering the execution of all Jewish people in his kingdom – *Esther* represents an originary scene in which both the human and divine ends for history seem possible. The potential tragedy that hangs in the balance is not simply the death or undoing of a single character but the threat of cutting off prematurely the historical continuum leading towards Christ.

This paper will examine how *Esther* dramatizes the struggle for the authority to determine the meaning of history. Racine portrays contemporary concerns about historiography – and the concomitant questions about individual and social identity that historiography poses – by depicting each biblical character as presenting a competing notion of the meaning and direction of history. Aman, the king's adviser, represents history as a series of battles to assert greater force; Assuérus depicts history as the sum total of his political successes and failures; and the heroine, Esther, sees history as the unveiling of a divine plan. What is remarkable about *Esther* is not so much the ultimate triumph of divine authority and eschatological history (this is to be expected since the story is taken from the Old Testament and Racine was fairly true to his source), rather, it is the fact that Racine stages the triumph of divine authority as politically efficient for Assuérus and, thus, desirable for the state. In the end, Assuérus realizes that monarchic authority – and his place in the history books – is best preserved through an assent to divine authority; he sees that he will be best remembered as king if he uses his authority to promote the divine ends for history.

Furthermore, it is striking that Racine would have all three major characters openly deliberate about how history will remember them. They are asking, in effect, what part their individual identities will have in the collective self-understanding of the history books. In this sense, the play puts into question not only how divine and political authority can coexist, but also how the individual fits into a world where history is often a question of a (purportedly) unified social identity. Racine highlights the negotiation between individual and social identity by making all three of the characters orphans – either literally, in the case of Esther and Aman,[2] or metaphorically, in the case of Assuérus, who was chosen to be king by the throwing of lots. As orphans, these characters need to assert their own identities from the very beginning. In each case, however, their individual identity eventually clashes with the collective identity: Aman's self-positioning as tyrant does not allow for a well-functioning, contractual society; Assuérus's desire for glory allows him to be duped into anti-social decrees; Esther's decision to hide her religion and marry the king leaves her people at risk of execution. The solution to this problem for the individuals, as well as the history books, is to submit to a single, higher authority that recognizes both their collective and individual identity. Ultimately, the tragedy's resolution will depend upon the recognition that each historical subject possesses autonomy on some levels, but must also *choose* to submit to an authority who will assure the individual's place in a collective identity.

Competing Models of Authority

In the biblical book of Esther, as well as in Racine's play, we learn early on that an evil adviser to King Assuérus,[3] Aman, has convinced the king to kill all of the Jews by claiming that the Jewish people were a threat to Assuérus's sovereignty. Both accounts attribute Aman's false representation of the Jews to his hatred for a single Jew, Mardochée, who refuses to bow down to Aman. When, in a private meeting, the king asks Aman's advice on how best to honour a subject who has done a good deed, Aman thinks the king is referring to him (Aman) and makes the mistake of suggesting that the king deck the subject in royal regalia and parade him around the town. When Aman discovers that Mardochée is the favoured subject, because he had unveiled a plot to assassinate the king, Aman's hatred and determination to execute the Jewish people is doubled. The only person capable of preventing the execution of the Jews is Esther, Assuérus's wife and Mardochée's adopted daughter. Assuérus does not know that Esther is Jewish; the height of the drama is the revelation of her true identity. Mardochée convinces Esther to go to the king unbidden (an act punishable by death) and plead for the salvation of the Jews. She goes to the king, receives his clemency, and reveals Aman's plot. Through Esther's actions, the king reverses the death warrant on the Jews and sends Aman to death instead.[4]

Aman, the character responsible for convincing Assuérus to order the execution of the Jews, represents domination by one group as the end of history. In the Bible story, Aman is said to be 'de la race d'Agog' (from the race of Agog) (*Esth* III:1),[5] and in the Apocryphal version of Esther, Assuérus writes in his letter condemning Aman: 'Nous avions reçu avec bonté auprès de nous Aman, fils d'Amadeth, étranger, macédonien d'inclination et d'origine, qui n'avait rien de commun avec le sang des Perses, et qui a voulu déshonorer notre clémence par sa cruauté' (We had taken in, with good will, Aman, son of Amadeth, a stranger of Macedonian inclination and origin, who had nothing in common with the Persians and who wished to dishonour our clemency with his cruelty) (*Esth* XVI:10). Racine adds to these limited details by describing Aman as an orphan who was sold into slavery and then rose to power in the land where he was initially purchased (II.i.451–2). Racine also emphasizes Aman's ethnicity as an Amalécite[6] which, in Aman's own words, makes him part of a long tradition of people who were at war with the Jews: 'Une éternelle haine a dû m'armer contre eux' (An eternal hatred drove me to take up arms against them) (II.i.483–5).

In keeping with the biblical account, Racine paints Aman's longstanding antipathy towards the Jews very specifically in the form of his hatred for Mardochée. Aman resents the fact that Mardochée refuses to lower his eyes when Aman passes by. Aman, talking to Hydaspe, an officer of Assuérus's court, says:

L'insolent devant moi ne se courbe jamais.
En vain de la faveur du plus grand des monarques
Tout révère à genoux les glorieuses marques;

> Lorsque d'un respect saint tous les Persans touchés
> N'osent lever leurs fronts à la terre attachés,
> Lui, fièrement assis, et la tête immobile,
> Traite tous ces honneurs d'impiété servile. (II.i.424–9)

> [The insolent one never bows before me.
> Despite receiving the favour of the greatest of monarchs
> Whose marks of glory are revered by all on bended knee,
> While the Persians, touched by holy respect,
> Do not dare to raise their faces, prostrate on the ground,
> He, proudly seated, head immobile,
> Treats all of these honours as servile impiety.]

Further on, Aman explains to Hydaspe that it is due to Mardochée's disrespect that he decided to convince the king to sentence all of the Jews: 'C'est lui qui, devant moi refusant de ployer,/ Les a livrés au bras qui les va foudroyer' ('It is he who, refusing to bow before me, / has delivered his people to the arm that will destroy them') (II.i.467–8). Aman thus justifies the murder of a race of people by virtue of his displeasure with one of its members, a displeasure rooted in Mardochée's failure to recognize Aman's position of political authority.

Aman expresses overt concern about how he will be remembered in the history books. At one point in the play, he quotes from the history book of the future, as he envisions it, where the elimination of the Jews and the triumph of the Amalécites have been achieved:

> Je veux qu'on dise un jour aux siècles effrayés :
> 'Il fut des Juifs, il fut une insolente race ;
> Répandus sur la terre, ils en couvraient la face ;
> Un seul osa d'Aman attirer le courroux,
> Aussitôt de la terre ils disparurent tous.' (II.i.476-480)

> [I would like, one day, for it to be said to the terror-struck generations:
> 'There once were Jews, they were an insolent race;
> Spread throughout the earth, they covered its face;
> One of them dared attract the wrath of Aman
> And with that, they disappeared from the earth.']

Aman's words point to how one's future renown (or infamy) equals one's present stature in importance in the play. This is a society that is

Reconciling Divine and Political Authority in *Esther* 143

self-consciously historical, aware of itself both in the present and as it will be remembered in the annals of history. And Aman's model of history, in short, relies on pure force for its institution. The history books, in this view, will remember those whose force enabled them to dominate, if not annihilate, others.

Earlier in the same scene of the second act, when Aman describes his historical antagonism towards the Jews, we learn of another historical model competing for dominance in the play: the political history of the monarch, King Assuérus. The scene begins with Hydaspe and Aman exchanging gossip about the king. Hydaspe reveals to Aman that the king has been lying awake nights in fear of an enemy who threatens his reign: 'Il s'est plaint d'un péril qui menaçait ses jours ;/Il parlait d'ennemi, de ravisseur farouche' (He complained of a peril that was threatening his days;/ he spoke of an enemy, an evil ravisher) (II.i.388–89). In order to chase the thoughts of these dangers from his mind, Assuérus orders that the *Annales* of his reign be brought to him:

> Enfin, las d'appeler un sommeil qui le fuit,
> Pour écarter de lui ces images funèbres,
> Il s'est fait apporter ces annales célèbres
> Où les faits de son règne, avec soin amassés,
> Par de fidèles mains chaque jour sont tracés :
> On y conserve écrits le service et l'offense,
> Monuments éternels d'amour et de vengeance. (II.i.392–8)[7]

> [At last, tired of seeking a sleep that eluded him,
> In order to drive away these funereal images,
> He had those famous annals brought to him
> In which the deeds of his reign are gathered,
> Recorded daily by faithful hands:
> They keep written there both service and offence,
> Eternal monuments of love and vengeance.]

These 'eternal monuments' to Assuérus, which chart all of history in relation to him, offer Assuérus solace in his anguish, as if the past could protect him from present danger. In this model of history, the *Annales* provide the image of the king that establishes his authority. Assuérus returns to that past image of himself in order to bolster his authority in the present. This gesture recalls Pascal's description of the authority of the king as derived from the crowds that surround him:

La coutume de voir les rois accompagnés de gardes, de tambours, d'officiers et de toutes les choses qui ploient la machine vers le respect et la terreur fait que leur visage, quand il est quelquefois seul et sans ses accompagnements imprime dans leurs sujet le respect et la terreur parce qu'on ne sépare point dans la pensée leurs personnes d'avec leur suites qu'on y voit d'ordinaire jointes. Et le monde, qui ne sait pas que cet effet vient de cette coutume, croit qu'il vient d'une force naturelle. Et de là viennent ces mots : le caractère de la divinité est empreint sur son visage, etc.[8]

[The custom of seeing kings accompanied by guards, drums, officers, and all things that move the machine towards respect and terror makes it such that the sight of the king's face alone, without his coterie, results in respect and terror in his subjects since one does not separate in one's thoughts the person from the coterie that is normally joined to him. And the world, which does not know that this effect comes from mere custom, believes that it comes from natural force. And from this follows sayings such as: the divine character is written on his face, etc.]

Similar to Pascal, Racine depicts King Assuérus as garnering his authority from the historical account that represents him. When Assuérus is alone and sleepless, he does not have his coterie of followers to transform him into a powerful monarch. He depends, instead, on the record of the history of his reign to perform that transformation.[9]

In response to Hydaspe's gossip, Aman asks exactly *which* historical account Assuérus is interested in. Hydaspe responds: '[Il revoit tous ces temps si remplis de sa gloire, / Depuis le fameux jour qu'au trône de Cyrus / Le choix du sort plaça l'heureux Assuérus] (He returns to those times, so filled with glory, / beginning with the famous day when the choice of the lots placed the happy Assuérus on the throne of Cyrus) (II.i.402–4). By highlighting the throwing of lots Racine draws attention to the fact that, like Aman, Assuérus is cut off from a rule of inheritance that would determine his identity as king. Assuérus ascended to the throne by chance and commands authority for no other reason than his own determination. The looming threat to that authority is all the more real, since it has no basis in blood.

After telling Aman his secret, Hydaspe then asks Aman whether he has a secret of his own. Aman proceeds to tell Hydaspe of how Mardochée has treated him disrespectfully and, because of this, how he persuaded the king to order the execution of the Jews. To convince Assuérus of the need for this order Aman says:

> Je prévins donc contre eux l'esprit d'Assuérus,
> J'inventai des couleurs, j'armai la calomnie,
> J'intéressai sa gloire : il trembla pour sa vie.
> Je les peignis puissant, riches, séditieux ;
> Leur dieu même ennemi de tous les autres dieux. (II.i.492–6)

> [I moved the mind of Assuérus against them,
> I invented stories, I described calumny,
> I invoked threats to his glory: he trembled for his life.
> I painted them as powerful, rich, seditious,
> Even their god as an enemy to all other gods.]

Aman thus constructs an image of the Jews as a threat to Assuérus's sovereignty. Ignoring his own history as an ethnic outsider to Persia, Aman describes them as 'étrangers dans la Perse, à nos lois opposés' (strangers in Persia, opposed to our laws) (II.i.499). As outsiders, the Jews are not subject to Assuérus's law and, thus, are immune to his authority. Any menace to Assuérus's authority must be eliminated in order for his vision of history, as a set of events leading towards his glory, to be realized.

The theme of the king's ability to sleep comes up again in Aman's speech '[les juifs] n'aspirent qu'à troubler le repos où nous sommes]' : ([the Jews] aspire only to trouble our current state of repose) (II.i.501). Assuérus responds: 'Assure ... le repos de ton roi' (Ensure ... the repose of your king) (II.i.507). This mention of the king's 'repose', as well as the earlier reference to his inability to sleep, calls to mind the historical *topos*, common in accounts of the kings of antiquity as well as medieval and early modern France, of the king sleeping well before a battle as a sign of his confidence and authority.[10] Aman's mention of the king's ill-repose insinuates not only that Assuérus's confidence and authority is at risk but also that his *Annales* will not remember him as one who slept well. In order to assure that Assuérus is thus memorialized, Aman is charged with the elimination of all threats to the king's repose, that is, the history of his reign.

Assuérus's anxieties about the recording of the history of his reign are played out in the scenes following Aman and Hydaspe's tête-à-tête when Asaph, another officer in Assuérus's court, reminds the King that he had already been saved from a potential assassination by the advice of one of his subjects (whom we know to be Mardochée). Assuérus, frustrated by his own forgetfulness, proclaims:

> O d'un si grand service oubli trop condamnable!

Des embarras du trône effet inévitable!
De soins tumultueux un prince environné
Vers de nouveaux objets est sans cesse entraîné;
L'avenir l'inquiète, et le présent le frappe;
Mais, plus prompt que l'éclair, le passé nous échappe. (II.iii.541–6)

[O the damnable forgetting of such a great service!
The inevitable effect of the difficulty of the throne!
A prince is constantly surrounded by tumultuous cares
Led without relief towards new concerns;
The future worries him, the present strikes him;
But, quicker than lightning, the past escapes us.]

Assuérus's fear that the past (history itself) is being lost translates into a fear that his glory and authority are being lost with it. Without a record of his reign, Assuérus is without purpose and meaning – he has no authority. Furthermore, Assuérus's forgetfulness reveals that he has no memory of his own, and thus none of his own means to assert his authority. If the king had remembered Mardochée's heroism of his own accord, he might not have been so gullible ('too credulous' [trop crédule] I.iii.172) as to have been convinced by Aman that the Jews were a dangerous race. The king's forgetfulness and inability to preserve his own history is indirectly the cause of the potential tragedy.[11]

Even though he fears for his future memorialization, Assuérus will achieve an identity as well as a place in the eternal history books by the end of the play through his union with his wife, Esther. Esther is the good double to Aman, who prevents the tragedy of history from occurring and reveals her true identity at the end of the play. Despite their diametric opposition in the play, both Esther and Aman started life in a relatively similar position. As orphans, they were both ripped from the line of tradition that should have guided them.[12] Without that link to their parents, they both needed more individual determination to achieve their positions in the world. In fact, they do well in life by pretending to be other than they are – Esther by posing as a Gentile and Aman by leaving his identity as a slave behind. Once established in their respective positions of power, however, the play shows how they both need to recuperate a tie to tradition or history in their actions. The collective identity from which they came triumphs over their self-determined individual identities.

Whereas the character of Aman represents a model of history that has ethnic domination as its end, Esther represents a model which has the preservation of the line of David as its end. More precisely, the entire focus of the play for Esther is the urgent need to reveal her identity and appeal to Assuérus's clemency; through that revelation, she will secure the preservation of the line of David. As opposed to Assuérus, whose place in history came by way of lots, Esther's historical model is in her blood; as a Jew, she bears the incarnate heritage of Christ in her body. Her faithfulness to that blood, at the moment she reveals her identity to Assuérus, will lead to the triumph of eschatological history.

Reasserting Divine Authority

In the play's opening scene, we learn that Esther is presumed dead by her people and that she is living as the wife of Assuérus, who does not know that she is Jewish. Her confidante, Elise, finds Esther after having received word from a prophet that Esther was still alive. The play's opening line, 'Est-ce toi, chère Elise?' (Is that you, dear Elise?), signals the first moment in the revelation of Esther's identity: Elise is the friend who recognizes Esther's true identity and starts the process of reasserting divine authority in history.

Upon finding Esther, Elise describes how a divine prophet came to tell her to seek Esther out at the palace of Assuérus. Not only did this prophet tell Elise of Esther's whereabouts, he also informed her that a day was near at hand when God was going to avenge his people. Elise tells Esther that this prophet said:

> Rassure ... les tribus alarmées,
> Sion: le jour approche où le dieu des armées
> Va de son bras puissant faire éclater l'appui;
> Et le cri de son peuple est monté jusqu'à lui. (I.i.19–22)

> [Reassure ... the alarmed tribes,
> Zion: the day approaches when the god of might
> Is going to make known the extent of his power;
> The cry of his people has risen up to him.]

By opening the play with Elise's testimony to divine intervention, Racine signals a divine 'prime mover' in the dialogic transmission of knowledge that will move the entire play. The prophet alerts Elise to important information which inspires her to find Esther; Elise, in turn, gives

Esther information that, when combined with Mardochée's revelations, will inform Esther's choice and assist her to act. Divine authority asserts itself openly in the play to promote the completion of the divine will in history.

Esther then describes to Elise the way that she came to be queen and laments her position of relative comfort while the nation of Zion has been enslaved:

> Esther, disais-je, Esther dans la pourpre est assise,
> La moitié de la terre à son sceptre est soumise,
> Et de Jérusalem l'herbe cache les murs !
> Sion, repaire affreux de reptiles impurs,
> Voit de son temple saint les pierres dispersées,
> Et du Dieu d'Israël les fêtes sont cessées ! (I.i.83–8)

> [Esther, I said, Esther is enthroned in purple,
> Half the world submits to her sceptre,
> And grass hides the walls of Jerusalem!
> Zion, repulsive refuge for the impure,
> Sees the stones of its holy temple dispersed,
> And the feast days of the God of Israel have ceased!]

The play thus opens with a scene of historical disorder: the ritual feasts have stopped; Jerusalem is in disrepair; the temple is desecrated; and the counter-positioning of 'Esther' and 'I' points to the distance between Esther's true self, the 'I,' and the self she pretends to be. Esther and her people, like the stones of the temple, have been dispersed and separated from their true identities – she to live as queen, they to live as slaves: 'Maintenant [la nation d'Israël] sert sous un maître étranger' (Now [the nation of Israel] serves a foreign master) [I.iv.259]). Esther takes her only solace in having filled the palace with the 'daughters of Zion,' whom she educates in the Jewish tradition. It is among them that Esther is able to reveal her identity: 'Et c'est là que, fuyant l'orgueil du diadème, / Lasse de vains honneurs, et me cherchant moi-même, / Aux pieds de l'Eternel je viens m'humilier, / Et goûter le plaisir de me faire oublier' (And it is there that, fleeing the pride of the diadem, / tired of vain honors, and searching for my true self, / at the feet of the Eternal, I come to humble myself / and to taste the pleasure of forgetting myself) (I.i.107–10). Esther's rhetoric mixes identity with humility: when she relinquishes her honour and authority, she finds herself. Her true identity is at the feet of

God, where she humiliates and forgets her regal self, revealing her true self which is subject primarily to divine authority.

We learn of the model of history that Esther will espouse when Mardochée comes to Esther to tell her of Aman's threat to the Jews. His speech to Esther reveals her responsibility within the present moment to preserve the divine will for history:

> Laissez les pleurs, Esther, à ces jeunes enfants.
> En vous est tout l'espoir de vos malheureux frères:
> Il faut les secourir; mais les heures sont chères:
> Le temps vole, et bientôt amènera le jour
> Où le nom des Hébreux doit périr sans retour.
> Toute pleine du feu de tant de saints prophètes,
> Allez osez au roi déclarer qui vous êtes. (I.iii.184–90)

> [Leave the tears, Esther, for these young children.
> In you lies the hope of your unhappy brethren:
> You must save them, but few hours remain:
> Time flies, and soon will come the day
> When the name of the Hebrews must perish without return.
> Filled with the fire of so many holy prophets,
> Go and dare to declare to the king who you are.]

All hope lies with Esther and her revelation of her identity to the king. The succession of temporal terms – 'few hours remain: / Time flies, and soon will come the day' – emphasizes the fact that this is the opportune moment in history for that revelation. Mardochée claims that she must preserve 'the name of the Hebrews,' the tradition that is at risk. She is moved to this by the 'fire of so many holy prophets' – those in the tradition who preceded her and foretold this moment. Thus, Esther bears the weight of saving not just the moment but all of history. She has been chosen to bear the divine promise for history and, thus, has an identity marked by the divine will.

Despite Esther's having been chosen by God, Racine's play stresses the fact that there is no absolute guarantee that God will protect the Jews if the divine will for history is ignored; the responsibility lies with the individual believers, who must protect the divine course of history. Racine emphasizes Esther's responsibility by omitting part of Mardochée's reply to Esther in the biblical account (which is via a eunuch, instead of in person) where Mardochée suggests that Esther is replaceable. In the Bible

story, Mardochée says: 'Ne croyez pas qu'étant dans la maison du roi, vous pourriez sauver seule votre vie si tous les Juifs périssaient; Car si vous demeurez maintenant dans le silence, Dieu trouvera quelque autre moyen pour délivrer les Juifs, et vous périrez, vous et la maison de votre père. Et qui sait si ce n'est point pour cela même que vous avez été élévée à la dignité royale, afin d'être en état d'agir dans une occasion comme celle-ci?' (Do not believe that because you are in the house of the king that you would be able to save yourself while all the Jews perish; for if you remain silent now, God will find some other means to deliver the Jews, and you will perish, you and the house of your father. And who knows if it is not exactly for this reason that you were elevated to royal stature, in order to be in a state that enables you to act on an occasion such as this?) (*Esth.* IV: 13–15). Racine's play places the entire burden on Esther and the imperative for her to choose freely to save the Jews, while the Bible story puts more emphasis on God's role as the one who predestines the end of the story, through whatever means possible. Racine's slight alteration has great implications, since it allows him to emphasize the role of human participation in eschatological history. In Racine's account, if Esther does not do this deed, no one will – the salvation of the line of David depends solely on her. This has interesting implications for the model of history that the play finally espouses. Eschatological history requires more than just submission to the divine will; it also calls for individual action and choice in keeping with that will. Racine depicts the play's events accordingly by emphasizing on the choice of a given character to act, rather than simply portraying the story's end as inevitable by dint of divine will. *Esther* thus adopts a historical model that seeks to balance the role of individual identity with that of collective historical purpose, individual authority with that of the social group and its leader.

Another aspect of Esther's model of history lies in her respect for the long-standing tradition of her ancestors bearing the divine promise for history, which influences her choice to reveal her identity.[13] In Esther's prayer after learning of the threat to her people from Mardochée, she says that she learned of God's promise to the Jews from her parents:

> Mon père mille fois m'a dit dans mon enfance
> Qu'avec nous tu juras une sainte alliance,
> Quand, pour te faire un peuple agréable à tes yeux,
> Il plut à ton amour de choisir nos aïeux :
> Même tu leur promis de ta bouche sacrée
> Une postérité d'éternelle durée. (I.iv.249–54)

[My father told me a thousand times during my childhood
That with our people you had sworn a holy alliance,
When, in order to make a people agreeable to your eyes,
It pleased you to choose our ancestors:
You promised them with your sacred mouth
Posterity of eternal duration.]

Esther is conscious of the *telos* of history of which her choice is a part. Contrasted with the 'eternal hatred' of the Amalécites, the Jewish people look forward to posterity of 'eternal duration' that God has promised them. The words of this promise are passed down verbally from generation to generation; the play depicts Esther's moment to transmit that promise.

Mardochée assures Esther that if she acts in a way that will help to preserve the Jews, God's grace will intervene sacramentally to ensure her success: '[Dieu] peut confondre Aman, il peut briser nos fers / Par la plus faible main qui soit dans l'univers; / Et vous, qui n'aurez point accepté cette grâce, / Vous périrez peut-être, et toute votre race' (God can overcome Aman, he can enable the weakest hand in the universe to break our chains; / And you who will not accept this grace, / you will perish perhaps, and your entire race) (I.iii.235–8). Mardochée suggests that God is offering Esther the necessary grace to achieve the defeat of Aman. God acts sacramentally through human beings by giving them the necessary grace to carry out an action that they have been chosen to perform; but the humans themselves must finally choose to act.[14]

The culminating moment of the tragedy is the revelation that Esther is Jewish and Assuérus's judgment of that revelation. After requesting an audience with both Assuérus and Aman, Esther's words to reveal herself are: 'Esther, seigneur, eut un Juif pour son père' (Esther, my Lord, had a Jew for her father) (III.iv.1033). The use of the past tense and the third person to describe herself signals both Esther's own distance from her identity and how her identity was determined by her predecessors, through her father's blood. She reveals the hidden God that she carries in her blood. Esther's revelation of her heritage thus suggests a sacramental transformation of her body. Even though she retains the accidents of her flesh, just as the host retains the accidents of the bread in the sacrament of communion, divine presence dwells within her blood and is called into history by her revelation.

After informing Assuérus of her heritage, she immediately makes a speech about how the Jews are different than Aman's depiction of them, appealing both to the historical level (the Jews are the chosen people) and to the individual level (Assuérus is married to a Jew and was saved by a Jew [Mardochée]). One ruler, she notes, Cyrus, considered the Jewish people to be a peaceable part of his kingdom: 'Cyrus, par [Dieu] vainqueur, publia ses bienfaits, / Regarda notre peuple avec des yeux de paix, / Nous rendit et nos lois et nos fêtes divines' (Cyrus, made victorious by God, heralded his good works, / regarded our people with eyes of peace, returned to us both our laws and our divine feast days) (III.iv.1070–2). Ester argues that the real threat to Assuérus's glory is Aman, whom she characterizes as 'un perfide étranger' (a perfidious stranger) and a 'Scythe impitoyable' (merciless Scythian) (III.iv.1093–1101). She thus appeals to a historical alliance between the Persians and the Jews under Cyrus, whose glory Assuérus surely envied, as well as to the fact that Aman, as a Scythian, is outside of this alliance. This knowledge ultimately works to effect Assuérus's conversion to Esther's cause and the tragedy is fully averted at the same time that Aman's tragic demise is made certain.

Racine stages the process of Assuérus's conversion in a manner that suggests that the king is also altered sacramentally. His initial reaction to Esther's revelation of her identity – 'Ah, de quel coup me percez-vous le coeur!' (Ah, with such a blow you pierce my heart!) (III.iv.1035) – points to his own flesh, which has suddenly been infiltrated by an 'impure source' (III.iv.1039). At that moment, Assuérus's very being is changed, as if his body has been transformed by his association with Esther. His comments that follow Esther's speeches are replete with references to flesh: 'Quel jour mêlé d'horreur vient effrayer mon âme! / Tout mon sang de colère et de honte s'enflamme' (Such a day filled with horror comes to frighten my soul! / All my blood with anger and with shame is inflamed) (III.v.1136–7); speaking of Aman, 'dans ses yeux confus je lis ses perfidies ... Qu'à ce monstre à l'instant l'âme soit arrachée' (in his confused eyes I read his perfidy; may the soul of this monster be taken instantly) (III.v.1169, 1171); 'Mes yeux sont dessillés, le crime est confondu' (My eyes have been opened, the crime is confounded) (III.v.1178). Despite his initial disgust, Assuérus is finally convinced by Esther's speech that his union with her is for the good; he is fundamentally transformed.

Moreover, it is through this transformation of his flesh that Assuérus gains his true identity as the king who protected the line of David. At the moment when Assuérus recognizes the virtue of the Jews and orders their preservation, the goal of his monarchic vision for history is realized: he will be memorialized for all of time because of his act. His identity shifts from one whose authority is founded on words alone, the *annales* of his reign, to one founded on flesh; as Esther's husband, he now belongs to the tradition which bears in its flesh the promise of an incarnate divine. We see this in Assuérus's declaration ordering the preservation of the Jews: 'Rebâtissez son temple, et peuplez vos cités; / Que vos heureux enfants dans leurs solennités / Consacrent de ce jour le triomphe et la gloire, / Et qu'à jamais *mon nom* vive dans leur mémoire' (Rebuild the temple, and people your cities; / May your happy children in their solemnities / consecrate this day to triumph and glory, / and may *my name* live forever in their memory) (III.vii. 1186–9, my emphasis). By preserving the name of the Hebrews, Assuérus also assures the preservation of his own name. The memory of the Jews will lend his name a permanency that even the *Annales* could not ensure. With this act, Assuérus joins the eschatological model of history, even if it is for his own ends.

These scenes provide the resolution for the historical disorder that had overtaken the Jewish people at the beginning of the play: Esther's identity is known, the Jews are freed from slavery, the temple will be rebuilt, and history will carry on. The revelation of Esther's identity and Assuérus's judgment of that revelation eliminated the threat to the continuation of eschatological history and the play can end. It is worth noting that, in the end, the authority to which Esther must appeal is not a figure of any special virtue or insight. Instead, Esther must be judged by the king, because the king has power and can preserve the Jews from their sentence. The monarch, although he lacks any outstanding virtue, possesses the necessary authority. Esther's words transform that authority, however, directing it to the service of the preservation of the Jews instead of simply the commemoration of Assuérus's reign. Moreover, through the marriage of Esther and Assuérus, the divine and the political models of history are united. In his consent to preserve their union even after he becomes aware of her identity, Assuérus embodies both the legal, contractual union (which is founded upon consent) and the sacramental union (founded on divine law).

The play closes with the chorus celebrating how God's hand played a role in the outcome of these events by transforming Esther into a tool of God's will. The transformative power of words evokes a final sacramental image in the play: 'De l'amour de son Dieu son coeur s'est embrasé; / Au péril d'une mort funeste / Son zèle ardent s'est exposé: / Elle a parlé; le ciel a fait le reste' (With love of God her heart is filled; risking a perilous death, / she exposed her ardent zeal: / she spoke, the heavens did the rest) (III.ix.1224–7). A flow of grace from God, once the individual had chosen to submit to divine authority, empowers the individual to act virtuously. The last words of the play, from Psalm 105, remind us of the primacy of God's history book, set up in the prologue: 'Que son nom soit béni; que son nom soit chanté; Que l'on célèbre ses ouvrages / Au-delà des temps et des âges, / Au-delà de l'éternité!' (May his name be blessed; may his name be sung; may his works be celebrated throughout all times and ages, throughout eternity!) (III.ix.1283–6). With Esther's act, history returns to the course of the eternal history book.

In *Tragedy and Truth*, Timothy Reiss proposes that tragedy makes a new form of discourse possible.[15] He contends that '[t]he periods in which tragedy has appeared have been notable for a profound reorganization of the political and social order.'[16] Racine's work, in particular, makes possible one aspect of the discourse of modernity wherein the individual and society are presumed to be mutually interdependent:

> Ultimately the character becomes a *person* endowed with psychological depth, and tragedy is taken as a container of certain knowledge showing the moral, psychological, and so forth functioning of society and the individual. In Racine, Dryden, and their contemporaries, the *development* of modern tragedy is concluded: the episteme no longer needs it. The absence of significance has been enclosed and meaning provided in the psychological identity of an individual place in the center of a web of societal relationships. In these writers the discourses that set forth our specific forms of knowledge and truth are (re)produced and represented: they elaborate economic individualism, the political theory and practice of the contractual state, of normative psychology, of the history and society of our modernity.[17]

At the end of the seventeenth century, in this view, tragedy reproduced a normative conception of the human being as embedded within an economic, political, and social reality that gave him or her individual as well as collective identity. As I have shown in this essay, the resolution of the struggle between the individual and collective forces in the social web requires a contractual conjoining of the forces – Assuérus and Esther together make up the new vision of history. The tragedy's resolution necessitates consent to the coexistence of individual and social identity.

While Racine's play represents the interconnectedness of social and individual identity by way of contractual conjoining, which is a symptom of modernity for Reiss, it would be difficult to say that the reconciliation of divine and political authority in *Esther* is also indicative of modernity. If, as Mitchell Greenberg argues, 'History colonizes the past with the present, while historical tragedy represents the present as past,'[18] then the Old Testament Persia of this play could be said to represent the state of French society at the end of the seventeenth century. The reconciliation between divine and political authority in the play echoes Louis XIV's attempt to achieve the same result with his 1685 revocation of the Edict of Nantes. In this way, *Esther*, like Louis XIV's ill-timed political decision, portrays a move away from modernity and towards a distant past where church and state could still be united. *Esther* seems to warn the spectator that a failure to recognize the divine will for and authority over history could lead to tragic consequences for the history of the world. Racine's turn towards biblical texts in his last two plays signals nostalgia for a world in which such unity was possible. By the time of the 1689 production of *Esther*, however, the disastrous effects of the revocation of the Edict of Nantes were surely already being felt.[19] The possibility of France being united under a single church was becoming an assured impossibility. The play's resolution in the sacramental union between divine and political authority, represented in the marriage of Esther and Assuérus, ultimately points only to the absence of such unions in what was becoming an increasingly modern society. In short, the calamitous consequences of the revocation of the Edict of Nantes underscored the failure of the legal, contractual world to achieve the same kind of sacramental transformation in its members as the union of Assuérus and Esther had achieved. Without the power to convince France's citizens that one church still possessed the authority to interpret the meaning and direction of history as well as the meaning and direction of each individual life, the king's authority over the 'web of societal relations' which constitutes modernity was fated to be fractured by the competing religious authorities who sought to interpret the divine will for history.

Notes

1 Jean Racine, *Oeuvres completes* (Paris: Seuil, 1962), 267. All quotations from *Esther* come from this edition. All translations from French in this paper are my own.

2 Since the Bible does not describe Aman as an orphan, this detail seems to be Racine's own invention and points to the play's thematic preoccupations.
3 In his preface, Racine says he modelled Assuérus on Darius. Assuérus is now considered to be Xerxes. Both figures were known to Racine from Herodotus's *Histories*.
4 Plays based on the *Esther* story were very popular during the sixteenth and seventeenth centuries. Three of the better known are André de Rivaudeau's *Aman* (1561), Pierre Matthieu's *Aman* (1585), and Antoine de Montchrestien's *Aman* (1601). Racine's version differs quite significantly from these predecessors. In calling his play *Esther*, Racine shifts the focus from the villain to the heroine. Racine's play also places less emphasis on Aman's inherently evil traits, focusing instead on his choices. This difference is reflected in the dramatic structure. The three earlier plays rely on lengthy monologues and the central theme of Aman's speeches is his egotism. In Racine, there are no real monologues except for Esther's prayer in Act I. Aman's character is revealed only through dialogue with other characters. Racine thus shifts the focus from Aman's egotism to his choices, which become more important in themselves. Instead of attributing Aman's actions to an inherently evil disposition, Racine makes Aman responsible for his own choices. See Jean Dubu '*Esther*: Bible et poésie dramatique,' *The French Review* 64 (1991): 607–20.
5 All Bible references are to Lemaître de Sacy's French translation (1657–96; repr., Paris: Robert Laffont, 1990). Since so many of the details and the phrasing of *Esther* and *Athalie* seem to be clearly indebted to this Jansenist translation of the Bible, I am confident that Racine made some use of it.
6 The Agagites are members of the Amalekite tribe.
7 Racine here slightly modifies the biblical account. According to Esther VI:1–3, Assuérus reads the *Annales* of his reign during a sleepless night and comes upon the record of Mardochée's heroic act of alerting the king to a plot on his life. This provokes his question to Aman as to how he should reward someone who saved his life. In the play, Racine separates out these two events. I would suggest he does so to give more force to the image of the king at risk of losing the past and the future of his reign.
8 Blaise Pascal, *Pensées* no. 25, in *Œuvres complètes*, ed. Louis Lafuma (Paris: Seuil, 1963), 503. For a detailed discussion of the mechanisms of representation used to express both the absolute power of the king and the absolute power of Christ, see Louis Marin, *Le Portrait du roi* (Paris: Minuit, 1981) and his article 'Le corps-de-pouvoir et l'Incarnation à Port-Royal et dans Pascal ou de la figurabilité de l'absolu politique,' in *Pascal et Port-Royal* (Paris: PUF, 1997).

9 Ultimately, this is a *mise en abyme*: the king's coterie and the *Annales* are each a reflection of a reflection, with no *real* king to fill the place of the thing itself.
10 '*Topoi*, those general truths applicable to all men in a similar situation yet true of a narrative about a specific time and place, became for all writers the favorite device refined and developed from the *ars historica*. In the prose of a mediocre writer such as Charles Bernard, the *topoi* thunder from the pages, creating a heavy *histoire sainte et moralisante*. In Jean Racine's prose they are used to transgress the boundaries of time and place in ways that add both psychological and moral dimensions to any subject,' Orest Ranum, *Artisans of Glory* (Chapel Hill: University of North Carolina Press, 1980), 19.
11 It is understandable that Racine, as *historiographe du roi*, should attribute the king's guilt to forgetfulness rather than to a conspiracy with Aman, like Montchrestien. The latter's *Aman* has been seen as criticizing a monarchy which he believed responsible for murdering so many Huguenots in the sixteenth century. Racine deflects this problem by inventing the character of Hydaspe to serve as Aman's interlocutor. His prologue, commonly viewed as an *éloge* of Louis XIV, may have been another effort to distance himself from his predecessor. See H.C. Lancaster, *A History of French Dramatic Literature in the Seventeenth Century*, Pt. 4, vol. 1 (New York: Gordian Press, 1966), 293.
12 According to Jean Rohou, the fact that Esther, like the Joas of *Athalie*, has only an adoptive father suggests that in his late plays Racine envisions fatherhood as a spiritual rather than carnal relationship. Relationship to one's spiritual father would more closely approximate the relationship one should have with God. Aman's lack of a spiritual father may also herald his doom. See Jean Rohou, *L'évolution du tragique racinien* (Paris: Sedes, 1991), 15.
13 Eléonore Zimmermann, in *La Liberté et le destin dans le théâtre de Jean Racine* (Geneva: Slatkine, 1999), suggests that the successful characters in Racine's dramas are always those who act strictly out of tradition. But even the choice to follow tradition must take circumstances into account. Esther might not have succeeded in her efforts had she gone to the king too precipitously or chosen to enforce her tradition too brutally or capriciously.
14 Racine's plays never assert unequivocally that human action or belief is contingent upon grace. Instead, Racine uses the device of the chorus or another character to suggest that God's grace was or will be at work in some human action.
15 Timothy Reiss, *Tragedy and Truth* (New Haven, CT: Yale University Press, 1980), 2.

16 Ibid., 282.
17 Ibid., 5.
18 Mitchell Greenberg, *Subjectivity and Subjugation in Seventeenth-Century Drama and Prose* (Cambridge: Cambridge University Press, 1992), 53.
19 The consequences of the revocation include the flight of many of France's most important Huguenot capitalists to countries that would allow them to practice their religion; an acceleration of the anti-papist sentiment in England, which may have contributed to the 1688 revolution; and an increase in Holland's aggressive stance towards France, since Holland took in the majority of France's Huguenot exiles. See François Lebrun, *La Puissance et la guerre, 1661–1715* (Paris: Seuil, 1997), 169–87.

chapter nine

Apostles and Apostates: The Court of Peter the Great as a Chivalrous Religious Order

ERNEST A. ZITSER

The language of a court coterie is always two-edged, by turns veiling and revealing. If the phrase of the worshipper is taken too seriously it immediately becomes a jest, but if it is treated merely as a courtly game it suddenly is fully and literally intended.

Ernst Kantorowicz, *Frederick the Second, 1194–1250*

At first glance, the strange discursive practices by means of which the royal entourage of Peter Alekseevich Romanov (the future Peter the Great of Russia, r. 1682–1725) enacted its vision of Orthodox imperial reform appear to have very little to do with this monarch's endeavour to transform Muscovy into a powerful member of the nascent 'concert of Europe' and to declare himself the first Russian emperor.[1] After all, what can a pilgrimage to some obscure, unaccredited Arctic shrine – the subject of the first section of this essay – tell us about the tsar's desire to emulate the example of other, 'modern' Christian princes? What, if anything, does the foundation of a mock order of chivalry – the topic of the second section – reveal about the grandiose imperial ambitions of the tsar and his entourage? Finally, what do these two seemingly unrelated events have to do with the playful role of the humble 'artisan tsar,' which the imperious young monarch adopted (and urged others to adopt) in the company of his most trusted advisers? It will be the purpose of this paper to demonstrate that such examples of royal play are not trivial or embarrassing asides in the teleology of Russia's 'modernization' but, rather, crucial constituents of a distinctively Petrine court culture, which is more complicated (and more interesting) – I would say more 'baroque' – than traditional descriptions of its supposed 'Westernizing' and 'secularizing' character would allow.[2]

As I will argue in this paper, the tsar's unexpected layover at the Pertominsk monastery in 1693, like his decision to create the first, Russian knightly Order (1699) and its mock counterpart (1709), all stemmed from the same source: namely, the desire on the part of tsar and his intimates to mobilize the loyalties of a committed group of disciples who could attest to the redemptive significance of Peter's mission and who could help him to realize the ideals, which were first formulated at the end of the seventeenth century, on the grounds of the suburban royal estate of Novo-Preobrazhenskoe (literally, New Transfiguration). Over the course of Peter's reign, this 'Transfigured Kingdom' – with its mock kings, knights, and clerics, its extravagant ceremonies of solidarity, and its imaginary and ever-expanding topography – served as an important reference point for every member of the tsar's inner circle. Simultaneously a geographical and a rhetorical common place (*topos*), the Transfigured Kingdom delineated the boundaries between those courtiers who belonged to Peter's select 'company' (*kompaniia*) and those who did not. Continuously invoked, presented, and re-presented by the organizers of Petrine court spectacles, both in public ceremonies and in private correspondence, this allegorical realm marked off those who had come to believe in Peter's personal gift of grace – that is, in his charisma – from those who remained unconvinced or hostile to the tsar's leadership style and his vision of imperial reform.[3]

Almost immediately after the foundation of the Transfigured Kingdom, the rituals of inclusion and exclusion into the entourage of the young Tsar Peter began to partake of both religious and chivalrous tropes. This orientation towards the ideal of the *ecclesia militans*[4] explains why, in the spectacles preceding the inauguration of the Order of St Andrew, as much as in those accompanying the foundation of its mock chivalrous counterpart, the 'Order of Judas,' the tsar's courtiers appeared as modern-day, Orthodox 'knights.' Precisely by affiliating themselves with a knightly order like those of other contemporary Christian monarchs, the tsar and his courtiers sought to prove that they were linked by these very institutions and traditions to the broader, pan-European court society. At the same time, in an effort to realize the Orthodox religious imagery associated with these two orders of chivalry, Peter's knights distinguished themselves from their European brethren by appearing as the apostles of the Russian tsar, in his capacity as the 'anointed one.'[5] Indeed, as I will argue in this paper, only after the idea of discipleship came to be accepted by the tsar's circle of intimates could other Muscovite courtiers begin to conceive of Peter as the divinely ordained, charismatic leader who was personally responsible for transfiguring his realm and inaugurating the renovation of a reformed, Russian Orthodox empire.

The Accidental Pilgrims

Although some of Tsar Peter's closest political advisers had toyed around with the idea of building a Russian navy as early as 1688, he did not get a chance to implement this bold, new approach to the program of Orthodox imperial reform until well after the court coup that transformed him into the de facto ruler of Russia.[6] Indeed, even after the coup of 1689, the ceremonial duties of his office, as well as the familial and political obligations that he owed to his kinsmen and their supporters, forced Tsar Peter to find ever more elaborate excuses for justifying his avid interest in the unrealized naval projects of his father.[7] In order to get around these restrictions on his freedom of movement, the young tsar hit upon a ploy to which even his mother could not object: whenever he wanted to make a trip to the dockyards of Iauza or the wharves of Pereiaslavl', Peter would offer to make a 'pilgrimage' to some nearby monastery. This pious desire was perfectly in keeping with established Muscovite traditions, according to which Russian tsars had made their political presence known by appearing before their subjects during pilgrimages to the most important holy shrines of the realm. Visits to the hallowed relics of such shrines not only demonstrated the Muscovite rulers' respect for the wonder-working saints of the Orthodox Church, but also made an important statement about their own role as intercessors between heaven and earth.[8]

It is not surprising, therefore, that in a letter addressed to his elder half-brother and co-ruler, Tsar Peter explained his desire to visit the port city of Arkhangel'sk – at the time, Muscovy's sole outlet to the sea – by referring to this very tradition.[9] In June 1694, on the way back from his second trip to the White Sea, Peter notified Tsar Ivan Alekseevich of the fact that, this time, he had finally fulfilled his earlier promise to visit the famous, northern monastery complex of Solovetsk and to pray at the shrine of Saints Zosima and Savvatii.[10] However, the young tsar failed to mention the fact he and his entourage had also paid an unscheduled visit to the (as yet unaccredited) reliquary of Saints Vassian and Iona of the Pertominsk monastery – a distant outpost (*scete*) of the

Solovetsk Monastery. Nor did the junior co-tsar ever mention that this unplanned pilgrimage resulted from the fact that the boat in which Peter was travelling had nearly capsized in the stormy waters directly off the coast of the church, which housed the relics of the two Arctic saints. As we will see below, the tsar's silence about his unexpected detour was motivated by more than a supposed desire to prevent his relatives from worrying about him.[11] Had the powers-that-be back in Moscow known about the meaning of the strange spectacle, which the tsar staged in order to commemorate his accidental pilgrimage to the shrine of Saints Vassian and Iona, they would have seen that Peter's pledges of brotherly obedience and paternal respect concealed bold assertions about his independent, personal rule. Clearly, then, the unscheduled visit to the Transfiguration Church of the Pertominsk Monastery was meant for an entirely different audience.

The real reasons for Peter's two pilgrimages to Arkhangel'sk (in 1693 and 1694) – to make contacts with foreigners, to test out the latest technological advances in the field of naval architecture, and to get his first real experience of sea travel – prefigured his eighteen-month trip to northern and central Europe in 1697–8 and hinted at the form which the tsar and his courtiers imagined his personal rule would take. During his first visit to Arkhangel'sk, in the summer of 1693, the Tsar had an opportunity not only to see but also to sail in the top-of-the-line vessels of the best sea powers in the world.[12] At this time Tsar Peter first sailed on the *St Peter*, a small, armed, patrol ship (Dutch, *jacht*), christened after his heavenly namesake.[13] By mid-September 1693, the tsar had already started making plans for a return trip the following year. Foremost among his plans lay his interest in sailing beyond the White Sea and into the Arctic Ocean with a proposed, grandly named, but as yet non-existent 'White Sea Fleet,' composed of the *St Peter* and two new ships. The names of these ships – the *St Paul* and the *Holy Prophecy* (Dutch, *Santa Proffeetie*) – were clearly intended to play off of the 'providential' name of the *St Peter*, in order to emphasize the fact that the young tsar was predestined for his vocation.[14] The trips to the northern port city of Arkhangel'sk thus not only offered Peter a chance to try out the best military hardware in the world, but also served to highlight the prominent role which the navy – and the political, ethical, and religious ideals associated with sea travel – was supposed to play in the new economic and foreign policies of the tsar and his entourage.[15]

None of these reasons appeared in the 1694 letter to Tsar Ivan Alekseevich. Instead, the anonymous author of the epistle explained Peter's visit to Arkhangel'sk by emphasizing the conventional political, religious, and familial obligations of a pious, seventeenth-century Muscovite tsar. Even in this politically expedient explanation, however, the letter writer was not willing to discuss Peter's unscheduled pilgrimage to the Pertominsk Monastery, despite the fact that this would only heighten the impression of the great lengths to which the junior tsar was willing to go in order to perform his official duties as a Muscovite head of state. For the unofficial saints of Pertominsk were the indirect beneficiaries of the patronage extended by the Russian royal house to the Solovetsk Monastery, and particularly to one of its most powerful abbots, St Filipp – the sixteenth-century metropolitan of Moscow and the reputed teacher of Vassian and Iona. In fact, in 1652, Tsar Aleksei Mikhailovich and patriarch Nikon supervised the posthumous rehabilitation of metropolitan Filipp, who had been imprisoned and executed at the end of the sixteenth century for standing up to Ivan the Terrible. Patriarch Nikon even accompanied Filipp's relics on their long trip from Arkhangel'sk to Moscow, where, during an elaborate ceremony, the tsar himself begged forgiveness from the saint for his 'great-grandfather's ire.' Aleksei's ritual contrition, like his deliberate conflation of the Riurikid and Romanov lines of the Russian royal house, thus pointed to the political significance of the transfer of St Filipp's relics, a calculated move on the part of the tsar and his spiritual advisers to sanctify the new royal-sponsored program of Orthodox imperial reform.[16]

The historical example provided by Aleksei Mikhailovich's posthumous rehabilitation of metropolitan Filipp helps to shed light on the active role played by the tsar's youngest son in the canonization of that saint's disciples. From one point of view, Peter's personal solicitude for the memory of Saints Vassian and Iona, during the tsar's unscheduled pilgrimage to the Pertominsk Monastery, was yet another reminder of the Romanovs' continuing support for the reformist agenda of the Orthodox Church. On the other hand, Peter's visit to the Transfiguration Church of the Pertominsk Monastery was also clearly meant to emphasize the legitimacy of Aleksei's youngest son, by underscoring the reciprocal relation between Peter and the unaccredited Arctic saints, each of whom refracted (and, therefore, 'proved') the other's sacrality. For until the retinue of the junior co-tsar visited the Pertominsk Monastery, Vassian and Iona remained saints only in name. According to their *vita*, sometime in the sixteenth century two dead bodies had washed up on shore near the Pertominsk Monastery – a shrine for the local inhabitants, who made their living by fishing the dangerous and icy waters of the Arctic Ocean. Monastic and local tradition immediately identified the bodies with St Filipp's disciples, the Solovetsk monks Vassian and Iona, who had drowned in 1561 in a storm that capsized their boat. The author of the *vita* described the vision of the fishermen who had found the bodies of the two drowned monks and recorded the saints' strict instructions about being buried on the spot where they had washed up. He also noted that later, a church dedicated to the Transfiguration of the Saviour had been built to house the relics of Vassian and Iona, whom the local population credited with performing miracles. In keeping with this established local tradition, the anonymous chronicler who recorded the details of Peter's unexpected pilgrimage to the shrine of Vassian and Iona attributed the survival of the tsar and his entourage in a storm off the nearby inlet of Unskaia Guba to the miraculous intercession of the miracle-working Pertominsk saints.[17]

Relying on a biblical proof-text from the gospel of Matthew (14:24–33), the Pertominsk chronicler made an implicit comparison between the panic assailing the passengers and crew of the *St Peter*, struggling against the storm which overtook the royal yacht on the Arctic Ocean, with the fear and doubt of the Apostle Peter, as he strode on the waves of the sea of Galilee. Just as the episode of Peter's walk on water served the gospel author with an allegory of the apostles' faith in the divinity of Jesus, so the Pertominsk chronicler used the story of the near-capsizing of the royal yacht in order to illustrate the power of Providence in human (as well as royal) affairs. According to the chronicler's account, even the administration of the sacraments of Penance and Holy Communion did not succeed in calming either the passengers aboard the royal yacht or the waters of the Arctic Ocean. And although the Pertominsk chronicler recorded that a local pilot finally managed to steer the royal yacht into the bay, he made it clear that the tsar and everyone on board the *St Peter* ultimately owed their salvation to God and the intercession of 'the two drowned monks who in death still live.'[18]

The tsar's own actions after this unexpected safe landing demonstrate that he accepted the Pertominsk monks' interpretation of the events and credited his salvation from the storm to the miraculous intercession of the two Arctic saints. During the course of his four-day layover at the Pertominsk monastery in June 1694, Peter ordered that the relics of Vassian and Iona be exhumed and examined in the presence of Archbishop Afanasii of Kholmogory – a reform-minded Orthodox cleric who accompanied the tsar on his voyage, but who, at least according to the chronicler, had not been well disposed towards the monastery or the two saints and even questioned their credentials. To the great joy of the Pertominsk monks, the tsar asked the archbishop to perform an ad hoc ecclesiastical investigation into the status of their (as yet) unattested local miracle cult. Despite the fact that only one body was found, Afanasii of Kholmogory succumbed to royal pressure and agreed to recognize the holiness of the relics, which were laid to rest in the chapel of the monastery. A service of thanksgiving was held and was followed by a solemn liturgy at which the tsar himself sang in the choir and read from the 'Book of the Apostles' (*Apostol*), that is, from the Epistles and Acts. In a final step of the traditional canonization process, the tsar made a gift of money, supplies, land, and fishing rights to the monastery, as well as provision for the extension of its buildings.[19]

The fact that Peter sponsored the immediate investigation into the sanctity of the reputed remains of Vassian and Iona testifies to the political significance that the tsar attached to the personal miracle ostensibly performed for him by these two new saints. Indeed, it appears that the process that resulted, finally, in the recognition of the saintly status of the Pertominsk relics was also meant to affirm his own gift of grace. In a move that echoed the *vita* of Saints Vassian and Iona, in their insistence on being buried where their bodies had been washed ashore, the tsar chose to consecrate the spot where he and his party landed. Using the language and the persona of the 'Great Skipper' (*bol'shoi ship'ger* or *shiper*) – the address used by the tsar's intimates in their correspondence with him during the trip to Arkhangel'sk[20] – the tsar commemorated his miraculous rescue by carving a ten-and-a-half feet (one-and-a-half *sazhen'*) high, four-limbed pinewood cross, on whose cross-beam Peter inscribed the following sentence, in Dutch: '*Dat kruys. maken kaptein Piter. van. a. Cht. 1694*' (This cross was made by Captain Peter in the year of our Lord 1694).[21]

To the monk who chronicled this episode, the unorthodox shape of the cross and its incomprehensible, 'Roman' (*rimskaia*) inscription highlighted the strangeness of the tsar's behaviour on the last day of his visit to the Pertominsk Monastery. The tsar not only stooped to perform the manual work of an ordinary carpenter, but also insisted on carrying the wooden cross on his own back before erecting it on the seashore where he and his entourage had disembarked.[22] In an obvious re-enactment of Jesus' procession through Jerusalem on the way to Golgotha, Peter appeared literally bowed under the weight of the cross that he had fashioned and willingly took upon himself. Unlike Jesus, however, Peter had not been abandoned by his disciples; the tsar's 'company' solemnly escorted Peter and helped him to carry his burden from the Transfiguration Church of the Pertominsk monastery down to the shore. Indeed, the conspicuous involvement of some of the leading 'clerics' of Peter's Transfigured Kingdom – including N.M. Zotov and T.N. Streshnev, respectively, the 'Prince Pope' (*kniaz'-papa*) and 'archpriest' (*arkhierei*) of the 'Most Comical and All-Drunken Council' (*vseshuteishii i vsep'ianeishii sobor*)[23] – shows that this ceremony had less to do with recreating the Way of Sorrows than with celebrating the fact that the royal entourage had survived a test of their faith in the charisma of the tsar. By accompanying the tsar on his 'pilgrimage' to yet another holy shrine named after the Transfiguration of the Saviour, the members of the mock ecclesiastical council playfully sanctified the tsar's undertaking, conveying in jest the serious political message that would have been taken as a joke had it been uttered with all the pomp of a royal proclamation back in Moscow.

Taking advantage of their accidental pilgrimage to the shrine of the Pertominsk saints, Peter and his entourage thus improvised a unique royal spectacle which was intended for everyone in the group, including the creators of the ceremony itself. The fact that this ceremony was new, ad hoc, unexpected, is not insignificant either. Indeed, it is a clear illustration of the sociological argument that there must constantly be demonstrations of the charismatic leader's special gift of grace, at unexpected and unusual times, for his followers to continue believing in his divine election.[24] We have no evidence that Peter planned this ceremony in advance. Certainly, the tsar and his entourage never intended to get caught in a storm, although it is not really surprising that a boat sailed by people new to the sea (and to this part of the realm) had nearly capsized. But if we look at what the tsar and his advisers actually did with this near-tragedy, this little-known episode in the tsar's second trip to Arkhangel'sk becomes a good example of the unique way in which Petrine court spectacles created a sense of community among the followers of a self-proclaimed charismatic young ruler with weak dynastic claims.

Such enigmatic assertions of royal charisma demonstrated that the tsar and his entourage sought to foster a particular kind of *esprit de corps* among those who witnessed and participated in the Pertominsk procession with the cross. Taking advantage of the fact that the entire royal retinue had personally experienced the near capsizing of the *St Peter*, the organizers of this spectacle attempted to transform the relief at their physical salvation (from a storm) into a re-affirmation of faith in the coming of a new (political) dispensation. Although shaken by an unexpected confrontation with their own mortality, the tsar's companions were urged to let go of the past, with all its fears and tribulations, and to commit themselves ever more strongly to the tasks set by their divinely appointed leader. Whether or not they actually believed in the ultimate success of the tsar's mission, all of his courtiers (*so vsem tsar'skim sigklitom*) had to participate in the procession with the cross, supporting Peter as he carried his burden (*na rame svoikh*) down to the sea.[25] In this way, the ceremony improvised on the last day of the tsar's visit to the Pertominsk Transfiguration Church enacted the scenario of power first articulated on the grounds of the royal suburban estate named after the new, Petrine transfiguration.

The procession with the cross – like the fact that at the liturgy following the canonization of Vassian and Iona the tsar chose to read from the 'Book of the Apostles' – thus affirmed the analogy between the tsar's entourage and Christ's disciples. Just as the stormy voyage of the *St Peter* suggested the biblical proof-text from the gospel of Matthew to the monk who described the royal retinue's miraculous rescue, so the inscription on the cross borne by 'Captain Peter' invited his naval entourage to make an implicit comparison between themselves and the followers of Christ – the divine helmsman.[26] The tsar bolstered that interpretation by carving a crucifix that looked more like a ship's mast than an eight-limbed Orthodox cross. If one recalls that Jesus was also a carpenter, Peter's personal efforts on the docks of his shipyards, a theme which is a recurrent motif in the tsar's correspondence with his intimates back in Moscow, suggest that the image of the 'artisan tsar' was initially based on an a deliberate analogy to Christ, the 'New Adam.'[27] In this case, working with wood, Peter transformed a poignant reminder of physical suffering and other-worldly redemption into a triumphal sign of earthly salvation for himself and his followers, and – through the building of a sea-worthy, imperial navy – of a political salvation for the realm as whole. The organizers of this impromptu ceremony thus affirmed that the tsar's mission to make landlocked Muscovy into a major maritime power, the burden that he personally took upon his shoulders, was no less miraculous than the safe landing of the *St Peter*. To those who had faith in Providence, the miracle-working Orthodox saints, and the divine gifts of the 'Great Skipper,' the unsinkable royal yacht proved that, even on his first ocean voyage, the tsar, like his saintly namesake, could also walk on water.

The Fishermen's Order

By commemorating the debt owed to the two fishermen's saints of Pertominsk, the ceremonial procession staged by the tsar and his entourage recalled those other fishermen who had abandoned their nets to follow a charismatic leader on his mission to transfigure the world as they knew it. Indeed, in light of the playful interchangeability of names and attributes common to the rhetorical conventions of the baroque,[28] Saints Vassian and Iona came to stand in for the pair of apostles who first followed Jesus. To anyone familiar with the tropes and techniques of courtly panegyrics at the end of the seventeenth century, the implicit evocation of St Peter in the ceremony honouring the two Pertominsk saints conjured up the image of that apostle's 'double' – his brother, the apostle Andrew. And while Andrew was also considered the patron saint of travellers and sailors, he was not merely a convenient allegorical substitute for the miracle-working Pertominsk saints. In fact, St Andrew was more familiar to Russian Orthodox Christians as the apostle who (according to tradition) had first introduced Christianity among the eastern Slavs, and therefore, as the patron saint of Russia itself. Reading the story of St Andrew typologically, Peter and his entourage could, therefore, invoke this 'national' saint in order to justify the tsar's desire to sail through the whole of Russia and out into the cold waters of the Arctic Ocean.[29]

According to the story recorded in the *Russian Primary Chronicle*, St Andrew had been preaching the gospel to the pagans living along the northern littoral of the Black Sea when he came to Chersonesus, a colony on the trade route that connected the 'Varangians with the Greeks.' While proselytizing in that city, the apostle 'observed that the mouth of the Dniepr [River] was nearby' and immediately 'conceived a desire to go to Rome' by way of the extensive river system of the Eurasian plain. Ascending the Dniepr, 'by chance' he halted on the shore beneath the hills upon which Kiev, the mother of Russian cities, was subsequently built. St Andrew prophesied to his disciples that 'the favour of God [shall] shine upon [these hills]' and that on this spot a great city with many churches should arise. He then 'drew near the hills, and having blessed them, he set up a cross.' After offering a prayer to God, he descended from the hill and continued his northern journey up the Dniepr.[30] For the retinue of Peter, unlike for the Russian chronicler who recorded this tale, the apostle's point of departure and his ultimate destination were less significant than the journey itself. In their typological reading, the trip of St Andrew had, in some sense, prefigured the pilgrimage of Peter and his entourage. Just like St Andrew, the tsar had navigated the Russian river systems in an attempt to find a northern outlet to the sea; and just like the apostle, the tsar's chance stopover resulted in the recognition of a neglected holy place, a recognition sanctified by the erection of a cross. However, whereas the ancient chronicler used the Andrew legend to highlight Kiev's role in fostering the religious unity of the Slavs who inhabited the plains along the trade routes between the eastern and western halves of the Roman Empire, Peter's sailing trip was itself an assertion of his grandiose, all-Russian, imperial ambitions. Indeed, it is precisely by founding a chivalrous knightly order named after the apostle Andrew that the tsar first attempted to institutionalize his vision of a Transfigured Kingdom.

The tsar's decision to name the first Russian knightly order after St Andrew highlights both the imperial aspirations and the polemical thrust of his court's political program. From at least the seventh century, the image of Andrew the Apostle had served as an important point in the debate over precedence between the imperial churches of Rome and Constantinople. The claims of Roman bishops to primacy in the Church were based on the fact that they were successors of St Peter, to whom Christ had entrusted the care of his Church. To counter these assertions, Orthodox clerics located a tradition for the apostolic source of the see of Byzantium in the investiture of St Andrew. Because Andrew was the first apostle to whom Jesus had addressed his invitation to become his disciple and because Andrew had introduced his brother to Christ (John 1:37–42), the defenders of Byzantine primacy asserted that they were entitled to regard their episcopal see as equal, if not superior, to that of Rome. By the time 'Second Rome' finally fell to the Ottomans, the debate over the apostolic foundations of the see of Byzantium had become moot and both Orthodox and Catholic sides had come to accept the authenticity of the Andrew legend.[31] But so long as Constantinople remained in the hands of the Islamic Ottoman Porte and the Habsburgs continued to claim to be the only Christian ruling house to embody the authority of ancient Rome, it appeared that there could be no *renovatio* of the eastern Roman Empire or the see of St Andrew. However, at least from the twelfth century, the Andrew legend had been transferred from Byzantium and adopted by Orthodox apologists for the rulers of Russia, who came increasingly to be identified as the founders of a new or 'Third Rome.' Indeed, the growing imperial pretensions of Muscovite rulers almost guaranteed that, in one form or another, the Andrew legend would re-appear in Russian political rhetoric. The foundation of the Order of St Andrew 'The First-Called' (*Pervozvannyi*) at the court of Tsar Peter thus signalled the revival, in secular and chivalrous guise, of the ancient religious rivalry between the defenders of the Catholic and the Orthodox imperial ideas.[32]

The earliest records of its (informal) institution[33] indicate that the Order of St Andrew was intended as an Eastern Orthodox counterpart to the Catholic knightly orders sponsored by the Holy Roman Emperor, and, particularly, to the crusading order of the sea-going Knights of Malta.[34] In March 1699, F.A. Golovin, the courtier who headed Peter's foreign policy establishment and who had recently led the tsar's 'Great Embassy' to Europe, boasted of his membership in the tsar's new order to Johann Georg Korb, the secretary of the Habsburg ambassador to Moscow.[35] In his 'Diary,' the Austrian diplomat claimed that the tsar founded this Order to reward those servitors who had distinguished themselves in battle against the Turks during the 1695–6 Azov campaigns, when Orthodox Muscovy was part of the Catholic Holy Alliance consisting of the Holy Roman Empire, Venice, the Polish Republic, and the Knights of Malta. Korb assumed that the turn to chivalry reflected the tsar's desire to imitate the trappings of other European Christian princes, and particularly of Korb's own sovereign, Emperor Leopold I of Austria. As evidence of this desire, the Habsburg diplomat pointed to the special favour shown by the tsar to General-Field Marshal B.P. Sheremetev, the Russian emissary who had returned from abroad as an honorary member of the Knights of Malta, the crusading Catholic order patronized by the Pope and the Holy Roman Emperor.[36] In fact, the motto of the first Russian order ('For Faith and Fidelity') did resemble the one used by the Maltese knights (*Pour la foi*). Even the name of the tsar's new Order appeared to have been borrowed from that of two earlier Catholic brotherhoods dedicated to St Andrew: one was an old Scottish order, also known as the Order of the Thistle; while the other was the Habsburg Order of the Golden Fleece, which was originally dedicated to the Mother of God and Andrew the Apostle.[37]

Despite its similarity to these Catholic brotherhoods, however, the insignia of the Russian order were actually modelled after the first and most ancient European knightly order, reputedly founded by the Byzantine emperor Constantine I 'The Great.'[38] The fact that Peter chose to emulate this particular emperor was not in itself that innovative; even before the collapse of the 'Second Rome,' the comparison to Constantine the Great had become a mainstay of the claim that the tsars of Russia inherited the imperial and religious authority of Byzantium. However, it was not the traditional image of the pious ruler who legalized Christianity, but that of the divinely ordained, chivalrous warrior-king which found favour at the court of Tsar Peter. In this, as in so many other innovations in Muscovite court culture, the son followed the lead of his father. During his long and controversial reign, Tsar Aleksei Mikhailovich had repeatedly invoked the martial imagery associated with the first Christian emperor, particularly the legendary Cross of Constantine – a familiar emblem in medieval European heraldry, representing the cross that had appeared in the sky above the armies of Constantine as a sign that he would defeat the usurper Maxentius. Aleksei Mikhailovich even went so far as to order that the 'relics' of the Cross of Constantine, supposedly housed in an Orthodox monastery on Mt Athos, be transferred to Moscow.[39]

The cult of the Cross of Constantine, associated with divine protection and victory, was picked up by Aleksei's successors, including his youngest son, who also continued his aggressive policies against the Muslim overlords of Constantinople, as well as his dreams about making Moscow the centre of a reformed, Orthodox empire. For example, in 1696, during Peter's second attempt to wrest the fortress of Azov from the hands of the Crimean Tatars, the Cross of Constantine decorated the standards of a newly organized 'Naval Regiment.'[40] After the initial failure to take the fortress by land the tsar and his military advisers realized the importance of a naval blockade and had formed this new regiment in the hopes of actualizing the motto on its standard: 'By this sign shall you win.' Indeed, the ideological origins of the insignia for the Russian first order of chivalry can be traced back to the tsar's 1696 triumphal entry into Moscow, during which the royal 'Captain' walked in the ranks of his Naval Regiment through an arch whose banners hailed 'The victorious return of Tsar Constantine' and 'Tsar Constantine's victory over the profane Tsar Maxentius of Rome.'[41] Although both Constantine and Maxentius were called 'tsars' (*caesar*), the designers of the banners for the first-ever Russian imperial 'triumph' clearly distinguished the Orthodox Byzantine emperor, the spiritual forefather of the Russian tsar, from his profane Latin counterpart, who represented the Austrian Kaiser. The decisive role of the tsar's new flotilla in his first major military victory thus provided the impetus for the foundation of an Orthodox order of sea-going knights, whose well-ordered military organization and Christian valour could rout the 'barbarous' hordes of

Muslim infidels while, at the same time, rivalling the Catholic brotherhood sponsored by the Holy Roman Emperor.

By founding Russia's first order of chivalry – a symbolic act which was the institutional equivalent of the 1694 Pertominsk ceremony – the royal 'Captain' thus transformed the Cross of Constantine into the *Cruz Decussata* of St Andrew, invoking the protection of the patron saint of sailors for the nascent Russian navy and his own imperial ambitions. As during the procession outside of the Pertominsk monastery, the tsar did not carry this weight solely upon his own shoulders. The first cavaliers of the Order of St Andrew included the tsar's most trusted geopolitical allies, particularly those who were involved in the secret diplomacy at the end of the seventeenth century, when Russia was building its coalition against Sweden, while ostensibly still part of the Holy Alliance and its crusade against the Ottoman Empire. Besides the Muscovite foreign minister (F.A. Golovin), the first two members of the Order included I.S. Mazepa, the hetman (Cossack leader) of Left-Bank Ukraine, and Constantine Brancovan, the Orthodox hospodar (prince) of Wallachia, the nominal vassal of the Turkish sultan who was covertly involved in recruiting sailors for the imperial Russian navy.[42] Both the honour and the burden of the tsar's personal trust in these men was embodied in the Order's medal, a representation of the crucified figure of St Andrew in the form of the characteristic diagonal cross, worn around the neck on a sash or chain. By accepting the cross of St Andrew, the men empowered to act as Peter's personal representatives on the stage of world politics took on the responsibility of fulfilling the words of the Order's motto, 'For Faith and Fidelity' (*za veru i vernost'*). Thus, like the courtiers who helped the tsar erect a cross in honour of the Pertominsk saints, the knights of the Order of St Andrew were urged to become the disciples of their royal patron and his heavenly intercessors.

The Uses of Apostasy

The impromptu ceremonies, which demonstrated Peter's personal gift of grace, were not confined to the early days of his reign. Indeed, as I will now demonstrate, the providential interpretation of Peter's imperial mission, as reaffirmed during the accidental pilgrimage of 1694, went on to inform the way the tsar and his courtiers handled what was perhaps the most embarrassing episode of the entire Northern War (1700–21): the unexpected defection of Ivan Mazepa, the second cavalier of the Order of St Andrew, to the side of King Charles XII of Sweden, in the fall of 1708. The relative success with which the tsar and his entourage transformed this potentially disastrous foreign policy debacle into the most important turning point of the entire conflict between Russia and Sweden once again serves to underline how easily the tsar and his company could integrate even this flagrant violation of Peter's new scenario of power into the royalist myth of Russia's anointed one. Playing on the religious and political connotations associated with membership in the tsar's self-styled, chivalrous fellowship of believers, Peter and his apostles would go on to compare Mazepa's defection to the apostasy of Judas Iscariot, the disciple who betrayed *his* Anointed One for thirty pieces of silver. In fact, this analogy would become one of the most prominent motifs in the shaming rituals staged by Russian diplomats, strengthening the impression that Peter's court had reorganized itself according to the ideals of a chivalrous religious order so as to demonstrate the charismatic authority of the divinely anointed Russian monarch.[43]

Although they have been obscured by centuries of confessional (and, later, nationalist) polemics, the reasons for the hetman's breach of faith are not hard to fathom.[44] Over the course of the long and costly conflict between Russia, Sweden, and Poland, Ivan Mazepa had become increasingly worried about the effects of Muscovite wartime exactions upon the military organization and morale of the Ukrainian political elite, as well as upon the security of his own position as hetman of the Cossack Host. Doubting that the tsar, who was beleaguered by the demands of war, would be able to protect Ukraine from the previously unbeaten (and seemingly invincible) armies of Charles XII and his Polish protégé (King Stanisław Leszczynski),[45] Mazepa stunned the tsar and his court by switching sides, just a few months before the fateful battle of Poltava. No one at the court of Tsar Peter expected that kind of behaviour from the faithful septuagenarian, who had successfully managed to serve both the interests of the Russian crown and those of the Ukrainian socio-military elite ever since his election as Cossack hetman in 1687. The shock was compounded by the fact that the hetman's defection came at a crucial point in the war between Russia and Sweden, on the eve of what promised to be the final showdown between the armies of Peter and Charles. Mazepa's betrayal caused a terrible panic among the Russian leadership, which now had to face the full force of the Swedish invasion without any allies.

News of Mazepa's defection spread very quickly and for months it appeared that this major diplomatic embarrassment would have catastrophic strategic and political consequences, not only for Russia's war effort, but also for the Russian court's whole program of reform. Mazepa had seriously challenged the tsar's authority in Ukraine and had gone unpunished. Worse still (at least from the Russian point of view), he continued to argue his case in numerous proclamations and manifestos, which were disseminated throughout Ukraine after October 1708. Clearly, the Muscovite tsar could not let Mazepa and his claims go unanswered. In November 1708, the tsar's diplomatic corps mounted an intense campaign to counter the literature produced in the camp of Mazepa and Charles XII.[46] The conclusions that the Cossack elite and the urban inhabitants of Ukraine were to draw from these broadsheets were dramatized during two remarkable ceremonies, in which the fugitive Cossack hetman and erstwhile cavalier of the Order of St Andrew figured prominently.

On 6 November 1709, A.D. Menshikov, the royal favourite who commanded the Russian forces responsible for the punitive expedition against Baturyn, the Ukrainian hetman's capital, and G.I. Golovkin, the vice-president of the Foreign Affairs chancellery, hastily gathered the remaining loyal members of the Cossack elite in the town of Glukhov (Hlukhiv). In the midst of the proceedings to elect a new hetman, the Russian military authorities built a large platform and a gallows in the centre of town. Accompanied by the sound of rolling drums, a life-size effigy of the treasonous Ukrainian hetman, adorned with the cavalier's medal and the blue sash of the Order of St Andrew, was brought out into the public square. Menshikov and Golovkin waited while the dummy was carried up the steps of the central platform. When the effigy of Mazepa was brought before them, these two cavaliers of the Order of St Andrew proceeded to tear up the official certificate that attested to Mazepa's membership in the tsar's knightly Order; immediately afterwards, the effigy was stripped of its chivalrous insignia. Then, after a public reading of the charges against the ex-hetman, the naked dummy was tossed into the hands of the executioner. The dummy was bound with ropes and dragged through the streets, unto the gallows set up for the occasion. The executioner tore up the Mazepa family seal, broke the sword that still hung at the dummy's side, and finally, without further ado, hung it from the gallows.[47]

A few days later, on 12 November 1709, in an act timed to coincide with the installation of Ivan Skoropads'kyi, the new Cossack hetman, the Russian tsar and his entourage personally witnessed the official ceremony during which the metropolitan of Kiev thrice anathematized the name of Mazepa. Less than a week later, in Moscow, Mazepa's anathematization *in absentia* was repeated by metropolitan Stefan (Iavorskii), the caretaker of the vacant throne of the Russian patriarch, in front of the heir apparent and all the leading political figures of the Russian capital.[48] Like the defamation of Mazepa, this ceremony was undoubtedly part of the diplomatic manoeuvring following Mazepa's defection; it too was designed to portray the hetman's actions as, first and foremost, a betrayal of the common Orthodox faith. But apparently for Peter and his entourage it was not enough to exclude Mazepa from the fold of the Russian Orthodox Church and to condemn him to eternal damnation. The humiliating ceremony in which Mazepa's effigy was stripped of his cavalier's sash and literally dragged through the mud emphasized the ex-hetman's betrayal of the common interest represented by membership in the tsar's knightly order. Peter's charge that Mazepa had 'turned traitor and betrayer of his [own] people' thus referred not only to the Ukrainian Cossack elite or to the Orthodox Slavs, but also to his fellow cavaliers of the Order of St Andrew.[49]

On 27 June 1709 Mazepa was with Charles XII during the clash in which the Swedish army, under the command of the young king himself, was routed by Muscovite forces near the Ukrainian town of Poltava. While most of the Swedish army was captured, Charles XII, Mazepa, and a small, but loyal retinue barely managed to escape from the field of battle. Throughout all of July 1709 the Russian tsar and his military advisers hoped to capture Charles XII and Mazepa before they managed to make their way to the court of the Ottoman sultan, and certainly before the Swedish king and the Ukrainian hetman had succeeded in persuading Ahmed III to enter into the fray on their side. In order to forestall the possibility of a two-front war, on 1 and 2 July Peter sent out two regiments of mounted cavalry, under the commands of Brigadier Kropotkin and Major-General Prince G.S. Volkonskoi, in pursuit of the 'remnants of Poltava' (*poltavskie nedobitki*). Prince Volkonskoi received detailed written instructions, signed by Prince Menshikov and composed by the tsar himself, about the manner in which Charles XII and Mazepa were to be transported back to Russia in the event of their capture.[50] In the meantime, Peter and G.I. Golovkin began an extensive diplomatic correspondence with the rulers of adjacent territories, encouraging them 'diligently to seek out, capture, and put under guard the traitor Mazepa,' and implicitly warning them against abetting the fugitives.[51] It is clear that in the beginning of July, the Russian tsar and his closest advisers believed that in one way or another, the Swedish king and the Ukrainian hetman would soon be brought to justice.

The attempt to bring the 'remnants of Poltava' to justice, however, necessitated more than a flurry of diplomatic activity on the part of the Russian court. Indeed, this manhunt also led to the creation of the 'Order of Judas' – a mock counterpart to the first Russian order of chivalry. During the course of the month-long chase across the steppe, A.Ia. Shchukin, the Russian official in charge of the Ingermanland Chancellery, the department responsible (among other things) for administrating the future site of Russia's new northern capital, received three letters, each more urgent than the last, about the minting of a special silver commemorative medal (*moneta*). The first letter, written just two weeks after the battle of Poltava, was sent by diplomatic pouch on 11 July 1709. Bearing the seal and signature of the head of the Ingermanland Chancellery, Prince Menshikov himself, the letter contained the following order: 'Mr. President. Upon receipt of this [dispatch] immediately make a silver medal weighing ten pounds and have engraved upon it [a picture of] Judas hanging on an aspen tree, above thirty pieces of silver lying next to a sack; on the reverse [the medal is to have] the following inscription: "The thrice-cursed [i.e. anathematized] fatal son, Judas, hanging [literally, choking] because of his lust for money." After a two-pound chain is made for that medal, have it sent to us immediately by special courier ...'[52] Menshikov repeated his injunction to hurry in two other missives to Shchukin. The last letter, dated 9 August 1709, was written just a week after the retinue of Charles XII had managed to cross into the Crimea and thereby to evade capture. However, although the sultan refused to hand the Swedish king over to their mutual enemy, Russian diplomats continued to hold out the hope that, as the subject of the tsar, the Ukrainian hetman would be extradited to answer the charge of treason.[53] Clearly, Peter and his royal favourite believed, even at this late date, that they could still get their hands on the fugitive Cossack hetman. And the heavy silver chain and medallion of Judas commissioned by Menshikov seemed to have figured prominently in their plans to avenge Mazepa's treachery.

According to the instructions later appended to the original decree, upon receipt of Menshikov's commission, the staff of the Moscow-based Ingermanland chancellery contacted a silversmith named Matvei Alekseev, who was charged with transforming twelve and a half pounds of silver coin into the medal described in the letter of the royal favourite.[54] However, in the eleven days between the time that the Judas medal was first commissioned and the time that Menshikov's letter appears to have been rewritten in the form of a royal decree, the reference to the 'thrice-cursed fatal son, Judas' was replaced by a quotation from the gospel of Matthew (Mat. 27:9).[55] The biblical proof-text of the later version of the medal – 'And they took the thirty pieces of silver, the price of the one on whom a price had been set, on whom some of the people of Israel had set a price ...' – comes from Matthew's description of what the chief priests decided to do with the 'blood money' inherited after Judas's death. So as not to sully the temple coffers with ill-gotten gains, the elders decided to use the thirty pieces of silver that Judas received for betraying Christ to buy 'Potter's Field' – a profane place on the outskirts of the Holy City – as a place to bury foreigners. Adapting this biblical story to contemporary events, the new inscription appears to have served as a warning to all of Russia's enemies that if they dare to engage in battle against the army of Russia's divinely anointed monarch, then they too shall inherit Potter's Field. In this reading, the Judas medal was intended to offer a prediction: just as Poltava had become a place for burying the Swedes, so any future engagement would end in the defeat of Russia's enemies. Judging by the actions of Menshikov, whose troops had recently razed the capital of the Ukrainian hetman, and who was now ordered to invade the territories of the Polish-Lithuanian Commonwealth in order to drive Leszczynski from the Polish throne, this was no idle threat.[56]

The new inscription on the Judas medal also played up the parallel between Christ, 'the one on whom a price had been set,' and Tsar Peter, the charismatic founder of the Order of St Andrew – a parallel that was fundamental to the chivalrous-religious organization of the Transfigured Kingdom. Like Jesus, the tsar had been betrayed by one of his own 'chosen people,' a disciple who belonged to the tight circle of believers in his divine gift of grace. As a result of this fundamental breach of faith, the traitor had become like one of those 'people of Israel [who] had set a price' on their Anointed One. Indeed, by betraying the chivalrous brotherhood committed to the cause of the Russian Orthodox tsar, Mazepa had also betrayed St Andrew, their patron saint, and by metaphoric extension, Christ himself. In retaliation, the Russian royal favourite and the rest of the tsar's disciples had enrolled the traitor into a diabolical counter-order, representing all the enemies of Christ – an Order of Judas.

Judging by the external and internal evidence contained in the original commission, it is not too far-fetched to suggest that the heavy silver medal and chain were intended as a humiliating replacement for the cross and sash of the Order of St Andrew, of which Mazepa was stripped, if only in absentia. In this light, the Judas medal would have served as a mock decoration for Mazepa, in his new role as the 'Cavalier of the Order of Judas.' Indeed, to the extent that the silver medal of Judas was intended as commemoration and commentary on an important aspect of the Russian military victory – Mazepa's betrayal – it served as a satirical counterpart to the campaign decorations for the battle of Poltava. In an ironic extension of the practice of awarding all the participants of a successful military campaign, the tsar and his advisers thus made sure that even the traitorous cavalier of the Order of St Andrew was to be recognized for his providential contribution not only to the victory at Poltava, but also to the apotheosis of Russia's anointed one.[57]

The Cavalier of the Order of Judas

If the primary purpose of the Judas medal was punitive, the tsar and his advisers failed to reach their objective. Indeed, despite all of their efforts, Mazepa escaped from Russian grasp – permanently. Having contracted some kind of illness during his flight across the border, the old Cossack hetman died, just a few months after finding asylum in the fortress town of Bendery. With him went all hope of stripping the real Poltava traitor, and not just his dummy, of the insignia of the Order of St Andrew, and of hanging the twelve-pound silver medal and chain of the Order of Judas around his neck. However, the mock order did not die with the Ukrainian hetman. Indeed, the fate of the Judas medal after the death of Mazepa only confirms the enduring connection between the idea of a knightly order, the tsar's geopolitical ambitions, and the exercise of charismatic authority at the court of Tsar Peter. Far from losing its entire *raison d'être*, the imaginary mock order represented by the silver medallion became, if only for a very short time, as much a part of the discourse employed at the early eighteenth-century Russian court as the annual commemoration of the victory at Poltava.

As early as the winter of 1709, just a few months after it was commissioned, the medal originally intended for Mazepa appeared in an impromptu skit staged by the tsar in front of Joost Jules, the newly appointed Danish extraordinary envoy to the court of Muscovy, who was sent to negotiate a new alliance between Denmark and Russia. During his first meeting with the Russian tsar, which took place in the recently reconquered city of Narva, Jules saw the Judas medal around the neck of a 'Prince Jacobskoy,' one of the titled 'court jesters' whom the tsar kept in his personal retinue and to whom he jokingly referred as 'patriarchs.'[58] In his diary the Danish diplomat recorded a story, which he claims to have heard from the tsar himself, about the origins of this mock chivalric order: 'The tsar told me that this jester is one of the wisest men in Russia, but despite that fact, he is seized with a spirit of rebellion. Once, when the tsar began a conversation with him about how the traitor, Judas, betrayed the Saviour for thirty pieces of silver, Jacobskoy objected that the price was too low and that Judas should have asked for more. Then, in order to poke fun at Jacobskoy, as well as to punish him – for it seemed from his words that had the Savior been alive today, he would not have been averse to betraying Him either, only for a bigger price – the tsar immediately commanded that the abovementioned Order of Judas be made, with a depiction of the latter preparing to hang himself.'[59] As will immediately become apparent to anyone familiar with the actual circumstances surrounding the origins of the Judas medal, the anecdote recorded by the Danish envoy was more of an allegorical commentary about Mazepa's treachery than an explanation of how this particular royal jester wound up wearing the commemorative silver medallion.

The jester's joke, as retold by the tsar himself at an informal diplomatic meeting at which the battle of Poltava was the main topic of conversation, had a contemporary political resonance.[60] The anecdote recalled the deeds of the former cavalier of the Order of St Andrew, whose betrayal had almost resulted in the death of Russia's 'saviour' and the loss of his crown. By hinting at the exorbitant price which he had nearly paid for his misplaced trust, the tsar made an implicit comparison between the inconstancy of the former Cossack hetman and that of Russia's potential new ally, the Danish king. The very fact that the Order of Judas was first shown to the Danish ambassador in Narva, the site of the disastrous defeat which befell Russia immediately after Denmark capitulated to Charles XII in 1700, emphasized the 'treasonous' actions of Frederick IV, who had already once, at the very beginning of the Northern War, betrayed the confidence of the Russian leadership by withdrawing from the secret alliance against Sweden and leaving Russia to face the army of Charles XII all by herself. By their insistence that the first meeting between the Danish diplomat and the Russian tsar should take place at Narva, after the tsar had returned from reaping the diplomatic fruit of the victory of Poltava, the tsar and his advisers meant to instil the belief that the Muscovites had overcome their initial problems and were capable of handling Sweden by themselves. If the Danes wanted to join in the dismemberment of the Swedish Empire they had to act on the terms set by the Russian tsar and his diplomatic corps, or else remain on the sidelines, in the camp of the enemy and of the traitors.

What Jules actually recorded in his diary was, therefore, a subtle dig at the honour of his king, orchestrated, at the expense of the Danish diplomat, by the Russian tsar and his court jester. However, whether the Danish envoy misunderstood the political significance of the tsar's practical joke, or simply decided not to record its real import in his diplomatic diary, it seems clear that he was not the primary intended audience for this impromptu little skit about faith, honour, and betrayal. In fact, if we analyse who 'Prince Jacobskoy' was and why the tsar chose this particular Russian courtier to succeed Mazepa as the first Cavalier of the Order of Judas, we will see that the full significance of this skit could only be understood by Muscovite insiders. Those courtiers who were able to recall the history of the complicated relationship between the Russian royal family and the Shakhovskoi princely clan and who understood the role of jesters at the early modern Muscovite court would surely have grasped that the 'spirit of rebellion' which had supposedly characterized the new Cavalier of the Order of Judas referred as much to events in his family's past as to the treachery of the former Cossack hetman or the inconstancy of the Danish king.

The Shakhovskois were a titled, princely clan, with a family history of rebellion against the House of Romanov. One incident, in particular, seems to have left a lasting impression in the collective memory of the Muscovite political elite. In the summer of 1620, several members of the Shakhovskoi family staged a parody of the 'election' of Mikhail Fedorovich, the first Romanov tsar. During a private gathering at the Moscow residence of a family acquaintance, Prince Matvei Fedorovich Shakhovskoi, the great-uncle of the future Cavalier of the Order of Judas, was named 'tsar' and invested with royal authority in what Muscovite officials later described as an 'intricate and rebellious manner' (*zateinym vorovskim obychaem*); meanwhile, his brothers and cousins styled themselves as top-ranking members of the mock tsar's royal council (*boiare*).[61]

This political burlesque, which recalled the installation of Mikhail Fedorovich by the 1613 'Council of all the Land,' underlined the fact that the lowly Romanovs were not God-ordained but men-made rulers, and hence could be replaced, especially by a titled family like the Shakhovskois. This was no idle threat, since another Prince Shakhovskoi, Grigorii Petrovich, was actively involved in organizing the Bolotnikov uprising during the 'Time of Troubles' immediately preceding the installation of the Romanov dynasty on the Russian throne.[62] After an official investigation, one of the first of its kind, into the Shakhovskoi princes' 'words and deeds against the sovereign' (*slovo i delo gosudarevo*),[63] the mock tsar and his company were found guilty of treason and demonstratively condemned to death by the royal council of Mikhail Fedorovich Romanov; however, at the request of patriarch Filaret, Mikhail's father and chief political adviser, the Shakhovskois' death sentence was commuted to exile and imprisonment in the towns of the Lower Volga and Siberia. The Shakhovskois were finally allowed to return into Muscovite court society fourteen years later, and then only after Prince Matvei Shakhovskoi and his mock royal council solemnly promised to 'pay off their great faults with [loyal] service' to the real tsar, the God-ordained representative of the Romanov dynasty.[64]

His family was still working its way back into prominence by means of faithful service to the Romanov dynasty when Prince Iu.F. Shakhovskoi (ca. 1671–1713) received the Judas medal from Tsar Mikhail's grandson. With this promotion to the imaginary Order of Judas, Prince Shakhovskoi acquired more than yet another in a long series of mock titles by which he was jokingly referred to at the court of Peter the Great. Indeed, if we now turn to Shakhovskoi's service career, we will see that despite the opinions of hostile contemporary witnesses, he was much more than a 'court jester.' The prince spent his entire political career at the Muscovite court, where he was an intimate member of the tsar's entourage. He began his career as an ordinary rank-and-file courtier in the retinues of various members of the Muscovite royal family. In 1687, Prince Iurii and his younger brother, Prince Afanasii Fedorovich, were transferred from the entourage of Tsaritsa Praskov'ia Fedorovna (*née* Saltykova, the wife of Tsar Ivan Alekseevich), to that of the two co-tsars. In 1696, following the successful second campaign to capture the fortress of Azov, he was appointed to the position of privy chamberlain at the court of Peter himself.[65] However, even before this promotion, Prince Iurii Fedorovich was already part of tsar's inner circle. Sometime after the formation of the mock ecclesiastical council of the Transfigured Kingdom, Prince Iurii Fedorovich adopted the title 'Archdeacon Gideon,' the pseudonym by which he was known among the tsar's personal entourage, many of whose members also assumed mock ecclesiastical titles in their intimate correspondence with the tsar. In this new 'ecclesiastical' capacity, Prince Shakhovskoi was the courtier responsible for drawing up the lists of participants in the tsar's annual Yuletide carolling processions,[66] in effect re-enacting the role of the divinely inspired biblical judge, whose trumpet called the righteous to their duty (Judges 6:34–35) and who 'sifted out' the Lord's true followers from 'the fearful and trembling' crowd simply by the way they drank (Judges 7:2–8).

Judging by the admittedly fragmentary evidence from the period of the Northern War, Shakhovskoi also seems to have served as a personal liaison between the tsar and two of his closest political advisers, A.D. Menshikov and I.A. Musin-Pushkin.[67] Besides heading up a department in Menshikov's Ingermanland chancellery[68] – the office responsible for minting the silver commemorative medal of Judas – Prince Shakhovskoi also acted as a personal intermediary between the tsar and Musin-Pushkin, the courtier who headed the Moscow-based Monastery Chancellery and who was rumoured to be Peter's illegitimate half-brother. In fact, Shakhovskoi seems to have spent the entire Northern War en route between the old capital and the new, and his constant travels, whether as part of the tsar's personal retinue or as Peter's personal emissary, may explain why so few of his own letters have come to light. Be that as it may, Shakhovskoi continued to serve in his capacity of privy chamberlain until 1710, when Peter bestowed upon him the highest (*boiar*) rank in the Muscovite royal council.[69] Despite its prestige value, it was clear that this appointment was more an honorary promotion than an actual advance in service rank. In fact, this was one of the last few promotions to the Muscovite royal council, whose aging membership was undergoing a natural decline and whose political authority was being usurped by new, foreign-sounding institutions, such as the Novo-Preobrazhenskoe 'consilium' presided over by F.Iu. Romodanovskii – the feared head of Peter's secret police and the 'Prince-Caesar' (*kniaz'-kesar'*) of the Transfigured Kingdom.

Prince B.I. Kurakin, a disaffected Russian courtier who penned a scathing portrait of the 'mediocrities' who composed the royal entourage of Tsar Peter at the end of the seventeenth-century, characterized Prince Shakhovskoi as the ultimate political creature, a man who was totally dependent on the good graces of, and willing to do anything for, his royal patron. According to Kurakin, Prince Shakhovskoi was 'a highborn court fool,' who allegedly earned his daily bread by spying on, denouncing, and humiliating the respectable members of the Muscovite elite during court festivities. Unlike some other jesters in Peter's royal retinue, however, Prince Shakhovskoi was not weak-minded. In fact, according to Kurakin, Prince Shakhovskoi possessed 'not a small intellect' and was 'an [avid] reader of books.'[70] Coming from a cosmopolitan polyglot like Prince Kurakin, this was indeed high, if backhanded, praise. Nevertheless, Kurakin immediately went on to qualify this already ambivalent characterization by describing Shakhovskoi as one of the 'most drunken and malicious vessels' in the tsar's entourage, a man 'who acted villainously towards everyone, from the lowest person [at court] to the highest.' As the unofficial eyes and ears of the tsar, Shakhovskoi was the 'channel' through which Peter was able 'to know everything.' In fact, Kurakin dubbed him 'Prince-Sticking Plaster' (*lepen'-prilipalo*),[71] presumably because Shakhovskoi would spy on important government officials, bring up their misdeeds during dinner, and reproach them in front of the tsar in the same way as a sticking-plaster draws out all the filth in a boil unto the surface of the skin. By this disgusting metaphor, Kurakin alluded to Shakhovskoi's idiosyncratic role in implementing what we would now call the anti-corruption thrust of Petrine legislation. For like the more formal guardians of probity at Peter's court (such as the so-called fiscals), in his unofficial capacity as the tsar's spy, Shakhovskoi made sure that courtiers were really loyal, doing their business, not embezzling, slacking off, or worse, plotting behind the tsar's back.

Knowing his family's history, as well as his work in the capacity of the tsar's private investigator, I would argue that Prince Shakhovskoi was given the Order of Judas in order to expiate his family's sins against the Romanovs. By serving to ferret out traitors, Judases against the Lord's anointed, Shakhovskoi not only made up for his family's checkered past, but also made sure that other courtiers would never take the tsar's name in vain. This hypothesis is strengthened by the fact that in 1711, two years after he received the Judas medal, Peter appointed Prince Shakhovskoi to the newly created post of 'General Gevaldiger,' or head of the military police.[72] In this capacity, Shakhovskoi was responsible for all the military policemen and executioners in every division of every regiment of the Russian army, as well as the instruments of their trade, such as the gallows, shackles, and armed mounted escorts. However, his most important duties consisted in judging, sentencing and, if necessary, organizing the execution of traitors, deserters, and anyone who caused disorder in the ranks during this important military campaign. In particular, Shakhovskoi was charged with carrying out investigations into breaches of discipline during the planned military marches through the

Balkans and with the responsibility for 'hanging, without any show of mercy,' anyone who 'willfully' deserted from the Russian ranks in the face of the enemy.[73] As the chief hangman of the Russian expeditionary army during the famous Prut campaign against the Ottoman Empire, this Cavalier of the Order of Judas – who wore a medal showing Judas hanging on a tree – was thus put in charge of the division responsible for executing deserters by hanging them on the gallows, in front of the troops, to teach future deserters a lesson. Obviously, this was no longer merely playful parody. Shakhovskoi's new, responsible position was deadly serious. And this, in turn, suggests that the role played by jesters at Peter's court should be redefined. Indeed, the example of Prince Shakhovskoi, the Cavalier of the Order of Judas, demonstrates that jesters were used as more than just a typical royal amusement. Or rather, these so-called amusements were, in fact, part of the very spectacle of power – a way of demonstrating and enacting the tsar's charismatic authority.

Prince Shakhovskoi played out the last years of his political career as a living representative of the Order of Judas, an institution that existed only symbolically, in the discourse employed at the court of Peter the Great, as a parodic counterpart to the Order of St Andrew. As the courtier actually entrusted with the task of locating and executing traitors to the Russian cause, this mock Cavalier enforced obedience to the ideals of faith and fidelity, associated with the tsar's knightly order. Even on the day of his funeral, Shakhovskoi was charged with performing the leading role, if only for one last time, in a ceremony which affirmed the chivalrous fellowship of believers in the tsar's charisma. The Cavalier of the Order of Judas was buried in St Petersburg, on 30 December 1713, with all the pomp and circumstance worthy of his rank in the mock ecclesiastical council of the Transfigured Kingdom. The coffin of Archdeacon Gideon was escorted by the 'entire [mock] Holy Council (*osviashchennyi sobor*),' which reconvened to honour the memory of one of its founding members. This Yuletide funeral procession was led by 'Prince-Pope' Zotov, the mock archpriest of the Transfigured Kingdom. He was followed by the 'Anti-Caesar' (*Antitsesar'*) (i.e., Prince F.Iu. Romodanovskii) and other 'spiritual dignitaries' (*dukhovnye osoby*).[74] The advent of the Anti-Caesar and the Prince-Pope, who represented the patrons of the mock Order of Judas, recalled the fact that the Order of St Andrew was intended as an Orthodox counterpart to the chivalrous brotherhoods sponsored by the Holy Roman Emperor and the Pope. In this way, the organizers of the grotesque funeral procession

Apostles and Apostates: The Court of Peter the Great   185

that escorted the coffin of Prince Shakhovskoi employed the corpse of the Cavalier of the Order of Judas in much the same way as the tsar had once utilized the relics of the Pertominsk saints, or as he would eventually use the bones of St Alexander Nevskii[75] – namely, to restate (in the 'two-edged language' of Kantorowicz's 'court coterie') the imperial pretensions and the polemical thrust behind the chivalrous religious organization of the Russian court.

Notes

1 On Russia's role in shaping the emerging pan-European balance of power between Christian monarchs, see M.S. Anderson, *Peter the Great*, 2nd ed. (London and New York: Longman 1995), 84; L. Jay Oliva, *Russia in the Era of Peter the Great* (Englewood Cliffs, NJ: Prentice-Hall, 1969), 29; and Lindsey Hughes, *Russia in the Age of Peter the Great* (New Haven, CT: Yale University Press, 1998).

2 For a pioneering attempt to situate Peter's reign within the context of a 'Russian Baroque,' see D.S. Likhachev, 'Byla li epokha petrovskikh reform pereryvom v razvitii russkoi kul'tury?' in *Slavianskie kul'tury v epokhu formirovaniia i razvitiia slavianskikh natsii XVIII-XIX vv. Materialy mezhdunarodnoi konferentsii IuNESKO* (Moscow: Nauka, 1978), 170-4; English translation by Avril Pyman, 'The Petrine Reforms and the Development of Russian Culture,' *Canadian-American Slavic Studies* 13, nos. 1–2 (1979): 230–4.

3 On the membership and political role of Peter's 'company,' see A.I. Zaozerskii, *Fel'dmarshal B.P. Sheremetev* (Moscow: Nauka, 1989), 200–6; and, more generally, Ernest A. Zitser, *The Transfigured Kingdom: Sacred Parody and Charismatic Authority at the Court of Peter the Great* (New York: Cornell University Press, 2004).

4 For an argument that the values informing the 'pillars' of the early modern state – 'the prince, the bureaucracy, and the army' – transformed them into an '*ecclesia militans*, a secular religious order, so to speak,' see Gerhard Oestreich, *Neostoicism and the Early Modern State* (Cambridge: Cambridge University Press, 1982), 72.

5 For an explicit defence of the idea that earthly tsars deserve to be referred to as 'gods' (*bozi*) and 'christs' (*khristy*), see the 'Sermon on Royal Authority and Honor [6 April 1718],' delivered by Peter's chief panegyrist, Archbishop Feofan (Prokopovich), 'Slovo o vlasti i chesti tsarskoi, iako ot samogo Boga v mire uchinena est', i kako pochitati tsarei i onym povinovatisia liudie dolzhenstvuiut; kto zhe sut' i kolikii imeiut grekh protivliaiushchiisia im ...,'

in *Sochineniia*, ed. I.P. Eremin (Moscow and Leningrad: Izd-vo Akademii nauk SSSR, 1961), here 84–5.

6 M.M. Bogoslovskii, *Petr I: Materialy dlia biografii* (Moscow and Leningrad: Ogiz, Goz. sotsial'no-ekon. izd-vo, 1940–8), 1:271–94; Edward Joseph Phillips, 'The Establishment of a Navy in Peter the Great's Russia: The Azov Fleet, 1688–1714' (PhD diss., University of North Carolina at Chapel Hill, 1990), 73–81; and Hughes, *Russia in the Age of Peter the Great*, 81–2.

7 For a discussion of the 'mercantilist' naval projects of Tsar Aleksei Mikhailovich, see Phillips, 'The Establishment of a Navy in Peter the Great's Russia,' chapter 1. On Peter's knowledge of his father's projects, see his autobiographical introduction to the 'Naval Statute' of 1720, 'Predislovie k morskomu reglamentu,' in N.G. Ustrialov, *Istoriia tsarstvovaniia Petra Velikogo* (St Petersburg, 1858), 2:399.

8 Nancy S. Kollmann, 'Pilgrimage, Procession, and Symbolic Space in Sixteenth-Century Russian Politics,' in Michael S. Flier and Daniel Rowland, eds., *Medieval Russian Culture* 2 [= *California Slavic Studies* 19], (1994): 163–81. For an insightful, comparative discussion of such 'political hierophanies,' see Clifford Geertz, 'Centers, Kings, and Charisma: Reflections on the Symbolics of Power,' in *Rites of Power: Symbolism, Ritual, and Politics Since the Middle Ages*, ed. Sean Wilentz (Philadelphia: University of Pennsylvania Press, 1985), 13–38.

9 Peter to Tsar Ivan Alekseevich (14 June 1694), *Pis'ma i bumagi imperatora Petra Velikogo* (St Petersburg, 1887), 1:21–2.

10 Ibid., I:21. Tsar Peter and his 'hundred-man retinue' first visited the port city of Arkhangel'sk in 1693. See Phillips, 'The Establishment of a Navy in Peter the Great's Russia,' 58–9.

11 The hagiographic trope of worrying relatives appears both in Peter's correspondence with his mother and in his autobiographical introduction to the 'Naval Statute' of 1720. Lindsey Hughes has recognized the 'implicit parallels' with the 'Lives of the Saints' in 'the fact that Peter's mother twice tried to dissuade him from his endeavour, first from sailing on a lake [Pereiaslavl'], then from sailing on the White Sea [near Arkhangel'sk].' She goes on to suggest that Peter's 'first visit to the latter [Arctic sea-port], and later to the West, is presented as a new sort of pilgrimage, not to holy shrines, but to maritime 'holy places' – harbours, shipyards, and docks.' See Hughes, *Russia in the Age of Peter the Great*, 81.

12 D.M. Posselt, *Admiral Russkago flota Frants Iakovlevich Lefort, ili nachalo Russkago flota* (St Petersburg, 1863), 18–19.

13 Phillips, 'The Establishment of a Navy in Peter the Great's Russia,' 58–9.

14 For a discussion of the allegorical significance of ships' names in Petrine court culture, see I.D. Chechot, 'Korabl' i flot v portretakh Petra I.

Ritoricheskaia kul'tura i osobennosti estetiki russkogo korablia pervoi chetverti XVIII veka,' in *Otechestvennoe i zarubezhnoe iskusstvo XVIII veka* (Leningrad: Izd-vo leningradskogo universiteta, 1986), 54–82; and Hughes, *Russia in the Age of Peter the Great*, 88.
15 For the ideological significance of the navy – and sea-travel in general – at the court of Peter the Great, see Evgenii Anisimov, *The Reforms of Peter the Great: Progress Through Coercion*, trans. J. Alexander (New York: M.E. Sharpe, 1993), 66; G. Kaganov, 'As in the Ship of Peter,' *Slavic Review* 50 (1991): 354–67; and Hughes, *Russia in the Age of Peter the Great*, 88–9. On the importance of maritime imagery during the baroque, see Peter N. Skrine, *The Baroque: Literature and Culture in Seventeenth-Century Europe* (London: Holmes and Meier, 1978), chapter 5, esp. 75–8.
16 For a discussion of this ceremony, see S.A. Zen'kovskii, *Russkoe staroobriadchestvo: dukhovnye dvizheniia semnadtsatogo veka* (Moscow: TSerkov', 1995), 182.
17 For the *vita* of SS. Vassian and Iona, see 'Skazanie o proiavlenii i obretenii i o chudesekh prepodobnykh otets nashikh Vasiana i Iony, izhe na Primorii Studenago moria, Velikago Okiiana, v Zatotse, vo Unskikh, naritsaemykh Rogakh Pertominskikh chudotvortsev,' *Rukopisnyi otdel Rossiiskoi natsional'noi biblioteki*, 'Solovetskoe sobranie' 181/182 (Sbornik zhitii russkikh sviatykh). Thanks to Eve Levin for providing me with a copy of her notes on this manuscript.
18 'Skazanie,' 197, 197u, 198.
19 On the attestation of the Pertominsk relics, see ibid., 198v–200u.
20 Posselt, *Admiral Russkago flota Frants Iakovlevich Lefort*, 37; *Pis'ma i bumagi*, 1:23–4, 495–6. The tsar even rebuked those courtiers who refused to play according to the rules of his 'company' and insisted on addressing their letters using the official royal titulature. See Peter to F.M. Apraksin (11 December 1696), *Pis'ma i bumagi*, 1:113; 2:97 (21 October 1702).
21 *Pis'ma i bumagi*, 1:21, 495. In 1805, Peter's cross was transferred to the main Orthodox cathedral in Arkhangel'sk. See N. Golubtsov, 'Krest Petra Velikogo, khraniashchiisia v Arkhangel'skom Kafedral'nom Sobore,' in *Petr Velikii na Severe. Sbornik statei i ukazov, otnosiashchikhsia k deiatel'nosti Petra I na Severe*, ed., A.F. Shidlovskii (Arkhangel'sk, 1909), 79–83; S. Ogorodnikov, 'Vtoroe poseshchenie Petrom Velikim Arkhangel'ska v 1694 g.,' in ibid., 28; and Bogoslovskii, *Petr I*, 1:181–2.
22 'Skazanie,' 200u–201.
23 For a partial list of the royal suite that visited the Pertominsk monastery, see 'Skazanie,' 196. For their roles in Peter's mock ecclesiastical council, see Zitser, *The Transfigured Kingdom*, Appendix 2.
24 Max Weber, 'The Sociology of Charismatic Authority,' in *From Max Weber:*

Essays in Sociology, ed. H.H. Gerth and C. Wright Mills (New York: Oxford University Press, 1958), 246–7.

25 'Skazanie,' 200*u*–201.

26 For a discussion of the patristic image of the Orthodox Church as the 'ship of Jesus,' see M.B. Pliukhanova, 'O natsional'nykh sredstvakh samoopredeleniia lichnosti: samosakralizatsiia, samosozhzhenie, plavanie na korable,' in *Iz istorii russkoi kul'tury: XVII-nachalo XVIII veka,* ed. A.D. Koshelev (Moscow: Shkola 'IAzyki russkoi kul'tury,' 1996), 3:408.

27 On Peter's labours as the redemptive work of a 'new Adam,' see the epistolary exchange between the tsar and 'arch-priest' T.N. Streshnev (6 and 12 March 1696), in *Pis'ma i bumagi,* 1:54, 547–8.

28 On the playful interchangeability of names as a rhetorical convention in Petrine court culture, see M.P. Odesskii, 'Khudozhestvennaia semantika panegiricheskikh imen sobstvennykh v teatre epokhi Petra I,' *Germenevtika drevnerusskoi literatury* 4 (1992): 370–97; and Grigorii Amelin, '"Se Moisei tvoi, O Rossiie!" (O semiotike imeni v 'Slove na pogrebenie Petra Velikogo' Feofana Prokopovicha),' in *V chest' 70-letiia professora Iu. M. Lotmana* (Tartu: Eidor, 1992), 20–9.

29 St Andrew was, in fact, often invoked alongside the tsar's name-day saints (Peter and Paul) as his other heavenly patron. See G.V. Vilinbakhov, 'Gosudarstvennaia geral'dika Rossii kontsa XVII-pervoi chetverti XVIII veka. (K voprosu formirovaniia ideologii absoliutizma v Rossii),' (Avtoreferat diss. kand. ist. nauk, Leningrad State University, 1982), 14; and 'Otrazhenie idei absoliutizma v simvolike petrovskikh znamen,' in *Kul'tura i iskusstvo Rossii XVIII veka. Sbornik statei* (Leningrad: Iskusstvo, 1981), 15, 17.

30 Samuel Hazzard Cross and Olgerd P. Sherbowitz-Wetzor, trans. and eds., *The Russian Primary Chronicle: Laurentian Text* (Cambridge, MA: Medieval Academy of America, 1953), 53–4.

31 Francis Dvornik, *The Idea of Apostolicity in Byzantium and the Legend of the Apostle Andrew* (Cambridge: Harvard University Press, 1958).

32 On the fate of the 'imperial theme' in early modern Europe, see Frances Yates, *Astraea: The Imperial Theme in the Sixteenth-Century* (London: Routledge, 1987); and B.N. Floria, ed., *Slaviane i ikh sosedi. Imperskaia ideia v stranakh tsentral'noi, vostochnoi i iugo-vostochnoi Evropy. Tezisy XIV konferentsii* (Moscow: In-t-slavianovedeniia i balkanistiki RAN, 1995).

33 Although the Order of St Andrew appeared at the end of the seventeenth century (ca. 1698–9), it did not become a 'monarchical order' in the full sense until 1720, when it acquired its own set of statutes (monarchical constitution). Until then, the Order of St Andrew can be classified as a 'cliental pseudo-order,' which has been defined as a 'princely order,' whose '"members" were bound by an oath of clientship to the prince who bestowed [the

order] in the form of a badge.' These 'pseudo-orders' were 'in effect glorified retinues, distinguished from other such groupings only by the misleading title 'order' applied to them by the prince who distributed the badge.' For a useful discussion of the distinction between various types of chivalrous orders, see D'Arcy Jonathan Dacre Boulton, *The Knights of the Crown: The Monarchical Orders of Knighthood in Later Medieval Europe, 1325–1520* (Woodbridge: Boydell, 1987), xvii–xx. For the text of the statutes of 1720, see E.E. Zamyslovskii and I.I. Petrov, *Istoricheskii ocherk rossiiskikh ordenov i sbornik osnovnykh ordenskikh statutov* (St Petersburg, 1892), 1 (2), 101ff.

34 On the Knights of Malta, see Boulton, *The Knights of the Crown*, 17, 17 n.25.
35 J.-G. Korb, *Diary of an Austrian Secretary of Legation*, trans. Count MacDonnell (London: Cass 1968), 135.
36 On the geopolitical significance of Sheremetev's trip to Malta, see Zaozerskii, *Fel'dmarshal B.P. Sheremetev*, 22–5.
37 On the Scottish Order of St Andrew, or of the Thistle, see Boulton, *The Knights of the Crown*, xx, 399, 399 n.8, and 499–500. For an extensive discussion of the Order of the Golden Fleece (*Toison d'or*), see ibid., chapter 13.
38 G.V. Vilinbakhov, 'K istorii uchrezhdeniia ordena Andreiia Pervozvannogo i evoliutsii ego znaka,' in *Kul'tura i iskusstvo petrovskogo vremeni: Publikatsii i issledovaniia* (Leningrad: Avuw, 1977), 153–5.
39 On the 'Cross of Constantine' and its veneration at the court of tsar Aleksei Mikhailovich, see Vilinbakhov, 'Gosudarstvennaia geral'dika,' 16–18. On the importance of the 'Cross of Constantine' in Muscovite political theology, see M.B. Pliukhanova, *Siuzhety i simvoly Moskovskogo tsarstva* (St Petersburg: Akropol, 1995), chapter 3.
40 Vilinbakhov, 'Gosudarstvennaia geral'dika,' 18.
41 For a description of the 1696 'triumphal entry' into Moscow, see Bogoslovskii, *Petr I*, 1: 344–7; V.P. Grebeniuk, 'Publichnye zrelishcha petrovskogo vremeni i ikh sviaz' s teatrom,' in *Novye cherty v russkoi literature i iskusstve (XVII-nachalo XVIII v.)* (Moscow: Nauka, 1976), 133–45; and Richard S. Wortman, *Scenarios of Power: Myth and Ceremony in Russian Monarchy* (Princeton, NJ: Princeton University Press, 1995), 1:42–4.
42 A.V. Viskovatov, 'Ob uchrezhdenii ordena sv. Apostola Andreia Pervozvannogo i o pozhalovanii sim ordenom v 1700 g. Multianskogo Gospodaria Brankovana, v kavalerskikh spiskakh nigde ne pokazannogo,' *Rossiiskii gosudarstvennyi arkhiv voenno-morskogo flota, f.* 315, *op.* 1, *ed. khr.* 47.
43 The analogy between Mazepa and Judas also informed the work of Peter's chief apologists. See Stefan (Iavorskii), 'Stikhi na izmenu Mazepy, izdannye ot litsa vseia Rossii,' in *Pamiatniki literatury drevnei Rusi: XVII vek. Kniga tret'ia* (Moscow 1994), 268; and Feofan (Prokopovich), 'Slovo pokhval'noe o preslavnoi nad voiskami Sveiskimi pobede ...,' in Eremin, ed., *Sochineniia*, 28.

44 My interpretation of Mazepa's motives during 1708–9 is indebted to the revisionist studies of Anisimov, *Progress through Coercion*, 112–16; and Orest Subtelny, 'Mazepa, Peter I, and the Question of Treason,' *Harvard Ukrainian Studies*, 2, no. 2 (June 1978): 158–83.

45 Stanisław Leszczynski was installed on the Polish throne by the Swedes after the forced abdication of Peter's ally, the elector of Saxony, August II 'The Strong,' in 1705. See N.N. Molchanov, *Diplomatiia Petra Pervogo* (Moscow: 'Mezhdunarodnye otnosheniia,' 1986), 188, 195.

46 This 'propaganda war' was treated by B. Kentrschynskyj, 'Propagandakriget i Ukraina, 1708–1709,' *Karolinska Förbundets Årsbok* (Stockholm 1958), 81–124; English-language summary in the *Ukrainian Quarterly* 15 (1959): 241–59.

47 For a first-hand account of Mazepa's shaming ceremony, see G.I. Golovkin to P.A. Tolstoi (undated), *Pis'ma i bumagi*, 8(2):910.

48 For the text of the anathema pronounced by metropolitan Stefan (Iavorskii), see *Polnoe sobranie zakonov Rossiiskoi imperii* (St Petersburg, 1830), 4:431–2.

49 Peter to F.M. Apraksin (30 October 1708), *Pis'ma i bumagi*, 8(1):253.

50 For Peter's instructions to Major-General Prince G.S. Volkonskoi, see I.I. Golikov, *Deianiia Petra Velikogo, mudrogo preobrazovatelia Rossii, sobrannye iz dostovernykh istochnikov i raspolozhennye po godam* (Moscow, 1789), 13:29–30; and *Trudy Imperatorskogo Russkogo voenno-istoricheskogo obshchestva* (St Petersburg, 1909), 3: 32, 304.

51 *Pis'ma i bumagi*, 9(1):242; 9(2):1013; and G.V. Zashchuk, '"Orden Iudy,"' *Voprosy istorii* 6, no. 6 (June 1971): 212–15, here 214.

52 This decree was found in a late-eighteenth-century manuscript, which was originally published in *Trudy Riazanskoi uchenoi arkhivnoi kommissii* 1 (1894), 69; the text of the decree was re-published by S.F. Platonov, 'Orden Iudy 1709 goda,' *Letopis' zaniatii postoiannoi istoriko-arkheograficheskoi komissii*, 1 (1927): 193–8, here 194; and Zashchuk, '"Orden Iudy,"' 212.

53 N.I. Pavlenko, *Petr Velikii* (Moscow: 'Mysl',' 1990), 320.

54 For the text of the instructions, see Platonov, 'Orden Iudy 1709 goda,' 194. It is unclear whether this silversmith was related to Fedor Alekseev, the master of the Admiralty Mint and the Russian medallion maker responsible for producing the first commemorative campaign medal of the Northern War. On Fedor Alekseev, see E.S. Shchukina, *Medal'ernoe iskusstvo v Rossii XVIII veka* (Leningrad: Izd-vo Ermitazha, 1962), 13ff.

55 The second version of Menshikov's decree, dated eleven days later (22 July 1709) than the one published by Platonov, was discovered by I.I. Sreznevskii. For the text of Sreznevskii's decree (and the accompanying drawing), see *Rukopisnyi otdel, Biblioteka Akademii nauk, Sbornaia rukopis'* 24.5.38, 75v.

56 On 15 July 1709, just four days after Menshikov first wrote to Shchukin about

the silver medal of Judas, the cavalry divisions of the royal favourite embarked upon a new campaign against the remnants of the combined Swedish-Polish forces. See Pavlenko, *Poluderzhavnyi vlastelin: istoricheskaia khronika o zhizni spodvizhnika Petra Pervogo A.D. Menshikova* (Moscow: Izd-vo polit. lit-ry, 1991), 153; and Pavlenko, *Petr Velikii*, 322–3.

57 On the Muscovite practice of awarding campaign medals to all participants, see Shchukina, *Medal'ernoe iskusstvo v Rossii XVIII veka*, 11–12; and V.A. Durov, 'Russkie boevye nagrady za Poltavskoe srazhenie,' *Numizmatika i sfragistika* 5 (1974): 63–4.

58 Iu.N. Shcherbachev, trans. and ed., 'Zapiski Iusta Iulia, datskogo poslannika pri Petre Velikom (1709–1711),' *Chteniia Moskovskogo obshchestva istorii i drevnostei Rossiiskikh*, 189, no. 2 (1899), here 91, 93.

59 Ibid., 92–3.

60 Ibid., 91.

61 A.I. Timofeev, ed., 'Zapisnye knigi Moskovskogo stola. 1633 sentiabr'-1634 avgust [7142],' in *Russkaia istoricheskaia biblioteka* (St Petersburg, 1884), 9: 529, 550–1, here 550.

62 E. Likhach, 'Shakhovskie,' *Russkii biograficheskii slovar'* (St Petersburg, 1905), 571, 578–9. For a genealogy of the Shakhovskoi clan, see A.A. Dolgorukov, *Rossiiskaia rodoslovnaia kniga* (St Petersburg 1854), 1: 168–9; and P.N. Petrov, 'Kniaz'ia Shakhovskie,' *Istoriia rodov russkogo dvorianstva* (St Petersburg, 1886), 1: 73ff.

63 For a work that places this skit in the context of other cases of *lese majeste* in seventeenth-century Muscovy, see I.I. Polosin, '"Igra v tsaria" (Otgoloski Smuty v moskovskom bytu XVII veka),' *Izvestiia Tverskogo pedagogicheskogo instituta* 1 (1926): 59–63.

64 Timofeev, ed., 'Zapisnye knigi Moskovskogo stola,' 9: 551.

65 For the service career of F.Iu. Shakhovskoi, see I.Iu. Airapetian, 'Feodal'naia aristokratiia v period stanovleniia absoliutizma v Rossii' (Diss. kand. ist. nauk, M.V. Lomonosov State University, 1987), 432, 336; and M.G. Spiridov, *Sokrashchennoe opisanie sluzheb blagorodnykh Rossiiskikh dvorian ... Sobrannoe iz stateinykh, razriadnykh, stepennykh, letopisnykh, sluzhebnykh i nekotorykh drugikh rodoslovnykh knig* (Moscow, 1810), 1: 252–3.

66 B.I. Kurakin, 'Gistoriia o tsare Petre Alekseeviche,' in L. Nikolaeva, et al., eds., *Petr Velikii. Vospominaniia. Dnevnikovye zapisi. Anekdoty* (Moscow: 'Tret'ia volna,' 1993), 81.

67 See the letters from Prince Shakhovskoi to A.D. Menshikov and I.A. Musin-Pushkin, published in *Opisanie dokumentov i bumag, khraniashchikhsia v Arkhive Ministerstva Iustitsii* (Moscow, 1888), 8: 169–73.

68 According to an unpublished document dated 16 August 1710 (Menshi-

kovskii arkhiv, *BAN*, 13-i *karton*, No. 211), *blizhnii boiarin* Prince Iu. F. Shakhovskoi is listed as serving at the Ingermanland chancellery. See Platonov, 'Orden Iudy 1709 goda,' 196.

69 Airapetian, 'Feodal'naia aristokratiia v period stanovleniia absoliutizma v Rossii,' 319, 110.
70 Kurakin, 'Gistoriia o tsare Petre Alekseeviche,' 80.
71 Ibid., 81.
72 On 2 June 1711, the 'high-born Prince, Privy Counselor and General-Gevaldiger' received a copy of the seven 'articles' according to which he was to exercise his new function. On 30 June 1711, Prince Shakhovskoi's new commission was confirmed by a royal decree, which was sent to all the field commanders of the Russian army. A copy of this royal decree can be found among the papers of the personal chancellery of General A.A. Weide, a German officer who headed an army division under General-Field Marshal B.P. Sheremetev. See 'Chernovye zhurnaly reliatsii i pisem kasaiushchiesia kak do voennykh deistv, tak i do ministerskikh negotsiatsii, 1711-go g. – Zhurnal iskhodiashchikh dokumentov [iz kantseliarii generala] A.A. Veide,' *Sankt Peterburgskii filial Instituta russkoi istorii Rossiiskoi Akademii nauk, f.* 83, *op.* 3, *ed. khr.* 3, 3–3v, 5–5v.
73 *Sankt Peterburgskii filial Instituta russkoi istorii Rossiiskoi Akademii nauk, f.* 83, *op.* 3, *ed. khr.* 3, 5v. On the duties of the 'General Gevaldiger,' and the Petrine military police in general, in keeping order within the ranks, see A.A. Preobrazhenskii and T.E. Novitskaia, eds., *Zakonodatel'stvo Petra I* (Moscow: Izd-vo 'IUrid. lit-ra,' 1997), 185–6; and John L.H. Keep, *Soldiers of the Tsar: Army and Society in Russia, 1462–1874* (Oxford: Oxford University Press, 1988), 108.
74 See the entry for 30 December 1713 in *Pokhodnyi zhurnal 1713 goda* (St Petersburg 1854), 53.
75 On the cult of St Alexander Nevskii, whose victory over the Swedes (1240), near the future site of St. Petersburg, was taken to 'prefigure' Peter's own victories, see Iu.M. Lotman and B.A. Uspenskii, 'Echoes of the Notion "Moscow the Third Rome" in Peter the Great's Ideology,' in *The Semiotics of Russian Culture*, ed. Ann Shukman (Ann Arbor: Department of Slavic Languages, University of Michigan, 1984), 57; and Hughes, *Russia in the Age of Peter the Great*, 276–8.

chapter ten

Self-Knowledge and the Advantages of Concealment: Pierre Nicole's 'On Self-Knowledge'

JOHN D. LYONS

The seventeenth century is sometimes viewed as an epoque in which the compromised, relativistic, and merely probable knowledge of the material and social world gave way to a pure, systematic, and certain knowledge sometimes known as the classical episteme. In recent years this overview has been increasingly questioned, and it now seems that in the heart of the seventeenth century many writers advanced a vision of inquiry in which truth and falsehood, far from being always and everywhere incompatible, must sometimes be combined in the search for knowledge. To understand this pleaching of truth and untruth, we need to consider how facets of the baroque interact. For instance, the baroque has long been associated with concealment – with masks and disguises of all sorts, with prevarication and mental reservation, with the distinction between the outer self and the inward self.[1] This masking of the inner self is seen as either commendable or as an inevitable and useful social practice by writers as diverse as Descartes, Pascal, Lafayette, and La Rochefoucauld. At the same time, in the natural sciences, direct experiential knowledge of the physical world was coming to be considered untrustworthy, while indirect knowledge acquired through the mediation of instruments (microscopes, telescopes, and laboratory apparatuses of various kinds) was presented as the path to verifiable facts.[2] The novelty of this mediated view of the world even, notoriously, found its way into the poetry and novels of the period. A third cultural phenomenon that is widely associated with the baroque – in France, particularly – is the growth of a category of writings with didactic or self-improvement themes based on empirical observation of humans in society authored by writers who have come to be called 'moralists' (or more exactly, *moralistes*) and are sometimes described as early social anthropologists.³ These three trends – concealment, mediated knowledge, and moralist writing – converge in paradoxical works in which the active and conscious construction of false appearances was sometimes motivated by the systematic search for truth. A good example of this convergence is Pierre Nicole's 'De la connaissance de soi-même,' a text little-known today but widely read in the seventeenth and early eighteenth centuries (mentioned frequently by Madame de Sévigné) and an influence on John Locke, who translated several of Nicole's essays.⁴

For Nicole the self is ugly and painful to know. Mankind has an inherent but imperfect sense of its fallen, corrupt nature, but this haunting intuition is too painful to bear. Humans thus resort to almost any expedient to distract themselves from it, thus avoiding accurate self-perception. The traditional counsel to know oneself, interpreted as introspection or direct self-observation, is thus useless, running totally contrary to human nature. Rather than turning inward, humans turn inevitably outward, seeking distraction from the sense of individual corruption in falsely laudatory images or 'portraits' of themselves in social interaction. The people who are the most successful in obtaining the anesthesia of fictive portraiture are powerful, wealthy, or active people surrounded by flatterers. Social institutions meant, apparently, to undo this flattery and to provide occasions for self-knowledge and self-improvement are easily manipulated to reinforce one's congratulatory image. While the practice of sacramental confession, for instance, should offer both frank self-discovery and appropriately harsh criticism and advice, people choose their confessors according to their taste in vices. A glutton might, therefore, locate a priest well known for concentrating on sexual transgressions and likely to overlook other sins (96). The least successful in obtaining the comfort of false 'portraits' are those whose favour is sought by few people, and who do not suffer the distorting effect of flattery, but even they create for themselves an illusory image, a 'vain phantom' constructed by their imagination (6).⁵ These portraits are not the only ones that exist. In fact, accurate portraits circulate on a third-person basis behind the back of the interested party. Therefore accuracy of representation increases in direct proportion to the distance from its object. First- and second-person discourse are inferior to the independent, third-person *bruit public* (public rumour). This unflattering report will not be heard by the main character of the rumor, and certain details may be distorted, but the principal, negative essentials will be accurate, since, in any event, the more vicious the report the more it corresponds to the evil that dominates human nature, the very nature that we cannot bear to see in ourselves.

How, then, can we acquire self-knowledge? And, to pose at a preliminary question, why should we want to know ourselves? Since the admonition to know oneself is, according to Nicole, universal in philosophy, it may seem that this question is not worth asking. Yet his argument in favour of self-knowledge merits attention because of its characteristic indirectness. There is no rational argument for self-knowledge on pragmatic grounds in everyday life. The immense effort and pain required cannot be justified by the corresponding gain enjoyed during man's brief lifespan. Therefore, only the hypothesis of a postmortal eternity during which the knowledge so carefully avoided during life would be forced upon us can justify the undertaking of trying to gain that knowledge now (actively) rather than suffer it later (passively). In short, not only can we not discover the truth about ourselves on our own, we cannot even justify the attempt. Only faith can make us want to transfer the moment of discovery from eternity to life – only the belief that self-knowledge is inevitable can move us to seek it.

Since introspection is useless, Nicole proposes that we turn the world into a laboratory for self-discovery by using other people.[6] The research required is indirect, empirical, and dependent on knowing the proper codes for interpreting the results. The first and easiest step is simply to observe other people and reassign the subject – a sort of rewriting process in which we switch third-person narratives and descriptions into the first person:

> comme il n'est pas défendu néanmoins de remarquer dans les autres certains défauts visibles, & qu'il est même impossible de ne pas voir ce qui frappe nos sens, il faut essayer de nous en servir pour nous mieux connoître, & afin d'en tirer cet avantage, il faut d'abord que nous appercevions quelques-uns de ces défauts, que nous nous demandions à nous-mêmes: Numquid ego unquam imprudens facio simile huic? (89)

> [since it is not forbidden, however, to notice certain obvious defects in other people and since it is in fact impossible not to see what is right in front of our eyes, we should try to make use of these occasions to know ourselves better, and in order to obtain that benefit, we must first perceive these faults and then ask ourselves: 'Might not I imprudently do something similar to that person?']

The faults of others, rather than exemplary virtues, therefore become the licit focus of our vicious curiosity (90). This curiosity is then redeemed by the humbling reascription of the actions to ourselves, actions that we confront stripped of their excuses. Or, in other words, the power of the narrative of observation comes from the lack of the 'explanatory' platitudes of intention, 'cette multitude de vûes et d'excuses artificieuses qui nous trompent dans les nôtres' (that myriad of perceptions and clever excuses that deceive us about our own actions) (90). On one hand, Nicole's approach is based on a simplification: we observe actions without intentions, crimes without extenuation. On the other hand, it requires a complication: to know ourselves we create a triangle in which the actions we see are 'our' actions but they are embodied by other people. Through our conceptual appropriation of the actions of others we are both the subject of knowledge and the subject of the action which appears in the lives of other people. However, the relation of these two subjects – of the 'I' as a doubled subject – traverses the object which is the life of another.

This is the first of the two major approaches to the self-knowledge that is available only when we have somehow evaded the protective toxins of self-love. Because the mystifying personal mythology of others is invisible to us, we see without these veils the ridiculous and repulsive actions objectively. Because the interiority of others is concealed from us – whereas our own exteriority is concealed to us – we can make use of their behavior to understand our own. Nicole's advice here is drastically different from that of our own time, with its usual appeals to understand the foibles of our fellow humans through empathic identification.[7] Instead of considering their probable motives, their feelings, and their 'needs,' Nicole's disciple will benefit from the natural disposition to objectify others and to see only their actions and the results of those actions. Then, in a subsequent and unique step, the Nicolian will cruelly recognize himself in that picture.

The second of Nicole's major approaches to self-knowledge goes beyond a certain way of seeing and requires physical action. We must learn to control our gestures, facial expressions, and language – not only at the verbal level but at the level of tone, rhythm, and inflection – to deceive others about our thoughts. We must, in other words, adopt the aggressive self-disguising posture that so many seventeenth-century writers describe.

The need to create a false image of oneself arises from the concept that truth increases with discursive distance. Each man's own natural self-description is the most false, because it is permeated by self-love. The descriptions of himself that one finds in conversation with others is only slightly less inaccurate, because this conversation is shaped by the self-love of social partners who fear the consequences of speaking frankly. The truest statements about someone are found in third-person descriptions that are normally not available to him. The challenge, therefore, is to become a spy in order to discover this publicly available knowledge that is hidden only to oneself. The pursuit of truth requires the active creation of falsehood. Deceit is, for Nicole, the most effective recourse for the discovery of truth.

Nicole thus endorses concealment and disguise. Unlike his contemporary La Bruyère, who deplores the hypocrisy of the court and city life and expresses a persistent nostalgia for a more sincere age and for the directness of provincial life, Nicole promotes artifice and deception. Convinced, like La Rochefoucauld, of the inevitability of deception, Nicole chooses to displace it, moving it from self-deception to the deception of others. The first step in encouraging the frank criticism that one needs is finding a *directeur,* the spiritual adviser known to us today primarily through Molière's darkly satiric *Tartuffe.* Since our *directeur* cannot see us all the time, we should make it known to everyone that we seek sincere commentary on our behaviour. Yet the weakness of this method is only too obvious, and may well remind us of some of the many appeals for forthright assessment that appear in the comedy of Nicole's day. We recall Oronte's appeal to Alceste in *Le Misanthrope.* The potential collaborators in self-discovery are forewarned against cooperating:

> Il faut supposer que chacun étant prévenu d'une part qu'on n'aime point à être averti de ses défauts, & n'étant pas bien-aise de l'autre de s'attirer notre aversion, est disposé par-là à s'exempter de nous rendre cet office de charité, & à ne nous rien découvrir de ce qu'il pense de nous & de ce qu'il sait que les autres en pensent. (100)

> [One must suppose that everyone, aware that people do not like to be told of their faults and, moreover, that no one wants us to have a grudge against them, is inclined to forego that charitable service and not to tell us what he thinks of us and what he knows that other people think.]

In order to make this simple plan work, Nicole recommends conveying the false impression that one feels no pain and has no resentment when people speak frankly. It is not enough to thank people for their help and to refrain from saying anything that reveals the inquirer's true, inward anger when he hears criticism. He needs to obtain an almost inhuman self-control over every conceivable sign of his feelings, for it is not enough to accept criticism without reacting emotionally and to thank people for their comments. This mastery of appearance must always set new records for deception, and since people are aware of the constraints of civility the inquiring self must be one step beyond the foreseeable gestures of false gratitude and acceptance in the face of sincerity.

> car tout le monde sait assez que comme il est honteux de témoigner de s'en offenser, on tâche de se faire honneur d'être civil en ces occasions: il faut persuader aux gens que ces civilités sont sinceres; & c'est ce qui ne se peut, à moins que d'éviter quantité de choses que le monde prend pour des marques d'un secret mécontentement, & d'un dépit que nous n'osons découvrir. (101)
>
> [for everyone knows that, since it is humiliating to show that one is offended, each takes pride in being civil on such occasions: one must persuade others that this civility is sincere – but that is impossible, unless one manages to avoid a lot of things that others will interpret as the signs of a secret irritation and of rancor that we don't dare reveal.]

Now, Nicole does not demand, and does not expect, that the inquirer achieve a degree of humility that would actually make him sincerely civil and unperturbed by this new knowledge. The secret vexation is still there; only the 'marks' of this vexation have been removed from the surface so that even the highly skilled observers who surround him and who are used to the complex and polished rhetoric of the court will not perceive it. This is, after all, the same society of which La Bruyère wrote 'La cour est comme un édifice bâti de marbre: je veux dire qu'elle est composée d'homme fort durs, mais fort polis' (The court is like a palace of marble – made of men who are very hard, but very polished).[8]

Almost like a skilled novelist – a comparison that would have revolted Nicole himself – Nicole sets out an inventory of plot elements that would reveal, through indirect ways over periods of time, the inquirer's deep and smoldering resentment of helpful comments. For instance, one might become more reserved, quieter, and less spontaneous when in the presence of the critic. Or one might deliberately misinterpret the criticism in order to find grounds to reject it or to encourage others to reject it (102). One might instead on other occasions affect certain apologies for the defect in question, and so forth. But even this is not enough, since the work of the inquirer – the spy of the self – demands no less than a lifetime commitment. Here is how Nicole describes the way the inquirer's discourse must be modified over a long period of time:

> C'est le sentiment d'un sage Payen, que celui que l'on avertit de quelque défaut, ne doit pas faire le même sur le champ à l'égard de celui dont il reçoit un avertissement, et qu'il doit attendre un autre tems à lui rendre cet office: mais il faut étendre cet avis beaucoup plus loin; car non-seulement il ne faut pas reprendre sur le champ ceux qui nous reprennent, mais il faut même éviter de les reprendre, lorsqu'il y auroit lieu de soupçonner que quelque dépit secret nous auroit ouvert les yeux sur leurs défauts, & nous auroit appliqués à les remarquer. (103)

> [A wise Pagan once said that someone who is informed of a fault of his, should not immediately reciprocate, but should rather wait for another occasion to return the favour. But we must take this advice a lot further, since not only should we refrain from criticizing right away those who have criticized us, we should avoid commenting on their faults altogether, when there might be a chance to suspect that some hidden spite might have opened our eyes to their faults and predisposed us to notice them.]

Advice like this, which presses us on to ever greater concealment of thought and emotion, prevents reciprocation and leads to increasing imbalance in social interaction. The inquirer withholds information that the people around him seek – namely, what does he think of what they do and what they say – in order to make sure that they do not withhold the equivalent information from the inquirer. The person who manages to be most covert, wins. The inquirer is constantly fearful that those around him will do exactly what he is doing. For if we show ouselves to be 'delicate' in receiving advice and too attached to our own opinions,

> personne presque ne se hazarde de nous contredire, principalement si nous avons quelque consideration qui porte les gens à se ménager avec

nous. Ainsi chacun se tient dans la réserve, & nous laisse croire ce que nous voulons, en s'en moquant souvent dans son coeur. (107)

[almost no one will take the risk of disagreeing with us, especially if we have a position of power that makes people want to stay on our good side. So everyone keeps quiet and lets us believe what we want, even though inwardly they are laughing at us.]

Yet concealment need not be seen as solely negative, for it produces as its by-product a false but satisfying appearance of sociability. Nicole counsels pointedly against allowing resentment of advice to appear in the form of constraint and reserve, so the inquirer necessarily creates an active disguise that can pass as 'une maniere libre & naturelle' (a free and natural manner) (102). The result is, logically, that the means adopted as camouflage to neutralize social resistance and to permit the inquirer to discover what others think of him and thus to gather or to approximate that third-person 'truth' about him that circulates in public will falsify that public report itself. If the inquirer has a consummate control of his every word and gesture, then other people will be providing frank information about a disguise, not about a person in the full sense. The more the inquirer resists the impulse to react to remarks that would correct him and the less he provides useful, but unwelcome, advice to others, the more the inquirer will skew public opinion. As a result, he will be able to gather large amounts of information about the impression people have of him, but that information will be less and less valuable.

Nicole does not appear fully aware of the dynamism of the system he theorizes – that is, the problem that we know as the observer's paradox. The act of observing is said to transform the phenomenon observed, and Nicole's construction of the self-spy shows how gaining access to the public discourse about the self inevitably modifies that discourse. Perhaps Nicole simply does not believe that the inquirer will really be able to transform himself enough to make a difference.[9] Apparently Nicole thought that a good deal of the inner self would still appear, for he supposed that our companions would still sense our resentment and he provided a guide for deriving useful information from deceptive and even absent statements. He tells his reader that 'on ne découvriroit pas seulement la verité au travers des petits nuages, dont l'honnêteté & la prudence se servant pour l'adoucir & la temperer, mais on sauroit même la discerner dans l'obscurité du mensonge & du silence' (one cannot only discover the truth behind the veils that good manners and prudence use to soften it, but one can even grasp it in the darkest lie and in silence) (112).

To use public discourse for self-knowledge, the inquirer needs to follow a set of interpretive rules, the 'Règles pour entendre le langage des avertissemens de la flatterie et du silence' (Rules for understanding the language of flattery and silence). These rules are based on the need to extrapolate from appearances:

> il faut que nous ajoutions de nous-mêmes ce qui manque à leurs paroles, et ne pas supposer que ces pensées leur naissent dans l'esprit avec tous ces temperamens et ces adoucissemens dont ils usent en nous les proposant. Faisons donc état qu'on ne nous dit jamais qu'une bien petite partie de ce qu'on pense de nous, et qu'il faut multiplier en quelque sorte tout ce qu'on nous en dit pour trouver le vrai ... Si l'on dit que l'on fait quelque difficulté sur quelque raisonnement, cela veut dire qu'on le croit faux et ridicule. (111)

> [we need to add what is missing from their words and not suppose that the words come directly from their mind with all the mitigation and softening that they put in when they speak to us. We need to realize that they tell us only a small portion of what they think of us, and that we need to amplify [multiplier] everything they say in order to discover the truth ... If someone says that they have a little problem with something we've said, that means that they think that what we said is false and ridiculous.]

There are four basic keys:

1. Social partners, 'flatterers,' believe the opposite of what they say.
2. Those who praise are sincere in their praise of the quality but insincere in attributing this quality to their interlocutor.
3. The flatterer believes that his interlocutor is benighted by illusion and vanity; the hidden thought of the flatterer is 'I view you with the scorn that you deserve' (j'ai pour vous tout le juste mépris que vous méritez).
4. Most instruction comes from decoding the language of silence – one only needs to 'notice what they avoid saying in front of us to discover what prejudices and defects they think we have' (remarquer les discours qu'on

évite devant [les personnes intéressées] pour savoir quelles préventions et quels défauts on leur attribue) (116).

There are, then, two hypotheses about the use of social intermediaries to study the self. In one case, the inquirer succeeds in concealing the self sufficiently to surprise others in frank statements about a person whom they at least partially misjudge, because if they knew that person they would realize that the benign outward presentation is deceptive. In the other case, the inquirer fails to conceal his avid self-love and receives deceptive information from those around him, but he is able to decode this deception and obtain useful information about himself. These two situations probably form a continuum, in Nicole's view, though presumably the inquirer who decodes the language of silence will use the information to acquire at least the outward semblance of virtues that are flatteringly (and thus ironically) attributed to him.[10] He will thus increasingly be in a situation in which social partners are less and less silent in speaking of his ever smaller and less perceptible vices.

The outcome of this process – and the process of self-discovery should be, according to Nicole, the life-long acquisition of self-portraits (78) – would seem to be a kind of photographic negative in which the 'inner' self becomes more and more conscious of its defects in proportion to the creation of an 'outer' self that at every point contradicts the spontaneous desires and beliefs of the inquirer. As this process continues, the division between the inner and the outer selves becomes more complete – though there will always be some gleam of the inner corruption that penetrates to the surface ('La vérité se fait toujours un peu de jour au-travers de tous ces nuages dont on s'efforce de l'obscurcir'. (25)) And it is only on such occasions of involuntary self-revelation that the inquirer can make progress by seizing the new information that of necessity can come only from social interaction. Considering the vertiginous implications of this always-unstable 'self' which is never fully known by anyone, it is not surprising that Charles de Sévigné, in the face of his mother's praise of Nicole's work, called it difficult to understand and nonsensical sophistry.[11]

Nicole's creation of the self-spy is part of the overarching anti-naturalism that he shares with most of the hyper-Augustinians of the late seventeenth century. The explicit preference of artifice over nature is taken farther in Nicole's work than in Pascal's, for the latter is concerned in part with helping his readers exploit some of the vestiges of the 'première nature' (first nature) that has been replaced by social convention and other habits that have formed mankind's 'seconde nature' (second nature). In part, of course, the seventeenth-century renunciation of direct knowledge of nature stems from Renaissance scepticism and from Descartes's construction of a system to combat scepticism at the cost of creating a highly indirect and counter-intuitive approach to the material world we might otherwise know through our senses. This logical or scientific anti-naturalism, which Bruno Latour, among others, has described, is expanded by Augustinian theology to everyday life.[12] Nicole's disciple therefore considers as suspect any movement that is spontaneous or apparently natural. Anything that appears 'obvious' to us should be suspect because 'nous nous trompons même dans le fond, & c'est l'aversion que nous avons pour la verité qui nous empêche de le reconnoître' (we are mistaken about the very substance of things, and it is our aversion to truth that prevents us from recognizing this) (74).

There are some surprising consequences of the preference for the artificial. One could say, indeed, that Nicole's system leads to an artificial irrationalism, quite different from the inspirational or poetic irrationalism sometimes found in the Renaissance and from the naturalistic or instinctive irrationalism of some Romantics. Whereas a principal Cartesian tenet is to disbelieve anything that has not been proven by the light of reason, in seeking self-knowledge the inquirer, says Nicole, should be guided by what other people say, however false it seems. This approach should be adopted because, with regard to the self, even 'just' people are blinded by self-love. Hence all their reasoning about the self is warped (49, 80) and as a consequence they need to suspend their usual critical stance vis-à-vis what people say about them. With regard to other matters, of course, such a systematic submission to the general, public view – and, hence, an abdication of individual judgment – is not absolutely obligatory, but since self-love is pervasive and since every perception and decision may affect us, all pretense to rational inquiry is ultimately suspect: 'le principal usage que nous faisons de cet amour de la verité, est de nous persuader que ce que nous aimons est vrai' (the main use we make of that love of truth is to persuade ourselves that what we like is true) (29).

Nicole's artificial irrationalism leads, thus, to a strange form of democracy, since the inquirer after self-knowledge must suspend his reliance on social hierarchy and also assume that he is wrong when he is frequently isolated in his views about anything. Accepting the observations and advice of everyone – 'amis, ennemis, familiers, étrangers, inferieurs, égaux, superieurs' (friends, enemies, acquaintances, strangers, inferiors, equals, superiors) – the inquirer will not filter what they say through an analysis of their motives, their individual limitations, their tone, or their style (58). Although there are apparent similarities here with the Cartesian provisional morality, these similarities are deceptive. Descartes explains in Part III of the Discourse that he resolved to adopt outwardly the customs and professed beliefs of the most moderate among the population in which he lived. However, this superficial abdication of a morality based on thorough, unprejudiced, rational examination of ethical questions in favour of simple conformity to the public will is specifically designed to permit introspective self-determination. Nicole, to the contrary, considers such individual self-determination through reason to be vitiated from the start by self-love.

Nicole also differs markedly with other writers associated with the Jansenist (or 'hyper-Augustinian') sensibility, like Lafayette and Pascal. While both of these better-known authors adopt one part of the program that appears in 'On Self-Knowledge' – the study of the self as it is revealed in others and then reattributed to the first person – neither follows to the radical consequence of surrendering individual judgment to a levelling, proto-democratic 'knowledge' gained from the public discourse. Lafayette's controversial heroine, the Princesse de Clèves, fought to preserve her singularity and finally to remove herself from public discourse.[13] And Pascal, in the account given by his sister Gilberte Périer, departed so far from the Nicolian model that he was a constant giver of stern advice, but never a receiver, willing himself a model of hyperbolic Christian virtue.

By fusing self-knowledge with social interaction and by fixing in advance the lesson that can be learned (history is only the study of a series of enormous wounds, the consequences of original sin), Nicole creates a picture that is both infinitely rich in minute variations and yet closed, without any room for significant change or progress. It is understandable that many of his contemporaries should have felt the sense of lateness that marked the fin-de-siècle in which he died.[14] Having destroyed the 'self' by making it accessible from both within and without, placing it unstably and uncertainly somewhere in-between, and creating the ideal of a duplicitous, alienated, and artificial humanity, Nicole no doubt helped precipitate the Romantic reaction, with its frequent insistence on self directly knowable through experience. But his description of the self – a self that works ceaselessly to prevent transparency – is quintessentially that of the baroque, the monad, as described by Gilles Deleuze: 'The monad is the autonomy of the interior, an interior without exterior. But the monad has as a correlate the independence of the façade, an exterior without an interior.'[15]

Notes

1 Among many studies that deal with disguise, concealment, and lying, noteworthy are Perez Zagorin, *Ways of Lying: Dissimulation, Persecution, and Conformity in Early Modern Europe* (Cambridge: Harvard University Press, 1990); Georges Forestier, *Esthétique de l'identité dans le théâtre français (1550-1680): Le déguisement et ses avatars* (Paris: Droz, 1988); Jean-Luc Nancy, 'Mundus est fabula,' *MLN*, no. 93 (1978): 635–53; Louis Van Delft and Florence Lotterie, 'Torquato Accetto et la Notion de "Dissimulation Honnête" dans la Culture Classique,' in *L'honnête homme et le dandy*, ed. Alain Montandon (Tübingen: Gunter Narr Verlag, 1993), 35–57; Emmanuel Bury, *Littérature et politesse: L'invention de l'honnête homme 1580–1750* (Paris: Presses Universitaires de France).

2 Historians of science and of epistemology have written extensively on the shift to an indirect and instrument-based approach to knowledge in the seventeenth century. Among the studies that most directly relate to the concerns of this article are Stephen Toulmin, *Cosmopolis: The Hidden Agenda of Modernity* (New York: Free Press, 1990); Thomas L. Hankins and Robert J. Silverman, *Instruments and the Imagination* (Princeton: Princeton University Press, 1995); Catherine Wilson, *The Invisible World: Early Modern Philosophy and the Invention of the Microscope* (Princeton: Princeton University Press, 1995); Bruno Latour, *We Have Never Been Modern*, trans. Catherine Porter (Cambridge: Harvard University Press, 1993); Michel Foucault, *Les mots et les choses* (Paris: Gallimard, 1966).

3 Louis Van Delft, *Littérature et anthropologie: Nature humaine et caractère à l'âge classique* (Paris: Presses Universitaires de France, 1993), and Louis Van Delft, *Le Moraliste classique: Essai de définition et de typologie* (Geneva: Droz, 1982).

4 Pierre Nicole, 'De la connoissance de soi-même,' in *Essais de morale, contenus en divers traités sur plusieurs devoirs importants* (Paris: Guillaume Desprez, 1730), 1–121. Nicole was an important member of the Jansenist or (to use Charles Taylor's term) 'hyper-Augustinian' current in French religion and literature. His collected essays, *Essais de morale*, published in six volumes beginning in 1671, were widely read and reprinted. Although a selection of the *Essais* has recently been edited by Laurent Thirouin, I have used one of the eighteenth-century editions. Page references in this chapter correspond to the 1730 edition of Guillaume Desprez. Locke's translation has been

reprinted (Pierre Nicole, *Discourses Translated from Nicole's Essays,* trans. John Locke, with a preface by John Locke (London: Thomas Hancock, 1828; repr. Thoemmes Antiquarion Books, 1991).

5 Nicole specifically dismisses the idea that the non-Europeans, who were the object of so much controversy concerning the 'savage' or the 'state of nature,' were any closer to self-knowledge (7).

6 Erec Koch shows convincingly that the self is not *known* or *knowable* only through the mirrors offered by society, it is fabricated by social interaction: 'Nicole's specular glance at the self reveals that there is no self without the Other, without the totalizing whole, and no whole without the self.' (Koch, '*Individuum*: The Specular Self in Nicole's *De la Connoissance de Soi-Même*,' paper presented at the conference of the North American Society for Seventeenth-Century French Literature, Arizona State University, May 2001.

7 For an excellent example of the appeal to empathy as basis of ethics see Martha Nussbaum, 'Invisibility and Recognition: Sophocles' *Philoctetes* and Ellison's *Invisible Man,*' *Philosophy and Literature* 23, no. 2 (October 1999): 257–83.

8 Jean de La Bruyère, 'Les Caractères Ou les Moeurs de ce Siècle,' 'De la cour,' in *Oeuvres complètes,* ed. Julien Benda (Paris: Gallimard, 1951), 216.

9 The shifting and unstable character of Nicole's thought in this essay is reminiscent of Pascal, in whose writing the desire for stability and the impossibility of locating truth through human means are intertwined. Sara E. Melzer, *Discourses of the Fall* (Berkeley: University of California Press, 1986), 75–108.

10 Irony is a fundamental component of Nicole's world-view, but through the program of self-concealment the proportion of irony shifts from the social partners (who ironically attribute virtues to the inquirer that they know he does not possess) to the inquirer, who increasingly feigns external goodness in an effort to gain access to the frank 'bruit public.'

11 'Pour les *Essais de Morale,* je vous demande très humblement pardon,' Charles wrote to his sister, 'si je vous dis que le traité «De la Connaisance de soi-même» me paraît difficile à comprendre, sophistiqué, galimatias en quelques endroits, et surtout ennuyeux presque partout.' (Marie de Rabutin-Chantal de Sévigné, *Correspondance,* ed. Roger Duchêne (Paris: Gallimard, 1972–8), 2:223–4.

12 Latour, *We Have Never Been Modern.*

13 On the heroine's deliberate singularity see Ralph Albanese, 'Aristocratic Ethos and Ideological Codes in *La Princesse de Clèves,*' in *An Inimitable Example: The Case for* La Princesse de Clèves, ed. Patrick Henry (Washington: Catholic University of America Press, 1992), 87–103; on her disappearance from

public view see Joan DeJean, 'Lafayette's Ellipses: The Privileges of Anonymity,' in ibid., 39–70.
14 Nicole died in 1695, La Bruyère the following year, and Charles Perrault in 1703. For the sense of the fin-de-siècle and its ideological implications see Joan DeJean, *Ancients against Moderns: Culture Wars and the Making of a Fin de Siècle* (Chicago: University of Chicago Press, 1997).
15 Gilles Deleuze, *Le Pli: Leibniz et le baroque* (Paris: Minuit, 1988), 39. My translation.

chapter eleven

The Baroque Social Bond in the *Memoirs* of the Cardinal de Retz

MALINA STEFANOVSKA

Society functions only by means of a misunderstanding. A universal misunderstanding is what enables all society to function harmoniously.
                                                                Baudelaire

A Baroque Fable

The *Memoirs* that Jean-François-Paul de Gondi, co-adjutor of the Archbishop of Paris and later known as cardinal de Retz, left of his life are among the best known in that literary genre in early modern France. As this controversial nobleman, high church figure, and faction leader reflects on his participation in the Fronde and on his later destiny during the triumphant era of Louis XIV's absolutism, he repeatedly returns to the issue of the bonds and conflicts at the heart of the civil war that shook France from 1648 to 1652 and develops themes that are emblematic of a baroque personal and political sensibility. Towards the beginning of his narrative, he recounts an event which deserves a closer look, since it illustrates his views on togetherness and communication.

In 1642 Retz, a young *abbé* at that time, was returning from Saint-Cloud at dawn in merry company, after a late night supper and dance. With him in the carriage were the duchesse de Vendôme with her daughter, Mlle de Vendôme, who was to become Retz's lover, M. de Brion (a suitor of the young lady), the famous maréchal de Turenne, the well-known man of letters Voiture, the Archbishop of Lisieux, and an elderly lady. At the bottom of a hill, the driver suddenly stopped the carriage and, upon Retz's prompting to continue, exclaimed 'Do you want me to run over all these devils in front of us?'[1] But the only scene that the proverbially near-sighted narrator could see was of the panic surrounding him: the six lackeys behind the carriage were screaming "Jesus, Mary"' and shaking; Voiture started an *Oremus*; the women "howled rather than screamed"'; Mlle de Vendôme prayed clutching her rosary; Mme de Vendôme began saying confession to M. de Lisieux; and the count de Brion, on his knees, chanted Hail Mary with the lackeys. All of this happened, Retz says, 'simultaneously and in no time at all.' Following Turenne, who jumped out of the carriage and stepped forward, Retz grabbed a sword from a lackey and drew it out blindly. He finally made out in front of him what appeared to be 'a long procession of black ghosts' and, though scared at first, immediately remembered that he had always wanted to see spirits.[2] When he rushed towards them, the cries of his fellow passengers were soon joined by those of the alleged devils. It turned out that these were only a few monks in black garb who were returning from an early morning bath in a nearby stream.

From the outset, Retz's story echoes a number of well-known baroque motifs such as the mixture of superstition and religious sentiment, the striking contrast between the perceived devils and the divinity that they recall to mind, the protagonists' acute awareness of the link between pleasure and sin, and their expectation that retribution follows on the heels of *divertissement*. Such are the psychological foundations of the dramatic display of devotion, the passionate conversions produced by fear, and the linking of death and eroticism that are the striking features of his narrative. Indeed, Retz recalls that, as he stepped back into the carriage, he immediately noticed Mlle de Vendôme's contempt for her suitor's conduct and her new attraction to himself and wasted no time in taking advantage of it. Retz's account, in which time seems to stand still, takes on the aspect of a *tableau*, almost a hypotyposis. One of his favourite techniques, this dramatization of the past rests on leaving out the causal relationship between the events or even their simple succession, and on compressing duration into illusory instantaneity.[3] This, too, was a technique perfected by baroque artists who represented Christ's agony on the crucifix as a simultaneous state of life and death.[4]

The awareness of a gap between appearances and reality pertains to the same sensibility: the devils turned out to be simple monks; the author's apparent courage stemmed from a combination of near-sightedness and excitement; Turenne's true valour was interpreted by the others as hesitation because of his naturally slow walk. Retz reports that, when he later exchanged impressions with Turenne, both men agreed that appearances are deceiving, and he concludes by exclaiming: 'Who can write the truth but those who have felt it?' His conclusion intimates that a better understanding can be reached in time by some, if not everyone, and that the communion between the two aristocrats runs even deeper, since both allegedly believe that history *can* be written by its protagonists. And yet, this conclusion acquires another unexpected twist as the reader learns that this event may never have happened to Retz himself, and that the dialogue may be entirely fictional. According to contemporary sources, it occurred to Voiture and Mme de Lesdiguières, who later told Retz the story. His role consisted simply in finding out, at her request, the identity of the apparent devils from the other participants.[5]

At this point, Retz's narrative transcends well-known baroque motifs and becomes exemplary of his understanding of social and political bonds at large. As a matter of fact, his final comments prompt several conclusions. First, all the relationships between the characters involved are based on a misunderstanding, including the newly hatched affair between Mlle de Vendôme and Retz as well as the general mistake regarding Turenne. In this story, the only communion that one can speak of is momentary, based on misperception and on the shared experience of a memorable event. Second, a similar blindness underlies the participants' relationship to themselves, as evidenced by the sudden and soon forgotten religious conversions. Third, even the *post factum* lucidity usually assumed by an author who reflects on his life is here illusory, or feigned. The striking realism of Retz's narration was perhaps no more than a *trompe l'oeil* used to legitimize memoir writing over official historiography. Unless, as it may well be, Retz's interest in the event made him forget twenty years after the fact that he only lived it vicariously and caused him to retell it in good faith, in which case he would simply be illustrating another baroque adagio: *life is but a dream ...*

If Retz's narrative is indeed a *feinte*, a simulation, it succeeds on several levels: in regard not only to the implied reader, but also to the real addressee of his *Memoirs*. For these are dedicated to an unknown woman to whom Retz promises he will unveil all the secrets of his life. In that respect, it is not insignificant to note that this anecdote does not end on history writing, but on a note of surprise at his own sincerity and at the pleasure felt in revealing to her 'tous les replis de mon âme et de mon coeur' (all the folds of my soul and my heart). What are we to conclude? Is the friendly complicity constantly stressed in his writing, which gives it the tone of an intimate, heart-to-heart conversation between old friends, yet another trick, another veil concealing his true self? Is Retz deluded or cynical in his contradictions?[6] Perhaps, for that matter, there is no true self to be disclosed through this autobiography. The narrator might ultimately be no more than a solitary magician who stages illusion as life and life as illusion: Shakespeare's Prospero, Corneille's Alcandre in the *Illusion Comique*, a memoir author as he invents himself under the façade of faked sincerity ... Whatever the case, his subjectivity keeps eluding the reader's will to stabilize it, thus perfectly illustrating Deleuze's formula: 'le trait du baroque, c'est le pli qui va à l'infini' (the baroque trait is the fold to infinity).[7] And maybe it is *le néant*, the nothingness of the self, which lurks under the folds of Retz's personal history, as death lurks under the still life of Holbein's *Ambassadors*.[8] To such a self, relating to others would appear as necessary as it is fake, and the anecdote above, as well as the entire *Memoirs*, could be read as a perfect enactment of what I will call Retz's baroque drama of the impossible social bond.

The Closest Confidante

That Retz is above all concerned with the experience of bonding is evident from the form that his *Memoirs* take from their very outset: that of a 'very long letter' addressed to an unnamed lady friend.[9] Their dedication is not a purely external, symbolic act, but one that is deeply constitutive of Retz's writing. The opening address thus not only starts his autobiography but shapes it:

> Madame, quelque répugnance que je puisse avoir à vous donner l'histoire de ma vie, qui a été agitée de tant d'aventures différentes, néanmoins, comme vous me l'avez commandé, je vous obéis, même aux dépens de ma réputation. Le caprice de la fortune m'a fait l'honneur de beaucoup de fautes; et je doute qu'il soit judicieux de lever le voile qui en cache une partie. Je vas cependant vous instruire nuement et sans détour des plus petites particularités, depuis le moment que j'ai commencé à connaître mon état; et je ne vous cèlerai aucunes des démarches que j'ai faites en tous les temps de ma vie. (127)

> [Madam, as reluctant as I might be to give you the history of my life, which has been tossed about for so many different ways, since you ordered me to do it, I obey you, even at the expense of my reputation. Fortune has graced me with many faults; and I doubt that it is wise to lift the veil concealing

some of them. I will, however, tell you plainly and with no detours of the most minute particulars of my life since the moment I became aware of myself; and I will not hide from you any of the acts undertaken at any time of my life.] (1)

The contract of trust and friendship established in these opening lines – a founding symbolic pact for the autobiographical genre, according to literary theorists – is reasserted almost in every sentence of the *Memoirs*. Indeed, when Retz continues the next paragraph by 'very humbly begging' her to forgive the lack of order in his writing, he starts weaving in an endless series of questions, addresses, remarks that will establish an implicit subtext for his writing. His interlocutor's role in it is manifold: she allows for interruptions of the narrative, provides agreement with the author, builds suspense, explains causal relations or clarifies the logic, and so on. Sometimes begging for attention, at other times for approval or patience, his appeals do more than provide an underlying justification for this anti-hero's life. They create and perform an intimate bond with the other. Most often, in fact, all other narrative functions seem subordinate to the phatic, which endlessly reasserts the linguistic bond between the narrator and his narratee, and through them between the writer and the reader: 'You have already seen ... I told you above ... as you can imagine ... you must suspect.' Page after page, these phrases act as a light and elastic scaffolding without which the history of the Fronde as well as Retz's autobiographical project might collapse for lack of support. This author thus fully realizes Barthes's observation that classical language is always reduced to a persuasive content, thus reaffirming dialogue and instituting a universe where 'speech is always the encounter with the other.'[10] Retz's desire for communication not only shapes his entire *Memoirs* into a dialogue, a friendly chat, a storytelling session, it inflects the tone, the depth, and the passion of his self-examination. It gives his narrative of the self the appearance of a communion with another being.

The presence of this female figure whose uncertain identity has been amply discussed but whose textual function has not been sufficiently underlined guarantees from within the text a perfect understanding, agreement, and complicity. She is an intermediary between the narrator and the reader, the main depository of his secrets. As the recipient of Retz's undivided sincerity, she is meant to redeem and exorcise the endless series of past lies and intrigues that constitutes his life. In this interlocution, Marc Fumaroli sees the formal innovation that decisively situates Retz's writing in the literary realm.[11] The gestures of constant exchange and bonding motivate him to view the *Memoirs* as a symbolic gift. In that respect, Retz's addressee also points to a higher agency. As indicated by the almost religious overtones in which she is addressed, his writing ultimately transcends interpersonal communication and takes the shape of a confession. The joy he feels in making it and the surprise he expresses reveal a sense of higher communion, in what constitutes, in all likelihood, the most authentic religious experience of his entire life.

And yet, there is another side to this exchange, made obvious by epistolarity. The unknown woman with whom Retz cultivates this purest friendship is also the victim of his lies and tricks. From an assistant in self-examination, she turns at times into an accomplice in self-delusion. The bond between them is predicated upon distance, a distance all the more apparent because of the author's constant invocation of her benevolence and friendship. In fact, Retz's writing may hinge precisely on the subtle interplay between distance and proximity, as shown by his exemplary, but probably fake, story and his professed, yet equally uncertain, sincerity. As a counterpart for his own elusiveness, it would only be fitting that his interlocutor's status rests on a lie as well – that, as some critics believe, Retz started his confession to Mme de Sévigné and ended it to her daughter (who in fact disliked him). If that were the case, her figure would come to resemble that of an abstract, impersonal confessor, standing for an increasingly Hidden God. The author's simultaneous gestures of communion and distancing, frankness and *feinte* would aptly designate his understanding that a perfect communion can only be based on illusion.

A Man on the Move

Retz's addressee is by no means the only figure with whom he establishes this type of relationship. Indeed, the *Memoirs* recount a whole series of such aborted or impossible encounters, both in the amorous and in the political realm. A few of his liaisons or pseudo-affairs are worth mentioning: the failed abduction of a pretty heiress, Mlle de Scepeaux, in Retz's youth; the union with the famous *Frondeuse*, Mme de Longueville, which remained strictly political though it was sealed with a flirtatious slap of her glove and the words, 'You understand me well'; an unsuccessful plot concocted by Retz's neglected mistress, Mme de Guéméné, to sequester him in her cellar for political reasons; a briefly contemplated liaison with the beautiful Mme de Montbazon, who unsuccessfully tried to persuade him to flee Paris.[12] These are not the only examples. In fact, transcending the erotic realm, the experience of establishing social or political bonds, often described as a failure, grounds Retz's history from its very outset. This motif might well be the only common thread between the handful of various episodes that Retz chose to represent his life before the Fronde in the first part of his *Memoirs*: the failed abduction mentioned above in which the erotic connection was revealed to others precisely as the inadvertent lovers were ascertaining their bond by exchanging glances in a mirror; two duels ending by a social exchange or bonding; two attempts at group conspiracy which, according to historians, Retz also largely invented; the shared experience of the ghosts; and his rejection of a useful political bond with Richelieu.[13] This series of aborted exchanges and missed encounters show that to Retz union appears generally as untenable as it is desirable. Communication, in his writing, might be limited to asserting the forms and circuits of exchange and to recounting their failure. This sentiment that union is bound to fail is central in his political thought and his interest in faction.

It is interesting to note that the baroque elusiveness in Retz's narrative strategy is paralleled by his restlessness as a protagonist of history. When at the very outset of his *Memoirs* he seals the 'auto-biographical pact' with his addressee-reader, by promising to unveil his entire life to her, the French term – *démarches* – he selects to designate the actions of his life strikes us as an odd, yet appropriate choice: stemming from *marcher*, to walk, it designates a gait or manner of walking, as well as an act or a formal procedure. Retz's choice expresses well the particular dynamics of his political experience, since the *Memoirs* trace step by step his endless errands, exchanges, and negotiations during the Fronde and give the picture of a man constantly on the move, if not on the run. Daily (and nightly!), Retz rushes through the streets of Paris lobbying the insurgents or the court, interceding between them, convincing one to act, and another to keep quiet. Literally, he never stops moving, as a contemporary pamphlet describes him: 'M. Le Coadjuteur ne perd point de temps de l'Autel au Palais, du Palais en la chaire, de la chaire en l'Hostel de Ville' (M. Le Coadjuteur wastes no time in rushing from the Altar to the Parlement, from the Parlement to the pulpit, from the pulpit to the City Hall).[14] Tallemant des Réaux, the famous gossip monger of the time, characterizes him with a witticism: 'Il a tousjours été d'humeur remuante' (His was a nature always on the go).[15] Retz himself explains his first participation in political faction as an illustrious 'way out' of a much disliked ecclesiastical career. Later, on the verge of joining the Fronde, the same dynamic terms describe his decision: 'j'abandonnai mon destin à tous les mouvements de la gloire' (I abandoned my destiny to all the movements of glory) (227). His spectacular escape from prison, and the eight subsequent years spent travelling in exile, are no less representative of him. In his peregrinations and flights, the cardinal de Retz uncannily resembles another baroque hero, Don Juan, whose endless search is also an endless flight.[16] Both are obsessed with bonding and breaking, practice seduction through hypocrisy, eschew religion, wear a mask, use secrecy, dissimulate and simulate. Both elude as well the ultimate confrontation with truth. The fugue, this most truly baroque musical form, aptly designates their common trajectory, which could also be described by another dynamic term, invented precisely during the Fronde, and used by Retz in the realm of the passions: *emportement* (being swept away).[17]

Of course, as with Don Juan, Retz's elusiveness has also been imputed to his ultimate individualism. This was the position of early literary criticism, which stressed his historical inaccuracies, as well as his tendency to exaggerate his role in the Fronde, lie about his faults, and rewrite history to his benefit. In literary histories, Retz is still accused of an 'exacerbated form of individualism,' 'an exaltation of the self'[18] representative of the entire Fronde with its 'epidemics of selfishness.'[19] Even when cited positively, it is for the same reasons: N.O. Keohane underscores that one of Retz's most distinctive themes is discussing the 'conflict and congruence of interest among the diverse parties;'[20] and Albert Hirschman, in *The Passions and the Interests*, praises him for analysing self-interest and placing it in men's unconscious inclinations.[21]

To a large degree, however, Retz's perceived self-centredness is due to the literary genre itself: personal writings reveal human egotism more easily than the novel, at the time not written in the first person, or than moralist writings, such as La Rochefoucauld's *Maxims,* in which the authorial *ego* is concealed under a rhetorical pronoun 'we' or the impersonal subject 'one.' It is also made apparent by Retz's formal innovations. In personal memoirs, dominated until then by an emphasis on action and a general lack of self-reflexivity, he pioneered the first-person narrative and a consciously assumed personal perspective. Individualism, however, cannot account for his constantly voiced obsession with communication, mediation, establishing relationships, defining and creating community. Its opposite, the passionate interest in the social bond and its baroque forms, is in fact a central element in his political views.

A Peculiar Political Theory

The motif of (failed) bonding links Retz's autobiography to most of his other writings. Such is the case with his earliest work, *La conjuration du comte de Fiesque* (The Conspiracy of the count of Fieschi) a history of a failed sixteenth-century insurrection in Genoa, composed in his early twenties after the Italian historian Mascardi. The text opens with a description of 'the lack of union that existed among [Genoans] and the seeds of hatred that the previous divisions had left in their hearts.'[22] Contrary to Mascardi, Retz uses this dissent to justify the conjurors. He also establishes a direct parallel between political tyranny in Genoa and the situation in France under Richelieu. The reader can sense his identification with the faction leader, described as a noble hero in search of glory. The theme of union and dissent, prominent in this work as well as in the political pamphlets composed by Retz during the course of the Fronde,[23] may help shed better light on his political ideas, representative of baroque thought at large.

These ideas remain largely implicit in the *Memoirs*. Since Retz saw himself primarily as a man of action, and a witness interested in historical truth, he did not elaborate any abstract model of the state of nature, the civil society or the origins of political power. Critics note for instance that he 'offers nothing precise in the way of a theory of sovereignty' or that his analyses 'pertain neither to history nor to political theory.'[24] The few general statements that accompany his explanation of the causes of the Fronde, and of the historical evolution of royal authority in France, are mainly grounded in the prevailing political thought of his time with its unquestioned foundation, the divine right of power. In its broadest terms, this traditional doctrine of the catholic Church drawn from St Paul's teachings via St Augustine can be summarized in the statement, *Non est potestas nisi a Deo* (there is no power that does not come from God). In other terms, political power – even if instituted by human acts such as a pact, a covenant, or an election – rests on the fact that God condones human choice. In this 'top-down' scheme, human decisions were seen as the 'channel' and God as the 'source' of sovereignty. This theory is, however, not to be confused with the doctrine of monarchical absolutism, since it applies to any kind of society, aristocracies as well as democracies.[25] It was accepted both by the defenders of absolutism, such as Bossuet (who wrote some time after Retz), and its detractors, such as the Protestant thinker Jurieu.

But while Retz undoubtedly subscribes to this commonly accepted general model, his views on the political bond are somewhat more peculiar. They are revealed in his lengthy analysis of the Fronde, which he sees as an inevitable response to the deteriorating bonds between kings and subjects over two centuries. For that situation he blames the kings' advisers or prime ministers: he accuses Richelieu of forming 'dans la plus légitime des monarchies, la plus scandaleuse et la plus dangereuse tyrannie qui ait peut-être jamais asservi un Etat' (194) (in the most lawful of all monarchies, the most scandalous and most dangerous tyranny, that has ever enslaved a kingdom) (82), and mocks Mazarin for trying to imitate Richelieu's acts without his savoir-faire and hence without success. Retz's descriptions of the tensions between the prince and his subjects show his understanding of the political bond at large. Not unexpectedly, for this nobleman interested in history, the ideal exists only in a distant past:

> Les rois qui ont été sages et qui ont connu leurs véritables intérêts ont rendu les parlements dépositaires de leurs ordonnances, particulièrement pour se décharger d'une partie de l'envie et de la haine que l'exécution des plus saintes et même des plus nécessaires produit quelquefois. Ils n'ont pas cru s'abaisser en s'y liant eux-mêmes, semblables à Dieu qui obéit toujours à ce qu'il a commandé une fois. (195)

> [Kings that have been wise, and that have known their true interests, have deposited their own ordinances in the hands of their parliaments, with a view chiefly of discharging themselves of part of the envy and hatred which the execution of these ordinances, even of those that are the most necessary and the most sacred, must sometimes occasion. They have not thought it beneath them, to bind themselves to the observation of them: like, in that case, God Almighty, who himself always follows what he has once decreed.] (83)

Contrary to expectations, Retz's comparison of the king with the Divinity serves here to infirm rather than to confirm the absolutist argument. An apparently Cartesian logical sequence where God is needed only to set the universe in motion according to immutable laws to which he then subjects himself, while it appears to express Retz's respect for the kings, also denies their independence, their position of being 'absolutus,' detached from law. Such reasoning puts in question both the primacy of faith over the mechanical, material world (as Pascal rightly pointed out in his criticism of Descartes) and any notion of a mystical political power. Retz's formulation also makes it clear that he views the relationship of ruler/ruled as one between two distinct and unequal parties. Absolutist doctrines insisted on a deep and constant agreement between the king's and the people's wills. For Retz, whose formulation here is rather exceptional among his contemporaries, their bond is characterized by inevitable envy and hatred and it requires the mediation of laws and their repository, the parliament. His phrasing insists on dissent and reciprocal obligations rather than on union and subordination, though the latter is certainly viewed as fundamental as well. The mediating role of the law comes to the fore when Retz attributes all past revolts in France to 'le renversement des anciennes lois, l'anéantissement de ce milieu qu'elles ont posé entre les peuples et les rois' (199) (the overthrowing of the ancient laws, the annihilation of that middle ground they have placed between the people and the kings) (89). His choice of terms underscores his views of the two parties in an inevitable, almost structural, conflict as well as the value he attaches to a 'middle ground.' Significantly, as well, Retz systematically uses the plural form, 'the kings,' when speaking of the social bond or pact. The singular form, generally used by theorists of absolutist monarchy, serves to represent the state (or king) as a singular, immutable, ideal construct, identical with itself. It anchors facts in rights and interprets history through ideology. In other terms, it transforms historical contingencies into an eternal edifice. Retz's underlying reasoning runs opposite: not unlike the sixteenth-century constitutionalist theorists, he grounds his vision of the state in French history, and describes the political bond as a its product rather than an ideal construction.[26] The kings are understood as historical beings in a succession and not as the eternal mystical construct expressed by the ritual formula '*Le roi est mort. Vive le roi!*'

It is worth noting that for Retz the quality of the bond between the ruler and the ruled is the factor that ultimately determines the state's well-being and safety. He elaborates on it elsewhere, in his recollections of the famous 'day of the barricades' in Paris. Facing popular insurrection, Anne of Austria had sent the co-adjutor of Paris (his title at the time) an envoy who begged him to calm the revolted populace. However, as Retz's earlier interventions on her behalf had brought him, instead of gratitude, accusations that he was actually fomenting the riots, he now refused to act and assured her messenger that he was powerless. Of course, both men knew perfectly well that his protestations of fidelity were faked and Retz concludes with the following remark: 'les favoris des deux derniers siècles n'ont su ce qu'ils ont fait, quand ils ont réduit en style l'égard effectif que les rois doivent avoir pour leurs sujets; il y a, comme vous voyez, des conjonctures dans lesquelles, par une conséquence nécessaire, l'on réduit en style l'obéissance réelle que l'on doit aux rois' (231) (The ministers of the two last centuries knew not what they did when they reduced to words only the true regard which kings ought to have for their subjects; there happens, you see, conjunctures wherein by a necessary consequence, the real obedience which is owed to kings, is reduced only to words) (126).

In his view, a defect in the political bond between the king and his subjects causes society's collapse. And though there is no suggestion in the *Memoirs* of the idea of a contract,[27] Retz emphasizes the need for mutual regard and sentiments of indebtedness by both parties, as well as their acknowledgment and respect of obligations. It is precisely to the decline of such feelings that he attributes the Fronde revolt. Citing the ill-famed Finance superintendent, Particelli d'Emeri, who ruthlessly increased taxes after promising the contrary and declared on that occasion that 'honesty befits only merchants,' Retz comments that the malady of the social body is at its worst 'quand ceux qui commandent ont perdu la honte, parce que c'est justement le moment dans lequel ceux qui obéissent perdent le respect' (200) (when those that command have lost all shame, because from that moment those who obey lose all respect) (90). The ideal political bond thus sketched out rests on linking sentiments to acts, on maintaining good faith through its external manifestations. But, in Retz's opinion, dissimulation and lies have long taken its place in France.

Reflecting on the respective roles of might and right in the political bond he further writes: 'Les monarchies les plus établies ... ne se soutiennent que par l'assemblage des armes et des lois; et cet assemblage est si nécessaire que les unes ne se peuvent maintenir sans les autres. Les lois désarmées tombent dans le mépris; les armes qui ne sont pas modérées par les lois tombent bientôt dans l'anarchie' (195) (The most established monarchies ... cannot subsist but by the union of laws, and of arms, and that union is so necessary that the one cannot be maintained without the help of the other. Disarmed laws fall into disrepute, and arms that are not tempered by laws turn quickly to anarchy) (84).

At first, his formulation appears very reminiscent of Pascal's famous fragment on might and justice.[28] What unites them is the awareness of a blurring between appearances and reality, the conviction that might ultimately comes to *constitute* its opposite, right. But whereas Pascal, from his juxtaposition of unarmed justice and disguised might, derives a positive if unjust solution and concludes to the actual supremacy of the latter, Retz simply deplores 'l'aveuglement de ceux qui ne font consister l'autorité que dans la force' (195) (the blindness of those who make authority consist in sheer force) (84). While in Pascal's thought the realm of politics is ultimately subordinated to the higher order of faith, which gives meaning to its (unjust) structure, for Retz there is no higher, transcendental agency. His formulation places him squarely in the non-dialectical political Imaginary of the baroque period.[29] His views imply an unmediated, unsolved antithesis, an aporia of a kind: for him the political bond, necessarily grounded in dissent and misunderstanding, is the highest truth.

A Baroque Political Pact

The most explicit development of this motif occurs as Retz describes how the Fronde insurrection was, paradoxically, started by the very institution meant to maintain the political order, the parliament. He asserts that the parliamentary debates on the lawfulness of levying new taxes were in themselves dangerous to the monarch, because they opened tacitly accepted practices and unwritten laws to public debate. He writes:

> Il gronda sur l'édit du tariffe; et aussitôt qu'il eut seulemet murmuré, tout le monde s'éveilla. L'on chercha en s'éveillant comme à tâtons, les lois: l'on ne les trouva plus; l'on s'effara. L'on cria, l'on se les demanda; et dans cette agitation les questions que leurs explication firent naître, d'obscures qu'elles étaient et vénérables par leur obscurité, devinrent problématiques, et dès là, à l'égard de la moitié du monde, odieuses. Le peuple entra dans le sanctuaire: il leva le voile qui doit toujours couvrir tout ce que l'on peut dire, tout ce que l'on peut croire du droit des peuples et de celui des rois qui ne s'accordent jamais si bien ensemble que dans le silence. La salle du Palais profana ces mystères. (201)

> [They grumbled at the tax edict; and no sooner was their rumbling heard, but every body began to awake. At their awaking, they groped in the dark to find out the laws, but no laws were to be found. People began to be

scared, and to call aloud for them; and in this agitation, the questions that arose because of the explanations provided, from obscure which they were before, and made venerable by their being so, became doubtful, and from thence hateful to half of the people. The populace penetrated the sanctuary, and there they pulled off the veil which must always cover anything one may say or believe about the respective rights of the people and of the kings, *rights which never agree better than when they are not spelled out.*[30] The lower house [of the parliament] profaned these mysteries.] (91)

This passage is crucial for understanding Retz's vision of the political bond. Indeed, the issue of the respective rights of the rulers and the ruled grounds all political theory. Retz does not discuss society *in abstracto*, nor does he go as far as to posit a state of nature in order to explain the origins of society, as did the natural philosophers of his time. The remarks on the bonds that constitute the French monarchy thus encapsulate his understanding of the social pact. As in the exemplary anecdote quoted earlier, Retz believes that the tacit agreement which creates a communion is in fact, necessarily, a misunderstanding. To put it in other terms, a well-managed misunderstanding provides the sole basis for society's union. This is diametrically opposed to absolutist political doctrines, based on the central postulate that the prince's will is identical to, *in itself constitutes*, the people's will. Such an identity, often naturalized in terms of paternal love, traditionally served to justify absolutism and distinguish it from tyranny; it was called the 'mystery of state.'[31] For Retz as well, the monarchy is founded on a secret, but it is one of dissent and not of self-identity. In spite of the religious overtones of his imagery (sanctuary, profanated etc.), there is nothing mystical about the state's founding secret. Beneath the veil of tradition lurks nothingness. In fact, to profane the state's founding mystery means for Retz not only, as it did for Augustinians, to uncover the violence of its origin, but to expose its inherent fragility. What should not be unveiled is that there is no social covenant, so to speak, since an agreement has no substance if the parties do not understand its clauses in the same manner. The reality of the pact lies in the subjects' right (and ability!) to break it if they so decided, as Retz states in the preceding paragraph: anger, which causes people to believe that they can raise a revolution, makes it really possible. Monarchy lasts only so long as no one dares contemplate revolt. Consensus is based on keeping the option of dissent secret. In fact, the only true agreement *is* that of concealment.

Further development of that political paradox is to be found in a speech Retz made to the prince de Condé to explain the conflict concerning the famous resolutions adopted at the meeting of the 'Chambre Saint-Louis,' with which the parliamentary Fronde began. Mazarin, in anger, provoked the parliament by asking: did they want to declare that they were setting limits to royal authority? The magistrates evaded answering, which Retz calls an act of wisdom. Had they answered positively, as they might have done in the heat of the argument, they would have toppled down the state. He then concludes:

> Chaque monarchie a le sien [mystère]. Celui de la France consiste dans cet espèce de silence religieux et sacré dans lequel on ensevelit, en obéissant presque toujours aveuglément aux rois, le droit que l'on ne veut croire avoir de s'en dispenser que dans les occasions où il ne serait pas même de leur service de leur plaire. (257)

> [Every monarchy has its mystery. That of France consists in a kind of religious and sacred silence wherein the people, by obeying the kings (almost always blindly) bury the right they believe they have to do otherwise; which right they are willing to take up only in such emergencies when their obedience would be a disservice to their Kings.] (155)

Retz's complex formulation, with its double negation, aptly expresses (and veils!) the state's mystical foundation. Here again, he affirms that it consists in keeping secret, concealing from others and from oneself, the right to disobey the kings' orders. Long rehearsed by nobility, the argument that subjects have the right to disobey when such disobedience is in the monarch's benefit was well known in Retz's time: Corneille too thought that obedience to the king without warning him of his true interest was courtly cowardice.[32] In the recent English revolution the disobedience argument had just been re-appropriated by the insurgents, who beheaded their king's mortal body in the name of the immortal one.[33] But Retz's ambiguous formulation can also be interpreted in a less restrictive sense, as the English translator did. In other terms, the subjects might believe that they *always* have the right to disobey, and yet, take advantage of that right only when they feel that it would be in the monarch's interest.[34] Retz foresees the revolutionary potential of voicing such a right, and he bases the very existence of the French absolutist monarchy on the necessity to keep it hidden from the public eye and even from oneself. In this respect, he could be called a Pascalian without Pascal's higher order of faith, a political cynic who understands both the arbitrariness and fragility of the political order and yet supports it. In his speech to Condé, Retz indeed laments the fact that the people started peering through the veil of the state's mystery, but he deems it much more dangerous that the veil be lifted by the parliament 'in due form and by decree,' as had almost occurred because of Mazarin's imprudence. Had it happened, Retz writes, the parliament would have made revered laws out of what used to be a secret, or at least treated as such: it is clear that he is speaking of the notion of political rights.

Retz's metaphors, borrowed from the religious cult, might indicate a close relationship between the secret and the sacred. The foundation of divine monarchy is its mystical character. But divinely willed mystery is not identical to the human strategy of concealment to which Retz alludes. For him, strategic secrecy about the founding pact allows for an understanding which, although fake, maintains the status quo in the monarchy. It hides the non-existence of the pact or, more precisely, its different interpretations by the parties involved. There is no intimation by Retz that a social contract exists or would even be desirable. But if the state's delicate, dynamic balance can only be upheld through a pretended pact, then the absolutist state exists only as an efficient illusion. Retz displays an acute awareness of the divine monarchy's theoretical fragility in a post-Machiavellian world which no longer rests on faith.[35] It may be that he is basically a social realist who presents the state of facts as a model, rather than the reverse. His social pact founded on a necessary opaqueness and concealment, needless to say, is the exact opposite of Rousseau's contract based on total transparency and openness.

Understandably, the same paradox – adequately rendered by the phrase 'together apart' – characterizes Retz's own conduct as he describes it in the *Memoirs*. On the one hand, he constantly highlights the need to maintain the social and political ties of a state: he criticizes the Queen Regent and Mazarin for not keeping their word and for mistrusting their subjects. In the prime minister's broken promises he detects the hidden rot that slowly and imperceptibly gnaws at the social fabric of the state. Justifying his own participation in the insurgency by his disgust at such behaviour, he stresses his own close ties with the Parisian clergy and people, as well as with his allies, and notes that he never gave his word if he could not follow through. Retz maintained a retinue of faithful men around him and had cordial relations even with some of his enemies, as both contemporaries and later historians have generally confirmed. This indeed made the prelate so influential in Paris as to arouse hatred in the young king. In the heyday of absolutism and long after Retz was dead, the famous Bossuet best summed up his enemy's integrity with the phrase, 'cet homme si fidèle aux particuliers, si redoutable à l'État' (this man so faithful to individuals, and so threatening to the State).[36]

On the other hand, however, from witnesses as well as from his own admissions, we learn that Retz cultivated duplicity and dissimulation. He remains, here again, exemplary of the baroque age defined by the proliferation of its outwardly appearances: its etiquette, its façades, its carefully choreographed dances, its mannerism in art. Craftiness, prescribed even in the friendly relations of equals, reigned supreme at the court. As apparent from Acetto's influential *Honest Dissimulation*, all manuals stressed the need to feign: both Baltasar Gracian's writings, widely read in seventeenth-century France, and Nicolas Faret's *L'Honnête homme ou l'art de plaire à la cour* underlined that crucial capacity of the courtier to read others while dissimulating himself. Notions of *feinte*, or *simulation* played an important role even in philosophy, as evidenced by Descartes's famous *Larvatus Prodeo* (I advance masked), his use of the hyperbolical *feinte* as the basis of the *Cogito*, or by the title of Francis Bacon's sixth *Essay*, 'Of Simulation and Dissimulation.' It is obvious that the political sphere, even more than the social one, had to rely on the art of concealment. Most treatises on politics construct the prince as a master (dis)simulator: *The Politician's Breviary*, apocryphal and sometimes attributed to Mazarin, thus opens with the following lines: '"Simulate and dissimulate," or "Know thyself and others," which unless I am mistaken amount to the same.'[37] And Bossuet defines the statesman as follows: 'On ne le découvre pas tant ses conduites sont profondes, mais il sonde le coeur des autres; et on dirait qu'il devine, tant ses conjectures sont sûres' (So deep are his strategies that he cannot be uncovered; but he scans others' minds and his conjectures are so reliable that he appears to read through them).[38]

When set in this context, Retz's conduct becomes more understandable: given that his notion of the founding political pact is defined by internal distance and hidden misunderstanding rather than by closeness and transparency, it becomes all the more important to multiply its outward signs. Such signs would in time come to constitute the very essence of the bonds he himself cultivated, as demonstrated by his epistolary strategy, his political allegiances, his friendships. An inward pessimism about the social pact might be precisely what motivated its eternal reaffirmation by means of civility and etiquette all through the baroque era. Retz's strategy of switching, making and breaking factions, amply illuminated by historians, thus amounts to valuing the forms and rituals of bonding over its substance. And all the protestations to the contrary that fill his *Memoirs* were perhaps necessitated precisely by this lucid understanding of the founding paradox of the monarchy.

For it is obvious that the Fronde *factions*, like the exemplary group described in our initial anecdote, or the founding political pact of the state, were fraught with the same concealed misunderstanding and dissent. The Enlightenment community would later define itself around a common project, but the baroque one – exemplified by the faction – delineated itself negatively, through failure, and empty forms: ostentatious exchanges of regards, soon to be broken public oaths, protestations of fidelity. These representations, endlessly staged and multiplied, would come to represent and replace for Retz the very substance of the desired bonds, and the principal thread of his narrative. In fact, as his *Memoirs* unroll, the real tenets of the insurgents' transactions fade in comparison with the description of their ever more flamboyant bonding rituals. Thus, at one point, when asked to keep his alliance with the rebel duchess de Bouillon, Retz swore that he would sign a promise to that effect with his blood. He recounts that she immediately took him up on his word, tied his thumb with a silk ribbon, drew his blood and made him sign it. Needless to say, the declaration, thrown into the fire by the duke de Bouillon who protested his unconditional trust of Retz's word, did not prevent their eventual breaking off of the political alliance and friendship. Significantly, in consistence with his obsession for the rituals of togetherness brought to light above, in which the (textual) representation is substituted for the missing communion, Retz reproduced in his *Memoirs* the entire oath word for word (337). The amplitude of the obsession illustrated by this episode testifies that the Fronde was indeed, as contemporary historians point out, a period of renegotiating the social bond in the absolutist monarchy. And Retz's baroque social pact, grounded in concealed dissent, may have been his ultimate coming to terms with the reality of absolutism.

Notes

1 Cardinal de Retz, *Mémoires*, in *Oeuvres* (Paris: Gallimard, 1984), 161–4; English translation by Thomas Evans: *Memoirs of the Cardinal de Retz: Contain-*

ing the Particulars of His Own Life, with the Most Secret Transactions of the French Court and the Civil Wars (London: T. Becket, T. Cadell, and T. Evans, in the Strand, 1774, 32–5). Translations are mine, modified from the English edition where appropriate, and indicated by the page number of the English and the French edition in the body of the text.

2 On the baroque belief in magic and in satanic rites see Robert Mandrou, *Introduction à la France Moderne (1500–1640): Essai de psychologie historique* (Paris: Albin Michel, 1961), 310–14.

3 See André Bertière, *Le Cardinal de Retz mémorialiste* (Paris: Klincksieck, 1977), 450 and 465.

4 Jean Rousset, *La Littérature de l'âge baroque en France: Circé et le paon* (Paris: José Corti, 1954).

5 That is the account given by the contemporary gossip monger, Tallemant des Réaux. See Retz, *Mémoires*, 254 (editor's note), as well as Derek A. Watts, who discusses at some length Retz's conclusion on history writing as 'the monopoly of an élite' in his *Cardinal de Retz: The Ambiguities of a Seventeenth-Century Mind* (Oxford: Oxford University Press, 1980), 49 and 120.

6 Watts makes ambiguity, tension, and paradox the central structuring principles of his important study of Retz. André Bertière, another distinguished Retz scholar, notes that his descriptions of people and events give ample room to the irrational and the baroque *Cardinal de Retz*, 206.

7 Gilles Deleuze, *Le Pli: Leibniz et le baroque* (Paris: Minuit, 1988).

8 For a similar analysis of moralist writings see Serge Doubrovski, 'Vingt propositions sur l'amour-propre: de Lacan à La Rochefoucauld,' *Confrontations* 3 (Spring 1980): 51–67.

9 Her identity has not been established so far, although critics speculate that she might have been the famous epistolary author, Mme de Sévigné, or her daughter, Mme de Grignan. From Retz's references, it is clear that this person really existed and he takes care to protect her anonymity. See Bertière, *Le Cardinal de Retz*, and especially Watts, *Cardinal de Retz*, 40.

10 Roland Barthes, *Writing Degree Zero*, trans. Annette Lavers and Colin Smith (London: Cape, 1984), 38.

11 Marc Fumaroli, 'Retz: des *Mémoires* en forme de conversation galante,' in *La diplomatie de l'esprit: De Montaigne à La Fontaine* (Paris: Hermann, 1994), 252.

12 Retz writes that, jumping on the occasion, he suggested that they retreat to her cabinet, to which she replied that it would have to follow their retreat from Paris; he concludes laconically: 'Thus ended our relationship.'

13 Instead of answering Richelieu's 'advances' and the recommendations that he was given to pay him homage, Retz 'paid him back with very bad excuses.'

14 Remerciement des bourgeois de Paris a M. le Coadjuteur, Paris (François

Preuveray, 1649), cited by H. Carrière, 'Sincérité et création littéraire dans les *Mémoires* du cardinal de Retz,' *XVIIe siècle* 94–5 (1971): 51. See also my article, 'Démarches et itinéraires de la Fronde: Paris dans les *Mémoires* du cardinal de Retz,' *Papers on Seventeenth-Century French Literature,* Biblio17, 131 (2001): 35–44.
15 Tallemant des Réaux, *Historiettes* (Paris: Gallimard, 1961), 2:305.
16 See Guicharnaud, *Molière, une aventure théâtrale* (Paris: Gallimard, 1963).
17 Retz, *Oeuvres,* 225.
18 Simone Bertière, Introduction to Retz's *Memoirs* (Paris, Garnier, 1987), 21. René Pintard, 'La conjuration de Fiesque ou l'héroïsation d'un factieux,' in *Héroïsme et création littéraire sous les règnes d'Henri IV et de Louis XIII,* ed. Noémi Hepp and Georges Livet (Paris: Klincksieck, 1974).
19 Kossmann, E.H., *La Fronde* (Leiden: Universitaires Pers Leiden, 1954), 151–4.
20 Nannerl O. Keohane, *Philosophy and the State in France. The Renaissance to the Enlightenment* (Princeton: Princeton University Press, 1980), 223–9.
21 Albert Hirschman, *The Passions and the Interests: Political Arguments for Capitalism before Its Triumph* (Princeton: Princeton University Press, 1977), 45.
22 Retz, *Oeuvres,* 3.
23 On these pamphlets, known as *Mazarinades,* see Christian Jouhaud, *Mazarinades: La Fronde des mots* (Paris: Aubier, 1985).
24 Watts, *Cardinal de Reitz,* 185; A. Bertière, *Le Cardinal de Retz,* 223.
25 Dérathé, *Jean-Jacques Rousseau et la science politique de son temps* (Paris: Vrin, 1970), 27–47.
26 His accusations of tyranny, as well as his references to the parliament, also bespeak of a constitutionalist bent in his thought.
27 Watts, *Cardinal de Retz,* 186.
28 Pascal, *Pensées,* #103–298, trans. W.F. Trotter (New York: E.P. Dutton, 1931): 'Justice without might is helpless, might without justice is tyrannical .... We must then combine justice and might, and for this end make what is just strong, or what is strong made just ... Justice is subject to dispute. Might is easily recognized and is not disputed ... And thus, being unable to make what is just strong, we have made what is strong just' (La justice sans la force est impuissante, la force sans la justice est tyrannique ... Il faut donc mettre ensemble la justice et la force, et pour cela faire que ce qui est juste soit fort ou que ce qui est fort soit juste ... La justice est sujette à dispute. La force est très reconnaissable et sans dispute ... Et ainsi ne pouvant faire que ce qui est juste fût fort, on a fait que ce qui est fort fût juste).
29 See Henry Méchoulan, *L'État baroque: regards sur la pensée politique de la France du premier XVIIe siècle* (Paris: Vrin, 1985).

30 My emphasis.
31 Roland Mousnier, *Les institutions de la France sous la monarchie absolue* (Paris: P.U.F., 1980).
32 J.T. Letts, *Le Cardinal de Retz historien et moraliste du possible* (Paris: Nizet, 1966), 152.
33 In France, it was to reappear in the early eighteenth century, when the chancelor d'Aguesseau claimed the right to disobey Louis XIV for his own good.
34 Significantly, critics have avoided the detailed interpretation of this much quoted passage, and Letts even misquotes it, omitting the dubious second '*que*' (*que dans les occasions*), which entirely changes its meaning.
35 On Retz's relationship to Machiavelli see Watts, *Cardinal de Retz*, 157–67. His relationship to the Hobbesian model merits further exploration, especially as Hobbes lived in France from 1630 to 1650, and was connected, as well as Retz, with the exiled court of Henrietta-Marie and Prince Charles II.
36 Bossuet, *Oraisons funèbres* (Paris: Garnier, 1961), 327. The oration was pronounced in 1688, at the death of the minister Le Tellier.
37 Jules Mazarin, *Bréviaire des politiciens* (Paris: Clima, 1984), 17.
38 Bossuet, *Oeuvres* (Paris: Firmin Didot, 1847), 472.

chapter twelve

A Different Kind of Wonder? Women's Writing in Early Modern Spain

LISA VOLLENDORF

> The true rule [of poetry] is to be able to break all rules at the right time and place, adapting oneself to current customs and to the taste of one's age.
>
> Giambattista Marino

As suggested by Giambattista Marino's assertion that poets must know how and when to break the rules, baroque authors demonstrated an intense self-consciousness with regard to the customs and taste of the age. Marino's comments gesture to literary tradition as well as to an emerging mass readership. Indeed, poetry, drama, and prose fiction had the consumer in mind. Writers sought a dense, intellectualized aesthetic aimed at subverting the overt accessibility of Petrarchan conventions; many were guided by the desire to provoke *admiratio* – admiration, shock, wonder. Concerned with linguistic variation and stylistic techniques in tune and in tension with that of previous generations, intellectuals throughout Western Europe pondered and practised the wonderful, convoluted art of baroque rhetoric. In Spain, authors cultivated every possible genre with baroque flair. Poets invented new words and wrote tangled syntax; popular plays frequently produced bleeding bodies or pale cadavers to audiences; and fiction relied on unlikely coincidences to move the plots forward. All in the service of wonder. And, I would hasten to add, all in the service of a burgeoning literary establishment primarily made up of men from similar class and educational backgrounds.

Scholarship has shown that we can understand much of the baroque by studying men's texts. Recent attention to marginalized or only recently recovered cultural production suggests a correlative argument: we cannot understand gender relations, class, and ideology without looking to the large numbers of texts written by women in the period. Although excluded from access to education, women produced literary and historical texts that still await recovery in the archives. The strategies used by women as they presented themselves to the public in fictional, autobiographical, and Inquisition texts have much to teach us about women's perceptions of authority and their place in Spanish culture of the seventeenth century.

In spite of the differences in writing for the public book market, for convent readers, and for Inquisition purposes, many women's texts self-consciously engage issues of authority and representation.[1] Of course, strategies of representation used by women in texts produced for the public book market differ from those used in texts produced for consumption by nuns and priests. Self-consciously literary texts tended to be written by the upper classes, while depositions and hagiographies capture a broader spectrum of society in terms of class, education, and ethnic backgrounds. Female writers of poetry, drama, and fiction experimented with long sentences, broken syntax, and intricate plots. Unlike their male counterparts, they also focused intensely on women's interpersonal relationships and perspectives. Fictional representations of female interpersonal interaction find their counterparts in accounts of women's life stories in Inquisition records and convent biographies. All told, this understudied body of literature provides rich information about women's attitudes and life experiences in the early modern period.

Hispanic women's cultural production has yet to be mined fully for its historical and cultural significance. What did it mean to be a noblewoman presenting one's work to the public book market? How did it feel to be a single woman defending one's occupation of matchmaking to an Inquisition tribunal? What did it mean to defend one's connection with God while also trying not to incur charges of illuminism or Protestantism? For women living in a period suspicious of female spirituality, autonomy, and intellectualism, these questions took on very specific meanings. By looking at how women sought authority and represented themselves and their issues to the world, I have come to question the gendered nature of the claims scholars make about the early modern period. Put simply, the shock, surprise, and aesthetic pleasure that constitute what we think of as the baroque poetics of wonder take on entirely new meanings in works produced by women. Tracing women's self-representational techniques in fiction, depositions, and biographies reveals that women of all backgrounds in early modern Spain employed highly self-conscious strategies aimed at legitimizing the position of woman as an authoritative position from which to speak and be heard.

Women in the Public Sphere

The handful of women known to have written for the emerging book market in seventeenth-century Spain produced texts that exhibit an acute awareness of the literary trends and rules of the period. The most popular female writer from the period articulated the amazement produced by the fact that she was a woman. María de Zayas writes in the preface to her 1637 novella collection, *The Enchantments of Love*, 'Oh my reader, no doubt it will amaze you that a woman has the nerve, not only to write a book but actually to publish it, for publication is the crucible in which the purity of genius is tested; until writing is set in letters of lead, it has no real value.'[2] Zayas also defends the biological similarities between men and women (based on the theory of humours) and claims intellectual equality. At the end of this philosophically and rhetorically complex preface, Zayas calls on consumers' chivalry, begging them to continue reading out of the obligation to treat women well.

Zayas's novellas incorporate the same complexity of style seen in other writers of the period. Yet in terms of their thematics, the novellas provoke a sense of wonder different from that seen in anything written by male authors. Zayas exemplifies the different kind of wonder that women writing for the book market evoked in their readers. A scene of wife-beating in one tale, 'The Power of Love,' captures this author's unique literary aesthetic. Zayas relies on Renaissance tropes of female beauty to generate sympathy for a woman whose husband, 'incensed in an infernal rage, began to beat her with his hands, so much so that the white pearls of her teeth, bathed in the blood shed by his angry hand, quickly took on the form of red coral.'[3] Laying bare the cruelty of early modern humanistic beliefs about gender relations, Zayas elicits wonderment through prose that relies on a subversion of poetic tropes normally used to capture female beauty.

In her direct treatment of domestic violence and social inequities, Zayas uses *admiratio* as a way to bolster her calls for women's inclusion in the workings of society. She depicts many a bleeding, beaten, and dying body. The character beaten by her husband in 'The Power of Love' also declaims the 'vain legislators of the world' for rendering women 'powerless and deny[ing] us access to pen and sword.'[4] Zayas's treatment of topics as wide ranging as sexuality, social exclusion, and violence led her to be branded lascivious, vulgar, and unfeminine by nineteenth-century critics. Many of her female characters are killed by their lovers or male family members, for example; two men have sex with each other; and a white woman's sexual appetite is so overwhelming that her black lover begs her not to take further advantage of him on his death bed. These issues – of sexuality, family politics, violence, and social justice – provide the key to understanding a female baroque aesthetic that relies more on an experiential than a rhetorical dimension of writing.

Zayas's would-be successor, Mariana de Carvajal, appeals to female experience in her 1660 collection, *Christmas in Madrid*. Reminiscent of Zayas's rhetorical manoeuvres, Carvajal's preface uses motherhood as the basis for the writer's authority. She refers to her book as a 'useless abortion of my small wit' and pleads for a sympathetic reading of texts that deal with widows and their children, since 'it is the pressing obligation of a noble heart to alleviate such disconsolate pain.'[5] While Carvajal's prologue calls on the reader's sympathy for mothers and widows, her detailed descriptions of household interiors, clothing, and food contribute to a unique style in what are otherwise quite conventional texts. In addition to being two of only a few examples of successfully published women, Zayas and Carvajal exemplify the thematic differences of early modern women's writing. Their fiction clearly brings a new perspective to bear on gender and family issues. First and foremost, their novellas show us that the rules of engagement were different for women, as Zayas and Carvajal express that their gender alone was cause for wonderment in the period.

One topic that illuminates the particularities of this female aesthetic is the issue of homosocialism. Zayas's emphasis on violence against women finds its complement in a strong endorsement of female solidarity. The female narrators often condemn those women who betray others, for example, and friendships cross class and ethnic lines in some of the tales. The focus on women's alliances and spaces is most apparent in the frame tale, but in the sixth story of *The Disenchantments* it metamorphoses to incorporate female homoeroticism as another facet of women's existence. In 'Love for the Sake of Conquest,' a cross-dressed suitor woos the young Laurela. The man successfully poses as a handmaid and manages to secure employment in Laurela's home. Like many literary examples of cross-dressing, Esteban/Estefanía's relationship with the pre-pubescent Laurela provides a front for a homoerotic exchange that culminates in an overt defence of same-sex erotic alliances. Esteban/Estefanía explains that his/her sex bears no relevance on his/her desire: 'since the soul is the same in male and female, it matters not whether I'm a man or a woman. Souls aren't male or female and true love dwells in the soul, not in the body. One who loves the body with only the body cannot say that is love; it's lust.'[6] In the end, Laurela discovers Esteban/Estefanía's true male identity and has sex with him. Then her family, in punishment for what they view as sexual corruption, kill her. While the gruesome outcome of the tale quashes any sense of idealism we might glean from the endorsement of homoeroticism, the first part of the tale probes female same-sex desire.

Mariana de Carvajal takes a different approach to female homosociality. As the beneficiary of her predecessor's successful intervention into the book market, this author produced a volume that strikes a balance between convention and innovation. *Christmas in Madrid* appears to deviate very little from the conventions of the genre; indeed, critics tend to see it as conservative in both ideology and style. The frame tale revolves around the affairs of an aristocratic household, for example, and the stories themselves explore the standard themes of marital and familial politics. The detailed descriptions of clothing and interiors constitute a unique domestic aesthetic for which Carvajal has been praised and condemned.[7]

Although Carvajal's writing has been viewed as politically disengaged and tediously detailed, the combination of her aesthetic with the focus on female friendship and desire gives her texts an undeniably different flair that distinguishes them from any other novella collection of the century. For example, the extensive descriptions of domestic space highlight the female focus of the frame tale, in which a widow gathers with her closest circle of friends to tell tales during the Christmas season. The emphasis on women's community shapes our reading of these tales, as it draws our attention to the female characters' experiences. While the mothers in the frame tale support each other as they make decisions on behalf of their unmarried children, for example, the women in the novellas have varying levels of support for (and control over) their decision making.

The stories that have been translated into English exemplify two common depictions of the female experience in Carvajal.[8] In the fifth tale, 'Virtue Is Its Own Reward,' women have little power over their circumstances. In the first, the protagonist Esperanza falls victim to domestic violence and to a nearly successful murder plot before finally marrying the man of her choice. Women's friendships form the backbone of the juxtaposed sixth tale in the collection. In 'Love Conquers All,' the strong-willed protagonist Narcisa surrounds herself with female friends and rejects the advances of all men but one. Disgusted with arrogant suitors and a justice system that fails to protect her from men's aggressive advances, Narcisa relies on a circle of women for friendship and support. Narcisa's suitors are disrespectful and inadequate, but she leads a fulfilled life surrounded by women whose friendships sustain her. Even when the inevitable knight in shining armour appears and Narcisa decides to marry, the tale emphasizes the important role of female friends. From making decisions based on her friends' wishes to responding to their desire to see her, Narcisa operates within a female-centred community of her own creation.[9]

Zayas's and Carvajal's engagement with female homosocialism, homoeroticism, and sexuality suggests that women writers dealt with some topics with a forthrightness and nuance not seen in men's texts. The authors anticipated the wonder that readers would experience when reading books written by women. By constructing fictional worlds based on the interpersonal relationships of female characters, Zayas and Carvajal refused to capitulate to a literary tradition that had little interest in women's concerns. Indeed, they showed themselves to be adept baroque writers who rewrote novella scripts to include a specifically female aesthetic attentive to a range of topics related to intimacy and gender relations.

Women and the Domestic Sphere

Familiar with literary stylistics and tradition, Zayas and Carvajal were unusually well educated. In truth, few women like them existed in the seventeenth century. Those with inferior educational backgrounds certainly did not employ literary techniques to challenge dominant gender ideology with the same intensity and complexity.[10] Yet women of varying class and ethnic backgrounds used different strategies to challenge male authority. One case in point is that of the Portuguese immigrant Bernarda Manuel, who was tried for Judaizing by the Inquisition in 1650.

A member of the merchant class, Manuel probably belonged to a *converso* family that immigrated to Spain after Portugal's annexation in the late sixteenth century. The Holy Office detained her husband, Antonio Borges, before arresting Manuel herself. In spite of the secrecy surrounding names of accusers and the nature of the accusation in Inquisition proceedings, Manuel rightly guessed that Borges had identified her as a fellow Judaizer. The formal accusation against Manuel was broad reaching. She was accused of observing the Law of Moses, proselytizing, and committing offences against the Catholic Church. These charges included wearing clean clothes, resting, and fasting on Saturdays; refusing to eat various foods prohibited by Judaism; attempting to flee the country; and conjuring a spell using a statue of Christ. Based almost entirely on the statements of Manuel's husband, the accusations only found marginal support in the testimony of one witness: their eleven-year-old daughter Inés testified that she had seen her father whip a small statue of Christ. This testimony implicated Manuel, her sister, and her brother-in-law, who were said to be present when the events occurred during a family Christmas gathering in Seville.[11]

In response to the accusations, Manuel did an unusual thing for a defendant of her class and gender: she wrote her own autobiographical statement (a *memorial*) and turned it in to the inquisitors as part of her defence. Inquisition trials always included questions aimed at determining biographical information, such as whether one's family was old or new Christian and whether any proof of their Catholicism existed. Very rarely did non-aristocratic defendants in Spain write their own defence. In the cases of upper-class and protected defendants (such as nuns in royal convents, for example), one might find letters of support from other nobles or functionaries. Some witchcraft cases might contain snippets of chants and spells confiscated from the prisoner's home. Other cases might include transcriptions of dictations given by the defendants. For the most part, though, the writing found in the records was done entirely by scribes.

Manuel, however, submitted a defence written in her own hand. In Portuguese-inflected Castilian, she wrote about her family's wishes that she not marry Borges and the accusations that he had killed his first wife. These details set the stage for the depiction of an unhappy marriage that grew worse as time progressed. Manuel attributed her husband's increasingly abusive, threatening behaviour to an illness described as palsy (*perlesía*). Whether a result of mental illness or a disease such as syphilis, the husband's behaviour included neurosis, physical threats, and accusations of extramarital affairs.

Borges initially accepted his sickness as divine punishment for having mistreated his wife. He later revised this account and blamed Manuel for making him ill in return for all of the bad things he had said about her. Then Borges became convinced that his wife would kill him. He moved his bed so he could sleep in a different room and locked Manuel and the children in a room to sleep together. Unsatisfied that this plan sufficiently isolated his wife from others, he made Manuel sleep downstairs with him again. He accused her of plotting his murder in conjunction with her brother-in-law. Manuel explains the extent of this neurosis when she indicates that Borges began to keep a dagger in his bed, 'saying that dagger was for killing me if he remembered at night and saw me in his room.'[12] Out of fear that she would poison him, he had the children drink and eat before he would touch anything Manuel prepared, and he even went so far as to place his medicine under lock and key so she could not tamper with it.

In addition to describing this physically threatening behaviour, Manuel also details the hardship she faced while living in Seville and the intensification of these problems when Borges later moved the family to Madrid. Once installed in the new city, he began to accuse Manuel of having an affair. Manuel presents this notion as irrational and hostile, and explains that it led her to fear for her life. Indeed, she says of this time, 'Many times I saw my death before my eyes.'[13] Borges, too, saw death before his eyes, but his anxiety about others pursuing him and plotting his death is depicted here as sheer paranoia.

Out of all the representational strategies that she could have used to argue for her innocence in this Judaizing case, Manuel chose to represent herself as a good wife and mother. Contrary to what we might expect, the defendant did not fill these pages with a discussion of the prayers she knew or with details about how many masses she attended a year. Instead, she told the story of a psychologically abusive marriage. Relying on the authority of her identity as mother and wife, Manuel wrote at length about her husband's strange, abusive behaviour. She noted that theirs was a Christian household, but she did not make religious observance the focus of her story.

Manuel relied on a strategy familiar to her, one that related to the primary source of authority (being a mother and a wife) that she had known. With this story she meant to shock the tribunal into letting her go. She attempted to show that she was an ill-treated wife and the only sane adult in her household. Without explicitly stating its goal, this strategy constituted a clear attempt to get the accusations of this crazy man struck from the record. In this regard, Manuel appealed to the logic of the *tacha*, the system by which defendants could remove hostile prosecution witnesses. Historians of the Inquisition have identified this tactic as one of the few resources available to defendants. As Renée Levine

Melammed explains, 'While the use of *tachas* was trying and often exasperating, it occasionally was successful, probably the only successful technique utilized by the defense.'[14] Manuel's desperate appeal to the *tacha* becomes clear at the end of the document, when she writes that her husband saw everything backwards, so if 'all that was good his imagination told him was bad, *how am I to blame?*' (*¿qué culpa tengo yo?*).[15]

In the end, the tribunal was not convinced by this plea. When Manuel faced the threat of torture, she finally confessed to Judaizing and repented for her sins. Had she refused to make such confessions, she could have been tortured, banished, or even relaxed to the secular arm of the law for public execution. As it was, her admission of guilt and her express desire for reconciliation with the Church led to considerably lesser punishments. The Inquisition confiscated all of her worldly goods, obligated her to wear a penitential garment (*sanbenito*), forced her to abjure heresy in the public spectacle of an *auto de fe*, and sentenced her to prison. It is unclear whether she had to serve this sentence; as a mother of five she probably would have been treated with some leniency. However, the subsequent whereabouts of Bernarda Manuel or her offspring are not known.

In addition to providing information about the education of at least some women of the mercantile class, Manuel's document points to an important insight: the strategy of representation that this woman thought most efficacious was that of the abused wife and mother. Manuel's choice coincides with many other women's views towards authority: in numerous records of women's voices and words, the experiences of marriage and motherhood emerge as two of the most common sources of authorization in women's texts. Narrow definitions of femininity attempted to confine women's worth to their roles as wife and mother, of course, yet women circumnavigated strict gender codes in inventive and even startling ways.

The *vida* of Sor Catalina de Jesús y San Francisco (1639–77) exemplifies the means by which women religious reinscribed the concept of motherhood in their spiritual communities. The intense pressures on women to comply with traditional gender expectations come to the fore in *Idea of Perfection and Virtues* (1693).[16] Written by Sor Catalina's son, Padre Juan Bernique, this biography makes use of autobiographical writings to construct a story of one woman's rejection of her role as secular wife and mother. Bernique purports to cite from his mother's autobiographical writings, including her letters, distinguishing her words by placing them in italics. This technique creates a dialogue between the biographer and his subject, yet it is one in which the biographer maintains clear control over the narrative. Bernique says little about his sources, except that he faithfully culled his mother's words from her letters and autobiographical *vidas*. A few points lead us to believe that the citations at least are based on her writings. The style and substance of the quotations seem to coincide with those of other religious women's writing. Perhaps more pertinent to the question of authenticity, Bernique discusses at length Catalina's rejection of sex, her husband, and child-rearing. Such details could not have been easy for a son to confront, and thus it seems even less likely that he would have invented them.

Idea of Perfection rests on a tension between Sor Catalina's rejection of her family and her son's desire to justify his mother's choices. The psychological complexity of the text is most apparent in the sections that reconstruct Sor Catalina's preference for a spiritual life. Sor Catalina is described as having a distaste for marriage, which she 'abhorred' because it was 'contrary to her plans.'[17] Bernique quotes her directly on the topic: '*I entered into marriage with such disgust and hatred that I cannot even truthfully say where this came from because by then I had forgotten my desire and plans that I had to maintain my chastity and become a nun.*'[18]

What was it like for this priest to confront his mother's life choices? Two conflicting perspectives emerge as the story progresses: that of a priest who supported chastity and religiosity and a son who was the offspring of an unhappy union. Sor Catalina's religious narrative takes precedence in the text, of course. From her adolescent aversion to marriage to her entry into the convent upon widowhood, she is depicted as having a natural inclination towards religious life. This imposition of a meta-narrative of predestined religiosity provides a solid structure to a life story that presents many challenges to the biographer. What can a biographer say about a woman who prayed for her husband's death? If that biographer is also the son, as in the case of Bernique, the problem becomes complicated. Bernique has to deal with the fact that, after Catalina begged San Diego to deliver her from her marriage, her husband died rather suddenly. As quoted by Bernique, Catalina wrote, 'The blessed saint answered my petition so quickly that within a month my husband fell ill and he died from that sickness, and then I came to Alcalá.'[19] Although it might seem impossible to put a good spin on this situation, Bernique manages to present his mother in a virtuous light, using various strategies to achieve a positive representation of his subject. Notably, he concurs with his mother's representation of the father's death as part of a divine plan: 'His Majesty disposed to deprive her of her husband.'[20]

Framing the narrative to express the opinions he shared with Sor Catalina, Bernique thus smoothes over the tension created by his mother's bad behaviour and by his relationship to the subject. By interpreting the longed-for death as a piece in the puzzle that God designed for the family, Bernique creates cohesion in the face of contradiction. Predictably, Bernique portrays his father as a martyr who only after death was appreciated fully by his wife. In this view, both mother and father are redeemed by their son's generous depiction of their troubled marriage: while Juan Bernique the elder died a martyr in the eyes of many, Catalina Bernique realized the error of her ways and repented for her bad behaviour in marriage. According to both mother and son, in other words, such behaviour could be attributed to the young woman's poor judgment *and* to God's plan for her. Moreover, Bernique emphasizes his mother's youth throughout the first section of the text, thus giving the impression that youth and inexperience led her to make mistakes in her secular life.

Upon widowhood, Catalina Bernique ignored the advice of those who insisted that she remarry. Instead, the twenty-six-year-old mother of three young children entered the Convent of Saint Claire in Alcalá. Making decisions that flew in the face of social norms regarding motherhood and widowhood, Catalina Bernique became Sor Catalina de Jesús y San Francisco and left her children to be raised by relatives in the secular world. Rather than leave behind her maternal identity, she refashioned it, positioning herself as a spiritual adviser and reformer, founding a school for poor girls and eventually taking her daughters in to be raised there. The reinvention of her maternal identity allowed her to become spiritual mother and counsellor to many girls and women throughout her life. Catalina Bernique's rejection of her secular maternal role freed her to realize her spiritual goals. What society would have viewed as a failure at mother- and wife-hood became the central problem not of her own life, but of her biographer's interpretation of that life. Faced with his mother's documented disregard for marriage, sex, and motherhood, Juan Bernique struggles to project an image of sanctity that downplays Catalina's failure in the realm of secular femininity and emphasizes her success as a religious mother and leader.

The complexities of Bernarda Manuel's and Catalina de Jesús's auto/biographies point to many contradictions in configurations of early modern femininity. Manuel and Sor Catalina recognized the authority accorded to mothers and wives – the only legitimate secular roles for women. Bernarda Manuel attempted to use this authority to bolster her defence in her Inquisition case, yet clearly the inquisitors were not moved. Catalina Bernique refused to capitulate to the pressures placed on her in widowhood and, instead, sought to free herself from what she viewed as the undue burdens of being a mother and a wife. Reinscribing motherhood within her religious order, Sor Catalina finally found a legitimate role that also gave her satisfaction. In the written records of their lives, both women left explicit information about their troubled relationships with their husbands. These records allow us to see the realities of women's social interaction and the limitations of their authority, and thus provide a counterpoint to some of the more idealized representations of women seen, for instance, in Zayas's defence of homoeroticism or Carvajal's safe female-centred world.

This overview of Zayas, Carvajal, Manuel, and Bernique provides only a brief introduction to the abundant literature and documentation that have yet to be examined in terms of women's writing and history. The experiential dimensions of women's texts offer surprisingly explicit information, as they often touch on the intimacies of everyday life. Catalina de Jesús wrote about hating sex and praying for her husband's death. Bernarda Manuel portrayed herself as isolated and mentions that she once forged a friendship with a woman who also practised Judaism. Witnesses in witchcraft cases often talked about mediocre sex lives or physically abusive husbands. Self-consciously literary texts by women also provide a new perspective on female sexuality and intimacy. Zayas's character explicitly defends female homoeroticism, for example, and Carvajal's builds a female-centred adult life.

These examples point to a pattern of thematic and ideological similarities found in a range of women's texts. Indeed, such topics suggest that women found ways to change the rules by expanding what was acceptable for public consumption and by portraying a female-centred view of the world. We can expand our vision of literary and cultural history by studying women's representations of themselves and the world. In the realm of self-consciously literary texts, we see that, rather than seek to amaze the reader through rhetorical dexterity alone, women writers provoked a different kind of wonder first by writing and also by drawing on topics neglected by men. Nuns provided insight into convent life, tensions in the church, and informal systems of education and advice giving. In addition to these literary examples, women whose words are recorded in autobiographies, Inquisition trials, and letters also give clues about an experiential aesthetic whose artistic, cultural, and historical merits we have yet to mine fully. Whether in front of inquisitors or confessors or when presenting fictional stories to the public, women often sought authority and legitimacy through the validation of personal experience.

This personal, experiential aesthetic serves as a reminder of the origins of our ideas about literary and cultural history: what we generally think of as the rules of baroque writing and what we know about the customs and practices of daily life often come from the study of male institutions, dictates, and literature. Varied in their purpose and content, the texts of an aristocratic, best-selling female author (María de Zayas), a widow turned writer (Mariana de Carvajal), a Portuguese immigrant (Bernarda Manuel), and a mother-turned-nun (Catalina Bernique) can lead us to a more profound understanding of gender, class, and authority. This, in turn, will allow us to revisit what we currently understand as *the* baroque aesthetic and to compare the different kinds of wonder evoked by women's texts from the early modern period.

Notes

1 These ideas are the basis for *The Lives of Women: A New History of Inquisitional Spain* (Nashville: Vanderbilt University Press, 2005), which analyses the texts mentioned in the present article. Research for the project has been supported by a Monticello College Foundation Grant through the Newberry Library; University Research, Minority/Women, and Humanities Center Grants from Wayne State University; and an Ahmanson/Getty Fellowship from the UCLA's Center for Seventeenth and Eighteenth Century Studies and William Andrews Clark Memorial Library.
2 María de Zayas, *The Enchantments of Love*, trans. H. Patsy Boyer (Berkeley: University of California Press, 1990), 1.
3 Ibid., 172.
4 Ibid., 175. For an analysis of Zayas in the context of other feminist novella writers, see Josephine Donovan, 'Women and the Framed-Novelle: A Tradition of Their Own,' *Signs* 22, no. 4 (1997): 947–80.
5 Carvajal, *Navidades de Madrid*, ed. Catherine Soriano (Madrid: Comunidad de Madrid, 1993), 5.
6 María de Zayas, *The Disenchantments of Love*, trans. H. Patsy Boyer (Binghamton, NY: SUNY Press, 1997), 224.
7 Until recently, most critics disparaged Carvajal's literary abilities, but some

have praised what they see as her realistic style. See Caroline Bourland, 'Aspectos de la vida del hogar en el siglo XVII según las novelas de Doña Mariana de Carabajal y Saavedra,' *Homenaje ofrecido a Menéndez Pidal*, Tomo II (Madrid: Librería y Casa Editorial Hernando, 1925), 331–68; Julio Jiménez, 'Doña Mariana de Carvajal y Saavedra, *Navidades de Madrid y noches entretenidas, en ocho novelas*, Edición crítica y anotada' (Diss. Northwestern University, 1974); and Evangelina Rodríguez Cuadros, 'Introducción,' *Novelas amorosas de diversos ingenios del siglo XVII* (Madrid: Castalia, 1987), 9–69. See Jiménez 'Doña Mariana de Carvajal, 15–16, and Cuadros, 'Introducción, 39–40, n.76, for discussions of previous criticism of Carvajal's work.

8 The translations appear in Noël M. Valis, 'Mariana de Carvajal: The Spanish Storyteller,' in *Women Writers of the Seventeenth Century*, ed. Katharina M. Wilson and Frank J. Warnke (Athens: University of Georgia Press, 1989), 251–82.

9 For a detailed analysis of homoeroticism in Carvajal, see Vollendorf, 'The Future of Early Modern Women's Studies: The Case of Same-Sex Friendship and Desire in Zayas and Carvajal,' *Arizona Journal of Hispanic Cultural Studies* 4 (2000): 265–84.

10 See Teresa Soufas, *Dramas of Distinction* (Lexington: University of Kentucky Press, 1999) for a study of female dramatists in seventeenth-century Spain.

11 I first came upon references to Manuel's document and to those of the next subject, Sor Catalina de Jesús, in María Isabel Barbeito's excellent book, *Mujeres del Madrid Barroco. Voces testimoniales* (Madrid: horas y Horas, 1992), 51–5 and 86–94. Manuel's trial record is housed at the Archivo Histórico Nacional in Madrid (Sección Inquisición, Legajo 164, Expediente 7).

12 'disedo q[ue] aquel punhal era p^a mi tirar a vida se acordase di note i me vise em su camara' (fol. 35v, l. 18–19). Manuel's own writing is transcribed verbatim here and line numbers from her text are given for ease of reference. All translations from the Spanish are mine.

13 On folio 34v of her 'memorial,' Manuel wrote: 'mutas vezes vi a morte diante dos oljios' (l. 28).

14 Renée Levine Melammed, *Heretics or Daughters of Israel? The Crypto-Jewish Women of Castile* (New York: Oxford University Press, 1999), 13.

15 'agora digo s[e]ñor q[ue] se su corasion lhe disia q[ue] a ropa susia q[ue] traia al sabado era lipa hi ... hi os aiunos verdaderas erão falsos hi todo lo q[ue] era bueno su maginision lhe disia q[ue] era malo *q[ue] culpa tiego io*' (fol. 38, l. 17-20, emphasis mine).

16 All citations from Bernique and Sor Catalina are taken from Bernique's biographical text (*Idea de perfección y virtudes. Vida de la V.M. y sierva de Dios Catalina de Jesús y San Francisco. Hija de su tercera orden y fundadora del Colegio de las doncellas pobres de Santa Clara de la Ciudad de Alcalá de Henares* [Alcalá: Con

licencia de Francisco García Fernández, Impresor de la Universidad, 1663]).
All punctuation and spelling have been modernized for ease of reading.
17 According to Bernique, the young Catalina had an 'inclinación nativa' toward chastity, and 'aborrecía el estado del matrimonio como contrario a sus designios'. *Idea de perfección y virtudes*, 18–19.
18 '*Entraba con tal disgusto en el matrimonio y con tanto aborrecimiento, que no puedo decir con verdad de adónde me venía porque los deseos y propósitos que antes tuve de guardar castidad y ser religiosa los tenía muy olvidados.*' Ibid., 19. I use italics to indicate the words that Bernique attributes to his mother's writings.
19 '*Cumplió el Santo Bendito ... mi petición tan presto, que dentro de un mes cayó malo mi marido y murió de aquella enfermedad y me vine a Alcalá luego.*' Ibid., 35.
20 'Dispuso su Magestad privarla del marido, o para aliviarla del estado para ella tan molesto o para confundir del todo su vanidad, imposibilitándola a seguir del mundo las locuras.' Ibid., 34.

Contributors

Paolo Cherchi is Professor of Italian Literature at the University of Ferrara. From 1965 to 2002 he taught at the University of Chicago, where he also taught medieval Spanish literature and romance philology. Among his books are: *Capitoli di critica Cervantina* (1977), *Enciclopedismo e politica della riscrittura: Tommaso Garzoni* (1981), *Andreas and the Ambiguity of Courtly Love* (1994), *La metamorfosi dell'Adone* (1996), *Polimatia di riuso – Mezzo secolo di plagio (1539–1589)* (1998), an edition of Tomaso Garzoni's works (1994), and *Piazza universale*, 1996. Forthcoming are books on Boccaccio and on philology and luck as well as works of fiction.

Massimo Ciavolella is Professor of Italian and Comparative Literature at the University of California in Los Angeles. He is the author of books and articles on Renaissance Italian literature and on the relationship between medical, philosophical, and literary ideas on love from ancient Greece to the seventeenth century. Among his books are: *La malattia d'amore dall'antichità al medioevo* (Rome, 1976); the English edition of Jacques Ferrand's Erotomania (Syracuse University Press, 1990: with D.A. Beecher); the critical edition of Gian Lorenzo Bernini's L'impresario (Rome, 1992).

Lorna Clymer is Professor of English at California State University, Bakersfield. In addition to editing a collection of essays on repetition in early modern British and European cultures, she is working on a book-length project on British didactic poems of the eighteenth century.

Patrick Coleman is Professor of French and Francophone Studies at UCLA. He is the author of *Rousseau's Political Imagination: Rule and Repre-*

sentation in the Lettre à d'Alembert (1984) and *Reparative Realism: Mourning and Modernity in the French Novel, 1730–1830* (1998), and co-editor of *Representations of the Self from the Renaissance to Romanticism* (2000) and *Montesquieu and Modernity* (2002).

Ann Delehanty is Assistant Professor of French and Humanities at Reed College. She has published articles on Racine, Pascal, Bakhtin, and Boileau. She is currently at work on a book which details the shift from poetics to aesthetics in France at the end of the seventeenth century.

Andrew Dell'Antonio is Associate Professor of Musicology at the University of Texas at Austin. He is the author of *Syntax, Form, and Genre in Sonatas and Canzonas, 1621–1635* (1997) and editor of *Beyond Structural Listening? Postmodern Modes of Hearing* (2004). His essays range from seventeenth-century musical traditions to twentieth-century musical historiography to MTV. He is completing work on a monograph that explores the role of listening as spiritual practice in early modern Italy.

Paolo Fasoli is Associate Professor of Italian and Comparative Literature at Hunter College and the Graduate Center of the City University of New York. His publications include articles and essays on late medieval literature, Aretino, baroque narrative prose, and lyrical poetry. He is completing a monograph on Gabriello Chiabrera and baroque 'classicist' poetry, and is completing, with Massimo Ciavolella, a critical edition of Battista Fregoso's *Anteros*.

John D. Lyons is Commonwealth Professor of French, University of Virginia. His books include *The Tragedy of Origins: Pierre Corneille and Historical Perspective* (1996), *Kingdom of Disorder: The Theory of Tragedy in Seventeenth-Century France* (1999), and *Before Imagination: Embodied Thought from Montaigne to Rousseau* (forthcoming).

Peter G. Platt is Associate Professor of English at Barnard College. He is the author of *Reason Diminished: Shakespeare and the Marvelous* (1997) and the editor of *Wonders, Marvels, and Monsters in Early Modern Culture* (1999). He has written articles on Shakespeare, Renaissance poetics, and rhetoric. He is currently completing a study of Shakespeare and the paradoxes of Renaissance culture.

Jon R. Snyder is Professor of Italian and Comparative Literature at the

University of California, Santa Barbara, as well as Director of the Italian Studies Program there. He recently served as founding director of the University of California's Rome Study Center. He has worked extensively on early modern Italian literature, particularly in the seventeenth century. His publications in the field include books and essays on such topics as Campanella, Florentine academies, Speroni, Accetto, theories of dialogue from Sigonio to Pallavicino, dissimulation in early modern Europe from Castiglione to Gracián, Salvator Rosa, and G.B. Andreini. He is currently at work on a book entitled *Estetica del Barocco* (2005).

Malina Stefanovska is Associate Professor of French and Francophone Studies at UCLA. In addition to her book *Saint-Simon, un historien dans les marges* (1998), she has published articles on French seventeenth-century court memoirs, history writing, anecdotes, and conspiracy plays. She is presently working on memoirs from the Fronde insurrection by Cardinal de Retz, and on literary representations of faction politics in early modern France.

Lisa Vollendorf is Associate Professor of Spanish at California State University, Long Beach. She is the author of *Reclaiming the Body: María de Zayas's Early Modern Feminism* (2001) and editor of *Recovering Spain's Feminist Tradition* (2001). Her latest book, *The Lives of Women: A New History of Inquisitional Spain,* was published by Vanderbilt University Press in 2005.

Ronald Vroom is Professor of Slavic Languages and Literatures at UCLA. He is the author of two books on the Russian avant-garde poet Velimir Khlebnikov, and numerous articles on the poetry and poetics of Russian modernism. His recent work focuses on the Russian baroque and neo-classicism, and he is currently completing the first volume of a monograph on the history of the Russian lyric sequence.

Ernest A. Zitser is Librarian of the Davis Center for Russian and Eurasian Studies, and Head of the Center for Government and International Studies Library at Harvard University. He is the author of *The Transfigured Kingdom: Sacred Parody and Charismatic Authority at the Court of Peter the Great* (2004). He is currently working on an annotated translation of the first secular autobiography in the Russian language, the *Vita* of Prince Boris Ivanovich Korybut-Kurakin.

Index

Accademia degli Incogniti 86, 89
Accademia degli Oziosi 86, 87, 89, 94, 101
Accetto, Torquato 86–7, 89, 95–101, 224; and *Della dissimulazione onesta* 87, 88, 94, 96, 98, 224; *Rime* (1621, 1626, 1638), 89
Addison, Joseph 44–5; and *The Spectator* 44
Adone, Marino 8
Afanasii, archbishop of Kholmogory 164, 165
Ahmed III, Ottoman Emperor 175
Alberti, Leon Battista 78
Alcandre, in Corneille's *Illusion Comique* 211
Alekseev, Matvei 176
Alekseevich, Tsar Ivan 161, 162
Aman, evil adviser to King Assuérus in Racine's *Esther* 139–46, 149, 151, 152
Anachreon 76, 77
Anne, Queen of Austria 218
Aquilano, Serafino 78
Aquinas, Saint Thomas 12, 15; and *Summa Theologiae* 12, 23
Aristotle 12, 13, 14, 15; and *Metaphysics* 12, 14; and *Parts of Animals* 15; and *Poetics* 12, 14, 15; and *Rhetoric* 15
Asaph, officer in King Assuérus's court in Racine's *Esther* 145
Assuérus, King of Persia in Racine's *Esther* 139–41, 143, 145, 146–7, 152–4, 155

Bach, Johann Sebastian 4
Bacon, Francis 13; and *Of Simulation and Dissimulation* 224
Barkan, Leonard 18
Barthe, Roland 212
Bartoli, Daniello 65, 74; and *L'ozio del saggio* 65
Battista, Giuseppe 86–7, 89–93, 95–7; and *Apologia della menzogna* 84, 87, 90, 92–6, 101
Bembo, Cardinal Pietro 78
Benjamin, Walter 5, 10
Bentley, Richard 49–50
Bernini, Gian Lorenzo 74
Bernique, Catalina 239, 240–1. *See also* Sor Catalina de Jesús y San Francisco
Bernique, Juan, the elder 239

Bernique, Padre Juan 237–9; and *Idea of Perfection and Virtues* (1693) 237–8
Bianconi, Lorenzo 107
Bisaccioni, Maiolino 86
Blackmore, Richard 30, 42–5, 47, 49–50, 52, 55; and *Creation; A Philosophical Poem. Demonstrating the Existence and Providence of a God. In Seven Books* (1712); 30, 43–4, 48, 54; *Eliza* (1705) 43–4; *King Arthur* (1697) 43–4; and *Prince Arthur* (1695) 43–4
Books [Acts] of the Apostles 165
Borges, Antonio 234–6
Boschloo, Anton 110
Bossuet, Jacques-Benigne 217, 224
Bouillon, duc de 225
Bouillon, duchesse de 225
Boyle, Robert 31
Brancovan, Constantine, Orthodox Prince of Wallachia 172
Brion, count de 209
Brion, Madame de 208
Brossard, Nicole: *Baroque d'aube* (1995) 7, 10
Bruni, Antonio 86, 90
Bulkeley, John 26
Burbage, Cuthbert 19
Burbage, James 19
Burbage, Richard 19
Burke, Edmund 55
Burnet, Thomas 31, 40; and *Telluris Theoria Sacra* (1681–9) 31

Caccini, Giulo 79, 113
Caesar, as discussed in Battista's *Apologia* 93
Caraffa, duke of 87
Caravaggio, Michelangelo Merisi 107
Carducci, Giosuè 78

Cariteo: *see* Gareth, Benedetto
Carter, Tim 113
Carvajal, Mariana de 232–4, 240–1; and *Christmas in Madrid* (1660) 232–3; and 'Love Conquers All' 234; and 'Virtue is its own reward' 233
Casali, Lodovico 108, 110; and *Invitation to the Greatness and Marvels of Music* 108, 109
Céard, Jean 19
Cebà, Ansaldo 74, 76, 77
Cellini, Benvenuto 75
Cesarini, Virginio 74
Charles Emmanuel I of Turin 74
Charles XII, King of Sweden 172–5, 176, 179
Charleton, Walter: *The Darkness of Atheism Dispelled by the Light of Nature: A Physico-Theological Treatise* (1652) 31
Cherso, Francesco Patrizi de 13, 16, 17, 18, 23, 26, 27, 65; and *Della poetica* (1587) 16, 64; and *La deca ammirabile* (1587) 16, 17, 64
Chiabrera, Gabriello 74–81; and *Adone* 74, 85; *Amedeide* 80; and *Crestomazia* 76; and *Dialogues on Poetic Art* 76, 77; *Firenze* 80; *Gotiade* 80; and *Maniere dei versi toscani* 77, 80; and *L'Orzalesi* 78–9; and *Vita* 75
Ciampoli, Giovanni 74
Cicero: *De partitione oratoria* 15
Clarke, Samuel 34, 49
Clèves, Princesse de 204
Collins, Richard: *Nature Displayed* (1727) 52
Columbus, Christopher 75
Condé, Prince of 222
Constantine I, the Great, Emperor of Byzantium 171

Cope, Sir Walter 19, 21
Corneau, Alain: *Tous les matins du monde* (1991) 3
Cowley, Abraham 38, 40, 52; and *Ecstasy* 42
Cyrus 152

Deleuze, Gilles 3, 7, 9, 80, 204, 211; and *The Fold: Leibniz and the Baroque* (1988) 3, 7, 9
D'Emeri, Particelli 219
Dennis, John 44
Derham, William 32, 51; and *Physico-Theology: Or, A Demonstration of the Being and Attributes of God, from his Works of Creation* (1714) 32; and *Astro-Theology* (1715) 32
Descartes, René 13, 23, 193, 203–4, 218, 224
Diruta, Girolamo: *Transilvano* 115
Domitian, as discussed in Battista's *Apologia* 93
Dony, G.B. 108
Dryden, John 154
Du Bellay, Joachim 77–8
Dubois, Claude-Gilbert 5, 10

Elise, confidante of Esther in Racine's *Esther* 147, 148
Esther, wife of King Assuérus in Racine's *Esther* 140, 141, 146–9, 151, 153–5
Estienne, Henri 77

Fairchild, Hoxie Neal 43
Faret, Nicolas: *L'Honnête home ou l'art de plaire à la cour* 224
Faust 75
Fedorovich, Prince Afanasii 181
Fedorovich, Tsar Mikhail 180, 181

Fedorovna, Tsaritsa Praskov'ia, wife of Tsar Ivan Alekseevich 181
Findlen, Paula 112
Florizel, son of Polixenes in *The Winter's Tale* 21
Foucault, Michel 13, 22; and 'The Masked Philosopher' 22
Frederick IV 179
Frescobaldi, Girolamo: *Primo libro* (1630) 111
Frye, Northrop 78

Gareth, Benedetto 78
Genette, Gérard 80
Gideon, Archdeacon 184
Giustiniani, Vincenzo 107–10
Golovin, F.A. 170, 172
Golovkin, G.I. 174–5
Gondi, Jean-Françoise-Paul de 208. *See also* de Retz, Cardinal de 208
Góngora, Luis de 65
Gracián, Baltasar 99, 100, 224; and *Oráculo manual y arte de prudencia* 99
Grebeniuk, V. 125
Greenaway, Peter: *Draughtsman's Contract* (1982) 3
Greenberg, Mitchell 155
Guéméné, Madame de 213
Gryphius, Andreas 5
Guarini, Guarino 78

Hakewill, G.: *An Apologie of the Power and Providence of God in the Government of the World* (1627) 31
Halliwell, Stephen 14
Hathaway, Baxter 16, 26
Hemmings, William 19
Henry VIII 19

Hermione, Queen of Sicilia in *The Winter's Tale* 21, 22
Hill, Aaron: *The Creation* (1720) 52
Hindemith, Paul 135
Hirschman, 215; and *The Passions and the Interests* 215
Hobbes, Thomas 3, 31, 47
Holbein 211; and *Ambassadors* 211
Holy Prophecy, the ship 162
Hughes, John 40–2; and *The Ecstasy. An Ode* (1720), 41–2, 52
Huygens, Christiaan 40
Hydaspe, officer of King Assuérus's court in Racine's *Esther* 141–5
Hymen, god in *As You Like It* 20

Iavorskii, Stefan 175
Istomin, Karion 123, 124, 126
Ivan the Terrible 163

Jacobskoy, 'Prince,' court jester of Peter the Great 178, 179
Jesús y San Francisco, Sor Catalina de 237–9
Johnson, Samuel 31; and *Rasselas* (1759) 52; and *The Vanity of Human Wishes* 36
Juan, Don 215
Judas Iscariot 173
Jules, Joost 178, 180
Jurieu, Pierre 217

Kalist, Bishop 129
Kantorowicz, Ernst: *Frederick the Second, 1194–1250* 159, 185
Karion, Istomin 131
Keill, John 40
Kempe, Will 19
Keohane, N.O. 215
Kierkegaard, Søren 64

Kochanowski, Jan 129–30
Korbe, Johann Georg 170; and *Diary* 170
Koyré, Alexander 48
Kristeller, Paul Oskar 16
Kropotkin, Brigadier 175
Kurakin, Prince B.I. 182, 183

La Bruyère, Jean de 197, 198
Lafayette, Madame de 193, 204
Lafew, old courtier in *All's Well that Ends Well* 20
La Rochefoucauld 193, 197, 215; and *Maxims* 215
Latour, Bruno 203
Law, William: *A Serious Call to a Devout and Holy Life* (1728) 46
Leontes, King of Sicilia in *The Winter's Tale* 21, 22
Leopardi, Giacomo 75, 76; and *Operette morali* 75; and *Zibaldone* 75
Leopold I, Emperor of Austria 170
Lesdiguières, Madame de 210
Leszczynski, Stanislaw, King of Poland and protégé of Charles XII 173, 177
Lily: *Early History of Rome* 138
Lisieux, archbishop of 208, 209
Locke, John 40, 194
Longueville, Madame de, the *Frondeuse* 213
Longinus 16, 26; and *On the Sublime* 16
Lord Chamberlain's Men 19
Louis XIV, King of France 8, 138, 139, 155, 208
Lucretius 40; and *De Rerum Natura* (ca. 50 BC) 44
Lugli, Adalgisa 1

MacGregor, Arthur 19
Mallet, David 30; and *The Excursion. A Poem. In Two Cantos* (1728) 52–4
Malvezzi, Virgilio 98
Manfred 75
Manso, Marchese Giovan Battista 85–6; and *Accademia degli Oziosi*, 85–6, 88; and *Poesie nomiche* (1635) 89
Manuel, Bernarda 234–7, 240–1
Maravall, Antonio 114
Maravall, José 7, 11, 80
Mardochée, Jewish subject of King Assuérus in Racine's *Esther* 140, 141, 142, 145, 146, 148–52
Marino, Giambattista 5, 63, 67–9, 71, 73, 78, 79, 81, 85, 89–91, 96, 229; and *Adone* (1623) 67–9, 71, 80, 85, 91; and *Fischiata 33* of the *Mutroleide* 73; and *Lira* (1614) 66
Martynov, Vladimir: *Song, Play and Prayer in the System of Russian Liturgical Chant* 122
Mascardi, Vitale 216
Maxentius, tsar of Rome 171
Mazarin, Cardinal 217, 222, 223; and *Politician's Breviary* 224
Mazepa, I.S., Cossack leader of Left-Bank Ukraine 172–80
Medici, Ferdinando II 111
Melammed Levine, Renée 236–7
Menshikov, A.D. 174, 177, 182
Meshikov, Prince 175, 176
Mikhailovich, Tsar Aleksei 126, 129, 163; and wife Maria 129
Milton, John 44, 52; and *Paradise Lost* 45–6
Molière 197; and *Le Misanthrope* 197; and *Tartuffe* 197
Montbazon, Madame de 214
Monteverdi, Claudio 4

More, Henry: *A Platonick Song of the Soul* (1647) 40
Morrice, Bezaleel: *An Essay on the Universe* (1725) 51
Moser, Walter 7
Murtola, *Creazione del mondo* (1608) 74
Musin-Pushkin, I.A. 182

Newton, Isaac 40, 42
Nicole, Pierre 8, 193, 195–200, 202–4; and *On Self-Knowledge* 193, 194, 204
Nigro Salvatore 87
Nikon, Patriarch 129, 163
Nores, Giason de 76

Ogilvie, John 36
Order of St Andrew 160
Order of St Judas 160

Paleotti, Gabriele 110; and *Discorso sopra le immagini* 110
Pallavicino, Ferrante 89
Parker, Samuel 40
Pascal, Blaise 9, 144, 193, 202, 204, 218, 219, 222
Paulina, friend of Hermione, Queen of Sicily, in *The Winter's Tale* 21, 22
Payne, William: *A Practical Discourse of Repentance ... and Demonstrating the Invalidity of a Death-Bed Repentance* (1708) 36
Perdita, daughter of the King of Sicilia in *The Winter's Tale* 21, 22
Peri, Jacopo 79
Périer, Gilberte 204
Peter the Apostle 164
Peter the Great 8, 159, 161–2, 164–73, 175–8, 182–3
Petrarch 76

Petri, Girolamo 73
Phillips, Augustine 19
Pindar, or Pindarus 76
Plato 12, 64
Platter, Thomas 19
Pléiade poets 77
Polixenes, best friend of Leontes, King of Sicilia, in *The Winter's Tale* 21
Pope, Alexander: *Scriblerus His Treatise of the Art of Sinking in Poetry* (1727/8) 44
Pope, Thomas 19
Pozzi, Giovanni 70–1
Primary Russian Chronicle 168
Prospero 211
Puliaschi, Giovanni Domenico 113
Purchas, Samuel 18

Quintilian: *Institutio oratoria* 15

Racine, Jean 8, 138, 139, 140; and *Esther* 138–41, 143, 147, 150, 152
Raleigh, Sir Walter 18
Ramus, Petrus 69
Ray, John 40, 49, 51; and *The Wisdom of God Manifested in the Works of Creation* (1691) 31, 45, 49
Reiss, Timothy: *Tragedy and Truth* 154; and *Esther* 155; and Racine 154
Retz, Cardinal de 6, 209, 210–15, 218, 221–4; and *La conjuration du comte de Fiesque* 216; and *Memoirs* 210–16, 218–19, 223, 225
Reynolds, John 30, 38–41, 49; and *Death's Vision Represented in a Philosophical, Sacred Poem* 38–40, 55
Richelieu, Cardinal 214, 216, 217
Rinuccini, Ottavio 74, 79
Robortello, Francesco 16

Romano, Giulio 21
Romanov, Peter Alekseevich 159. *See also* Peter the Great
Romodanovskii, Prince F. Iu. 182, 184
Ronsard, Pierre 77–8
Rousset, Jean 80
Rousseau, Jean-Jacques 223

St Alexander Nevskii 185
St Andrew 168, 169, 170, 172
St Augustine 15
St Daniil of Moscow 131, 133
St Donatus 131, 133
St Filipp 163, 164
St Hypatius 131, 134
St Iona 161, 162, 163, 164, 165, 167, 168
St John the Warrior 134
St Paul, the ship 162
St Peter 168
St Peter, the ship 164, 166
St Vassian 161, 162, 163, 164, 165, 167, 168
Sappho 76
Scepeaux, Mademoiselle de 213
Scève, Maurice 78
Seneca, as discussed in Battista's *Apologia* 93
Sévigné, Charles de 202
Sévigné, Madame de 194, 213
Shakespeare, William 9, 19, 20, 211; and *All's Well That Ends Well* 20; and *As You Like It* 20; and *Cymbeline* 22; and *Love's Labour's Lost* 19; and *Midsummer Night's Dream* 20; and *Pericles* 22; and *The Tempest* 22; and *The Winter's Tale* 20, 22
Shakhovskoi, Prince Grigorii Petrovich 181, 182

Shakhovskoi, Prince Iu. F. 181, 183, 184, 185
Shakhovskoi, Prince Matvei Fedorovich 180, 181
Shchukin, A. Ia. 176
Sheremetev, B.P., General Field-Marshall and Russian emissary 170
Simeon, of Polotsk 123–9, 131, 134; and *Rifmologion* (*Rhyme-Book, or Book of Verses, Containing Verses Composed in Equal Measured Lines and Rhyme, Suitable for Various Needs. To the Glory and Honor of God, One in the Trinity, the Immaculate Mother of God and the Saints Well-Pleasing to the Lord. For the Benefit of Young and Old, for the Comfort and Consolation of both Clerics and Laymen of various Ranks, Expressing Thanksgiving, Praise, Greetings, Etc.* 124, 125; *Rhymed Verses on the Nativity of the Christ* 127–8
Simonides 76
Skoropads'kyi, Ivan 174
Socrates 12
Sohm, Philip 114
Speroni, Sperone 76
Spinoza, Baruch 3, 31, 47
Sponde, Jean de 5
Stefani, Gino 116
Streshnev, T.N. 166
Summers, David 12

Tagliabue, Guido Morpurgo 80
Tans'ur, William 36
Tasso, Torquato 64, 78
Tassoni, Alessandro 78; and *Querelle des anciens et des modernes* 78
Taylor, Jeremy: *The Rule and Exercise of Holy Dying* (1651) 35

Tesauro 85; and *Il cannocchiale aristotelico* 85
Testi, Fulvio 74
Theotokos 130
Thomson, James: *The Seasons* (1726–46) 54
Tolomei, Jacomo de' 78
Tradescant, John the elder 19
Trapp, Joseph 36
Trimpi, Wesley 14, 23
Trissino, Gian Giorgo 78
Turenne, maréchal de 208, 209, 210

Vasari, Giorgio 75
Vendôme, duchesse de 208, 209
Vendôme, Mademoiselle de 208, 209, 210. *See also* de Brion, Madame de
Vergil, a.k.a. P. Vergili Maronis, 65; as discussed in Battista's *Apologia* 93
Villari, Lucio 97
Voiture, Vincent 208–10
Volkonskoi, G.S., Major-General Prince 175
von Gardner, Johann 123

Watts, Isaac 36

Young, Edward 36; and *The Last Day* 37

Zacconi, Lodovico 108
Zagorin, Perez 97
Zayas, María de 231–4, 240–1; and *The Disenchantment* 232; and *The Enchantment of Love* (1637) 231; and 'Love for the Sake of Conquest' 232; and 'The Power of Love' 231
Zotov, N.M. 166

www.ingramcontent.com/pod-product-compliance
Lightning Source LLC
Chambersburg PA
CBHW030312080526
44584CB00012B/541